KU-821-361

LIVERPOOL JMU LIBRARY

3 1111 01456 0161

Workplace Learning in Physical Education

Pre-service and beginning teachers have to negotiate an unfamiliar and often challenging working environment, in both teaching spaces and staff spaces. *Workplace Learning in Physical Education* explores the workplace of teaching as a site of professional learning. Using stories and narratives from the experiences of pre-service and beginning teachers, the book takes a closer look at how professional knowledge is developed by investigating the notions of 'professional' and 'workplace learning' by drawing on data from a five-year project. The book also critically examines the literature associated with, and the rhetoric that surrounds 'the practicum', 'fieldwork' 'school experience' and the 'induction year'.

The book is structured around five significant dimensions of workplace learning:

- Social tasks of teaching and learning to teach.
- Performance, practice and praxis.
- Identity, subjectivities and the profession/al.
- Space and place for, and of, learning.
- Micropolitics.

As well as identifying important implications for policy, practice and research methodology in physical education and teacher education, the book also shows how research can be a powerful medium for the communication of good practice. This is an important book for all students, pre-service and beginning teachers working in physical education, for academics researching teacher workspaces, and for anybody with an interest in the wider themes of teacher education, professional practice and professional learning in the workplace.

Tony Rossi is with the School of Human Movement Studies at the University of Queensland in Australia. He researches workplaces associated with human movement studies, particularly schools, where he pays close attention to the changing nature of teachers' work, specifically where it relates to the health of young people. In addition, he has directed his research towards Sport for Development projects in marginalized and underserved communities in Australia and elsewhere. From

January 2015 he will be in a new position in the School of Exercise and Nutrition Science at Queensland University of Technology in Brisbane.

lisahunter is with the Department of Sport and Leisure in the Faculty of Education at the University of Waikato, New Zealand. She has an eclectic range of research interests including surfing festivals and female surfing; female experiences of physical activities; young people and embodied subjectivities, and has methodological interests in visual methods, narrative and ethnography.

Erin Christensen is with the Faculty of Education at the University of Newcastle in Australia, a position she took up after completing her Ph.D. at the University of Queensland. Her research focuses on the micropolitics of teachers' workplaces as well as on children's voices in sport, physical activity, adventure education, and school physical education.

Doune Macdonald is with the School of Human Movement Studies at the University of Queensland in Australia where, at the end of 2013, she completed a ten-year tenure as the Head of School. She is internationally recognized as a curriculum scholar and theorist and recently led the development of the Australian Curriculum for Health and Physical Education. Her research interests span education, physical activity and youth, educational and health policy, and her current projects focus on the outsourcing of the physical education curriculum and the health work of teachers.

Routledge Studies in Physical Education and Youth Sport
Series Editor: David Kirk
University of Bedfordshire, UK

The *Routledge Studies in Physical Education and Youth Sport* series is a forum for the discussion of the latest and most important ideas and issues in physical education, sport, and active leisure for young people across school, club and recreational settings. The series presents the work of the best well-established and emerging scholars from around the world, offering a truly international perspective on policy and practice. It aims to enhance our understanding of key challenges, to inform academic debate, and to have a high impact on both policy and practice, and is thus an essential resource for all serious students of physical education and youth sport.

Also available in this series:

Children, Obesity and Exercise
A practical approach to prevention, treatment and management of childhood and adolescent obesity
Edited by Andrew P. Hills, Neil A. King and Nuala M. Byrne

Disability and Youth Sport
Edited by Hayley Fitzgerald

Rethinking Gender and Youth Sport
Edited by Ian Wellard

Pedagogy and Human Movement
Richard Tinning

Positive Youth Development Through Sport
Edited by Nicholas Holt

Young People's Voices in PE and Youth Sport
Edited by Mary O'Sullivan and Ann Macphail

Physical Literacy
Throughout the lifecourse
Edited by Margaret Whitehead

Physical Education Futures
David Kirk

Young People, Physical Activity and the Everyday
Living physical activity
Edited by Jan Wright and Doune Macdonald

Muslim Women and Sport
Edited by Tansin Benn, Gertrud Pfister and Haifaa Jawad

Workplace Learning in Physical Education

Emerging teachers' stories from the staffroom and beyond

Tony Rossi, lisahunter, Erin Christensen and Doune Macdonald

LONDON AND NEW YORK

First published 2015
by Routledge
2 Park Square, Milton Park, Abingdon, Oxon OX14 4RN

and by Routledge
711 Third Avenue, New York, NY 10017

Routledge is an imprint of the Taylor & Francis Group, an informa business

© 2015 Tony Rossi, lisahunter, Erin Christensen and Doune Macdonald

The right of the editor to be identified as the author of the editorial matter, and of the authors for their individual chapters, has been asserted in accordance with sections 77 and 78 of the Copyright, Designs and Patents Act 1988.

All rights reserved. No part of this book may be reprinted or reproduced or utilized in any form or by any electronic, mechanical, or other means, now known or hereafter invented, including photocopying and recording, or in any information storage or retrieval system, without permission in writing from the publishers.

Trademark notice: Product or corporate names may be trademarks or registered trademarks, and are used only for identification and explanation without intent to infringe.

British Library Cataloguing-in-Publication Data
A catalogue record for this book is available from the British Library

Library of Congress Cataloging in Publication Data
Rossi, Tony, 1955–
Workplace learning in physical education : emerging teachers' stories from the staffroom and beyond / Tony Rossi, lisahunter, Ern Christensen and Doune Macdonald. – 1st edition.
    pages cm. – (Routledge Studies in Physical Education and Youth Sport)
    Includes bibliographical references and index.
    1. Physical education teachers–Training of. 2. Physical education teachers–Professional relationships. I. Title.
    GV363.R67 2015
    796.07–dc23   2014024406

ISBN: 978-0-415-67365-5 (hbk)
ISBN: 978-0-203-13356-9 (ebk)

Typeset in Times New Roman
by Wearset Ltd, Boldon, Tyne and Wear

Printed and bound in Great Britain by
TJ International Ltd, Padstow, Cornwall

Tony

For mum – from whose memory we all faded, but never she from ours. Thanks for being there ... all the many times I fell off of life's bike.

And for my brother Paul, who was the rock when I needed it.

lisa

For elke.

Erin

For my beautiful friends and family.

Doune

For Steven ... once and always a wonderful teacher.

Contents

x   *Contents*

Foreword

This book is full of stories, so I thought I might tell one of my own. Back in 2005 I was visiting a student/pre-service teacher (let's call her Penny) in her final year practicum at an elite Brisbane private boys' school. The health and physical education (HPE) facilities at the school were outstanding and they had a large all-male PE staff who seemed to have a good reputation 'around town'. As a university supervisor my role was not to offer a specific judgement on Penny's developing teaching competence, but rather to watch her teaching and talk to the HPE staff about her progress, and basically 'see how she was getting on'. If the HPE staff expressed any concerns about her then I would arrange a return visit to observe her teaching again.

Penny taught a volleyball lesson to year 10 boys and, in my view, she handled the lesson quite well. Discussion with the HOD confirmed the fact that Penny was thought to be 'doing fine'. While in the HPE staffroom/office I noticed that, as an all-male preserve, it was rather 'blokey'. It was just a feeling I had and my intuition told me that Penny was having some difficulties in this context. When I had finished my official visit I asked Penny to walk with me to my car parked in the visitors' car park on the other side of campus. We had only walked about 50 metres from the gym when I remarked to Penny that the HPE staffroom conversations seemed rather testosterone fuelled. Penny responded by bursting into tears. It seemed I had touched a sensitive nerve and Penny then began to tell me how alienated she felt in the staffroom. The teaching was OK but the culture of the staffroom was sexist, homophobic, elitist and in her view basically toxic.

Of course this raises questions as to why we sent a young woman into such a space in the first place, but this school was generally considered a good practicum site for our students. No one else had complained. And Penny had not complained either; it was just that when the official visit was over she couldn't hold back her emotions.

This episode got me thinking about the practicum experience in general, and the HPE staffroom/office in particular, as a site of learning. Colleague and friend Lindsay Fitzclarence (1993) had many years earlier introduced me to the term 'poisonous pedagogy' originally coined by psychoanalyst Alice Miller (1987) to describe some of the more pernicious pedagogical work that occurs in some families. Lindsay had used the term to refer to certain forms of hyper-masculinity, violence, homophobia and misogyny that may be produced in certain youth sport contexts. Juan-Miguel Fernadez-Balboa (1999) later used the same term in talking about certain PE contexts. It seemed to me that we might be sending some of our students into practicum sites that might also be characterized by episodes of poisonous pedagogy. Moreover, while many have lauded the practicum as the place where it 'really happens' with regard to authentic learning for prospective teachers, little, if anything, was known about the nature of the HPE staffroom/office work culture and what student teachers might learn from it.

Not long after the episode with Penny another pre-service teacher, a male, also related stories about the toxic nature of the PE staffroom in which he found himself on practicum. The significance of this issue was reinforced, and accordingly, in 2005, we conducted a small pilot project to investigate the nature of the HPE staffroom culture and the learning that it facilitated for student teachers. Data from the pilot study revealed that, although some pre-service teachers experienced very positive subject department cultures, others experienced a negative context that some even described as nothing less than toxic. Some student teachers reported having to 'bite their tongues' (on matters such as sexual harassment, racism and homophobia) and to 'play the game' in order to be accepted in the subject department. Without acceptance, their judged performance on the practicum (and subsequent employment ratings) could be seriously compromised. While such 'playing the game' is not new, the significance and the power of the subject department as a site for learning and developing an emerging identity as a teacher has not been seriously studied in PE or its Australian equivalent, HPE. My early work on the nature of the practicum (Tinning, 1984) and then on social task systems (see Tinning and Siedentop, 1985) within the practicum had convinced me that, in addition to teaching skills and competencies, there was much to be learned on the practicum that had nothing to do with teaching per se.

As a consequence of this pilot work a more extensive research project began in 2008 to investigate the secondary school PE subject department as a professional learning community. Initially using a social theory of learning (Wenger, 1998), workplace learning (Billett, 2001) and task systems (Doyle, 1977) as the theoretical frames, the study investigated how the culture of a secondary school HPE subject department culture works to facilitate or compromise the process of becoming a professional teacher. The project, funded by the Australian Research Council, was completed in 2010.

As the project evolved, the initial social task theory took us only so far, and co-researchers Tony Rossi, lisahunter and Erin Christensen (née Erin Flannagan and a Ph.D. student at the time), and supported by Doune Macdonald, all brought new theoretical lenses to the project. Tony was interested in the work of Goffman and the practicum as a site for performance. Lisa was interested in how pre-service teacher identities and subjectivities influence, and are influenced by, the practicum and brought the work of Bourdieu and Butler to the project. Later both she and Tony introduced the ideas of spatial theorists Henri Lefebvre and Edward Soja. Erin was particularly interested in the micropolitical context of the staffroom and the idea of using narrative to explore micropolitical experiences within the staffroom. In 2006 we were also privileged to have Canadian Karen Sirna work as a post-doctoral researcher in the developing project, and her research skills and energy helped immensely in moving the research project forward as well as contributing significantly to some of the early publications.

All this meant that the project evolved into a more theoretically robust exploration of workplace learning in HPE. This book is a representation of this work and it makes interesting reading. Importantly, the book reveals that the practicum in general, and the (health and) physical education staffroom (variously described) more specifically, is a highly problematic and sometimes even destructive site of workplace learning for future teachers. Against the ever-burgeoning backdrop of new public management and what Stephen Ball calls the neo-liberal imaginary where the audit culture reigns, the message in this book is all the more important. Not only would it be nice if policy-makers and the teacher education 'industry' took the messages of this book seriously as an intellectual exercise; they should also take it seriously, as a matter of some urgency, as an important policy issue.

Professor Richard Tinning
May 2014

Preface

This book is drawn from a funded research study that took place in Australia. To be more accurate, the book is about the story of the research study, which if the pilot and the Ph.D. attached to the study are included, lasted nearly six years. It is a story that could not really be told in its entirety through the traditions of journal article publishing, simply because the story is more than the sum of its parts. The direction we ultimately decided to take with the book is a little different from our original plan, which included cross-cultural and a broader transnational analysis. In the end we decided against some aspects of this, since that would have taken us away from the central narrative contained in these pages. We therefore kept fidelity with the original study and its findings and outcomes considering what we offer here to be generative rather than generalizable. That said, it was important to place the study within the international context of (health and) physical education. We therefore make wide-ranging reference to policy issues that exist beyond the borders of Australia. Readers within their own jurisdictions will therefore judge and connect with the parts of the book that resonate most and from which they wish to take any important messages. This made more sense to us rather than trying to create a text that considered every nuance from every setting possible. Not only that; the research study we report on here and of which we tell the tale was precipitated by real events in a university department. We attempt to capture these events through small narratives early on in the book. The reason for revealing this is that at the time of the beginning of the study we were not contemplating a research study at all. We considered that enough had been written about the practicum as a site for learning within the context of teacher education. In addition, plenty had been written about some of the dubious practices within physical education teaching and one need only go back to Pat Dodds' work of the mid-1980s (1986) to see how persistent these have been. What happened in our situation was that the tales coming back from the practicum (teaching practice or teaching rounds at it is variously known around the world) were stories of success mixed with stories of deep foreboding. We realized that the ugly 'isms' Dodds referred to were alive and well not just in the classroom (at least we anticipated this would be the case) but in the Health and Physical Education Department office or room – the very space into which we were sending pre-service teachers to learn how to become members of the teaching profession. It was at that point that we considered it important to know more about this workplace as a learning space and so began what was a near six-year journey. Inevitably the players in this story changed over time for a number of reasons but for the record those involved to varying degrees were: Richard Tinning,[1] Karen Sirna,[2] Tony Rossi, lisahunter, Doune Macdonald[3] and Erin Christensen (née Flanagan).[4] Richard and Karen appeared on early work written about the project (See Sirna *et al.*, 2008, 2010; Rossi *et al.*, 2008), and Richard penned the Foreword. We all featured on various conference presentations around the world, and the project was brought to its conclusion by Tony, lisa Erin and Doune. It probably comes as no surprise that the study had an evolutionary quality to it and this was indeed the case. So, as different intellectual resources were brought to the project the dimensions by which we tried to understand the data expanded. The consequence is a book on workplace learning that is rather different from other books associated with workplace learning in that there is not a single theoretical framework that binds the entire book; rather there are five. Although this was somewhat messy to try to bring together, the result we believe makes a unique and an ambitious contribution to the literature. We hope you will enjoy what we have to say.

Tony Rossi
lisahunter
Erin Christensen
Doune Macdonald
May 2014

Notes

1 Emeritus Professor Richard Tinning was the original project leader and was the stimulus for the research programme. It is an important legacy as this research has extended into allied health professional learning and even medical training. While he is an Emeritus Professor at the University of Queensland and continues to work and write with us, this status as well as his outstanding reputation in the field takes him around the world as a visiting scholar.
2 Dr Karen Sirna was a visiting Research Fellow (from Canada) in the School of Human Movement Studies at the University of Queensland; she is currently with Douglas College in Vancouver Canada.
3 Professor Doune Macdonald was, at the time of writing, completing her final year as the Head of School, School of Human Movement Studies, the University of Queensland She fulfilled a ten-year tenure in that role by the end of 2013 during which time she led the School through a time of turbulent change, major review and extraordinary fiscal constraints. In spite of these exacting demands she moved smoothly into the writing team to bring the book to its conclusion.
4 There is no particular political motivation or otherwise to include Erin's original family name in parentheses. Rather, this note is included because since being married she chose to accept her husband's family name and consequently now publishes under it. Therefore readers need to be mindful that when Flanagan and Christensen are cited in the text they are one and the same person.

Tony Rossi

NB: Throughout the text, readers will notice we use the term Health and Physical Education, which is shortened to the acronym HPE. We do this because in Australia the name of the curriculum subject in schools is *Health and Physical Education* (though physical education can be studied in its own right at the senior level of schooling – perhaps equivalent, for example, to A levels in the United Kingdom). We do not dwell on the history of this subject name; rather, for the purposes of this book we take it to be the same as *Physical Education* in other jurisdictions.

Acknowledgements

The authors would like to acknowledge the Australian Research Council for funding the project (Teachers' professional development, communities of practice, and the secondary school subject department: The case of Health and Physical Education – ARC Discovery Project 2008–2010) from which this book draws.

We also acknowledge the emerging teachers who gave willingly of their time to make this project possible. We hope their journey, wherever it has taken them so far, has been a satisfying one.

Some of the material in this book has appeared in print in other outlets and the authors would like to thank the following publishers for the generous approval processes to use material from the research articles listed below.

Taylor & Francis

lisahunter, Rossi, T., Tinning, R., Flanagan, E. and Macdonald, D. (2011) 'Professional learning places and spaces: The staffroom as a site of beginning teacher induction and transition', *Asia-Pacific Journal of Teacher Education*, 39(1), 33–46.

Rossi, A. and lisahunter (2013) 'Professional spaces for pre-service teachers: Sites of reality, imagination and resistance', *Educational Review*, 65(2), 123–139.

Sirna, K., Tinning, R. and Rossi, T. (2008) 'The social tasks of learning to become a physical education teacher: Considering the HPE subject department as a community of practice', *Sport, Education and Society*, 13(3), 285–300.

—— (2010) 'Social processes of health and physical education teachers' identity formation: Reproducing and changing culture', *British Journal of Sociology of Education*, 31(1), 71–84.

Elsevier

Christensen, E. (2013) 'Micropolitical staffroom stories: Beginning health and physical education teachers' experiences of the staffroom', *Teaching and Teacher Education*, 30, 74–83.

Rossi, T., Sirna, K. and Tinning, R. (2008) 'Becoming a health and physical education teacher: Student teacher "performances" in the HPE subject department office', *Teaching and Teacher Education*, 24(4), 1029–1040.

Dr Tony Rossi

I would like to thank all of my close and immediate family, wherever they are in the world – they continue to be a source of inspiration, support, laughter and tears, and hope and aspiration, and were so at a time for me of excruciating loss. Mostly though I would like to thank them for being, above all else, a source of love – there is no greater gift. I want especially to thank my partner, Associate Professor Mary Ryan for her unbending love, support, guidance, and in particular her tolerance … to say that at times I was (and probably still am) like a 'bear with a sore head' would be the mother of understatement. I would also like to thank my co-authors lisa, Erin and Doune. Between us within the space of writing this book we managed to accommodate most of life's 'big events' and traumas: running a large university school/department at a time of fiscal restraint, job changes, country changes, family illness, loss of parents, Ph.D. completion, marriage, pregnancy and childbirth. Somehow we managed to support each other through all of these events to see this book to a conclusion. This was testimony not only to their professionalism, but more importantly their comradeship. Finally, I would like to thank my two close mentors, colleagues and friends, Richard Tinning, and one of my co-authors Doune Macdonald for their support, guidance and encouragement, in Richard's case across my entire academic career, and in Doune's case as the Head of the School of Human Movement Studies, at the University of Queensland in Australia. There is no measure as to how lucky and privileged I have been in this regard.

Dr Erin Christensen

Acknowledgement and a heartfelt thank you to my beautiful friends, family and husband for their unconditional love and support not only throughout my doctoral study and the writing of this book but also in my transition from Ph.D. student to early career academic. It is your unwavering love and support that keeps me grounded. To my co-authors Tony, lisa (who were also my Ph.D. co-advisers) and Doune, thank you for your research guidance, understanding and belief in me not only as your student but also as an early career academic 'feeling her way'. I feel very fortunate to have had the opportunity to work with such a strong research team made up not only of my co-authors but also my Primary Ph.D. adviser Richard Tinning. Richard, and for your support and guidance, I thank you. Finally to the participating pre-service and beginning Health and Physical Education teachers: without your time and willingness to share your stories this book would not have been possible – thank you.

Dr lisahunter

In a period where my academic career was shattered I was fortunate enough to be invited to work with Richard Tinning and Tony Rossi on this project. The project took me into new research territory, that of staffrooms, but enabled me to draw on my expertise of pre-service teacher education, geography, transition, human movement studies identities, and experiences in schooling, teaching and teacher education. Not only did Richard and Tony recognize this, but they also valued my input in a timely way. Their recognition, in the Butlerian sense, was not just professional however, it was also personal and I am extremely grateful for that, as it seems sadly uncommon in contemporary academic work. Tony has continued to be a wonderful colleague to work with on this book and beyond, and Richard continues to be the supportive and encouraging mentor that many academics should aspire to be. As a consequence I also had the privilege to work with Erin Christensen in her doctoral work. Her warmth and curiosity did much to sustain me and it is with great pleasure that I see her participating in this book as an early career academic and as my colleague. She has much to contribute if her wider 'staffroom' permits. The person who has never stopped encouraging me to participate in this project and book through the wild times of academic work and life, elke emerald, is by no means the last person for me to acknowledge but the pivotal person to acknowledge. Thank you all for your humanity.

Professor Doune Macdonald

Over the period of the project and subsequent writing of this book my engagement was less than anticipated or hoped. Clearly the talented and flexible project team was able to adjust to this while as Head of School I attended to growing staff and student numbers, a budget under pressure, structural reforms and floods, as well as accepting a role in the writing of the new Australian Curriculum for Health and Physical Education. I am therefore most appreciative that Tony, Erin and lisa invited me to participate in the creation of this significant manuscript as its questions of teachers' work, education policy and equity have been enduring professional interests. Tony has been particularly skilful in managing the course of this project, and his academic integrity and collegiality are highly valued by us all.

The author team

Finally, all the authors would collectively like to thank our colleagues at Routledge publishers for their tolerance. This book took longer than anticipated to come to fruition for all the complicated reasons indicated above. The flexibility in timelines demonstrates a finely tuned understanding of the complexity of the human condition – it was greatly appreciated by all four of us.

Projects and books like this rely on myriad support workers, contributors, advisers and friends, and we thank them all. As always however, we take full responsibility for the text that appears in these pages.

Part I
The study

1　Learning to be a teacher

Introduction

The *basic* mechanics of becoming a teacher may not have changed all that much over the past 40 years. As we discuss later, but for a few pockets (in the developed world at least), the experience of those wishing to be teachers approximately resembles a common structure. Generally it is made up of a period of formal university education; this might be a three-year baccalaureate degree in a particular area of study (in a disciplinary subject area like history or mathematics) followed by a programme of professional learning sometimes at the same university or sometimes at a different university but most commonly in a school or faculty of education. Alternatively it might be an integrated degree that includes the study of education that might run for four or five years. In among these configurations of structure are periods that are allocated to professional experience; that is, 'work' in schools to allow the life of schools to be experienced from the perspective of being a teacher. The allocation of time and how it is organized and governed (and indeed assessed) varies, but what can be said with some certainty is that learning to be a teacher always involves doing the *work* of a teacher. In some cases (though Furlong (2013) would argue that it is relatively few), learning to be a teacher after successfully completing a first degree consists almost *entirely* of doing the *work* of a teacher.

Potential changes to teacher education in Europe signalled by the Bologna Accord, an agreement among participating member states to standardize tertiary education to a point where university credits can be exchanged across international borders and the length of time in university programmes is the same, are yet to become clearer. However, the effect of the accord is being felt further afield; the University of Melbourne in Australia has adopted some of the Bologna Agreement structures in its professional preparation degrees. Readers will have already noted that this forms just the beginning of the learning process required to *be* a teacher and that being a teacher requires 'learning' to continue across the span of a career. One of the steepest learning curves is in the first year post-qualification or what our American colleagues refer to as the 'rookie' year. This transition year presents a number of challenges not least of which is the propensity for isolation, a plotline evident in the stories that follow later in this book. It was this notion of learning while *working* as a teacher (workplace learning) that intrigued us in the first instance, and then, based on some of the stories of our students (we will refer to them as pre-service teachers from here), in those workplaces, provoked the research agenda that forms the context for this book. This was where we came in.

The genesis of a research agenda

It is reasonable to suggest that teacher education, as it has always done, continues to attract attention regarding the need for revision and reform (Cochran-Smith and Fries, 2001; Darling-Hammond, 2000; Ferfolja, 2008; Smyth, 2006; Tinning, 2004; Zeichner, 2003). In Australia, for example, there are continuous calls for improved (new) teacher abilities in personal literacy levels, subject matter knowledge and pedagogical skill. Such accounts are prevalent in most Western developed countries and they tend to underline the sensitive and contested ideological terrain of teacher education that results in deeply divided opinions about it.

Similarly, arguments prevail around the significance of the practicum[1] in terms of impact on pre-service learning, its place in teacher education and the amount of time allocated to it within programmes. In addition, the role and indeed effectiveness of the initial year of teaching, as we suggest above referred to often as the induction or transition year, is also regarded as crucial in teacher development. We acknowledge that these issues are clearly of great national and even international importance, certainly in the developed world. However, the purpose of this book is not specifically to engage in polemic discourse about the place, role and function of these particular stages of teacher development. Admittedly the project (and therefore this book) came into existence against the policy backdrop of such contested discourse. The ebb and flow of such discourse given its inherent political nature, we are sure, will continue unabated. Rather, our interests across the nearly six-year life of this research project (comprised of a one-year pilot study, more than a year of development work, a three-year nationally funded research project, and the conclusion of a Ph.D.) were in delving more deeply into what is *actually going on*, and *where*, in terms of the school as the place of work-based learning for emerging teachers. In other words, we wanted to attempt to document the nature of the experience of final year Health and Physical Education[2] (HPE) pre-service teachers as they engaged in their final practicum and then transitioned into the profession and undertook the 'induction' year as beginning teachers. Readers, we are sure, will acknowledge that the arguments for more workplace time in schools for pre-service teacher learning (Colquhoun, 2005) are rife and imbued with (as we have observed) more than just a little partisan politics. We argue that such a discussion needs to be far more informed by the nature and quality of such professional learning rather than simply (and complacently in our view) assuming that more must surely be 'better', a position which attracts various levels of support around the world. We were far more interested in the school as a place of work for *emerging* teachers (we refer here to both pre-service teachers and beginning teachers) where we assumed that learning to become a member of a profession takes place.

Where do we learn?

It is argued that we live in a pedagogized society (see Bernstein, 1996; Singh, 2001). This means not so much that the world is full of teachers (even though we could think of the world this way – or at least view pedagogical work as ubiquitous); rather it means that the opportunities to learn are more widely distributed than ever before. However, at the same time there is a form of centralized control over what is learned, whether this is through an accredited (national) curriculum, the selected 'science' that allegedly endorses a product on a billboard or in a television advertisement, or electronically based information. This abundance of information and its relative ease of access affects not only children in school but also university and college students, trade apprentices and those in a range of professional preparation programmes (invariably but not exclusively in higher education) or in early career contexts. This may seem to have little resonance with the central plot of this book at this stage but consider this little example. We would argue that any keen exercisers out there, at the point of injury, use the Internet to self-diagnose. It may well be that this is purely a precursor to seeking professional help. Nonetheless, it is a practice that until a few years ago was mostly absent. In the days before electronic media and information availability, very few people self-diagnosed by going to the local library and borrowing or consulting a book on functional anatomy, much less sports medicine. The same may be said of building a cabinet, learning a language … the examples are almost endless. There is no suggestion here that this is either good or otherwise; rather it is an observation of the widespread, almost universal availability of information, (so-called) facts or knowledge, instructions, guidance, advice and so on. Moreover, it is an acknowledgement of the ubiquity of pedagogy … a pedagogized society if you will.

One might think that this digital revolution would have a profound effect on how people become educated and qualified in the professions that leads to accreditation and therefore being granted a 'licence' to practise. To some extent this is true and in some cases professional education has become (not always for educational or pedagogical reasons), an 'online' experience (see Metzler (2009) for the case of Western Governors University or WGU, accredited to deliver totally online teacher education programmes). Rizvi and Lingard (2010) talk about the globalization of knowledge but at the same time how the control of that knowledge has certain centralized features (for example, through large media companies or more increasingly Internet-based companies like Google). This leads, they argue, to a globalizing of policy-making, invariably informed by the neo-liberal imaginary (see Ball (2012) for more on this topic). An outcome of this is the almost excessive degree of what we will call 'policy cloning' in social, monetary and inevitably education (including higher education) policies.

How much change?

In some senses (and contexts), however, the opportunities for professional learning have not changed much. They may be enhanced with all sorts of online and digital opportunities and support mechanisms, but for the most part the structural constraints for learning in the professions are based on an industrial model. Thus, if we return to the 'professionals-in-training' referred to earlier, time in the workplace 'practising' craft is regarded as non-negotiable. Indeed, those who might choose to argue otherwise would be quickly labelled heretics or loonies, or some other epithet. Hence in medicine (in particular) – time on the wards is seen almost as a rite of passage or, better still, a baptism of fire (see Cooke *et al.*, 2010). Similarly, in nursing, teaching, social work, etc. the *practicum* as we have suggested holds particular privilege.

We use the word 'practicum' (or descriptions of it) with caution. This is because increasingly around the world within the context of teacher preparation (sometimes referred to as Initial Teacher Education or ITE) or teacher education (some still use the term teacher training) which is the subject of our focus, time in the workplace is seen as the *only* or the *best* way to learn how to be a teacher. In other words, time in the workplace (regardless almost of the quality of that time – see some of our earlier work) is how learning to be a teacher is conducted. In the United Kingdom this is a hotly debated and hotly contested policy issue. We will talk more about this later; for now it is important to acknowledge this as an example of what we suggested earlier as the globalization of policy (Rizvi and Lingard, 2010) or, as we suggest, 'policy cloning'. In other words, policy enactment in education in particular around the globe is predicated on the mores of the polity rather than on evidence. These mores are invariably informed by a neo-liberal, free market-inspired agenda that is monitored via managerial regulatory practices (Apple, 2004). It is an approach to education generally, and the preparation of teachers specifically, that ties education squarely to the economy. Educational policy then is the contested terrain upon which arguments about how best to educate teachers are played out and, within the context of these arguments, the role of work-based experience (and therefore potentially learning) is debated and it is clear that in some jurisdictions the cleaving of teacher education away from universities, to be placed in schools, is a stalking discourse.

Educational policy and learning to be a teacher: reform, reform and yet more reform

As we have indicated already, there is little doubt that teacher education around the world, for much of its recent history, has been mired in controversy. Primarily the controversy is ideological (see Cochran-Smith and Fries (2005) for an American account of this controversy). For the most part, teacher education seems to be regarded as a hotbed of radicalism that needs to be exorcised to enable more sensible programmes to be developed around the principles of technical skill, competence and subject matter knowledge. We are pretty convinced that it would be hard to find an argument against such principles. However, most researchers in teacher education would regard such principles as important but mostly insufficient for the preparation of teachers to meet the needs of twenty-first-century schoolchildren, especially since it seems almost impossible to predict the kind of world children will be a part of by the time they leave school. This is not how the situation might be perceived by various sections of the media. It will come as no great surprise to learn that a newspaper like the *Daily Telegraph* in the UK would lead its education editorial emphasizing subject matter knowledge and suggesting that teacher education students receive far too much 'classroom theory' (see Paton, 2011).

It may well be that the interlocking contestations around teacher education are examples of what Cuban (2008) calls *tame* problems. That is, they are relatively procedural and a large number of solutions may be brought to bear to address them, such as better training in classroom management, a more content-based curriculum, increased 'practice' in pedagogy and so on. In truth, education, including teacher education, is more likely to be a *wicked* problem. This is an intractable concern that has no end-point solution and one that can only be managed, often it would seem, in the developed world at least, within the context of the electoral cycle. Cuban prefers the term 'dilemma', in that the dilemma of education – and, we would argue, of teacher education also – can only be managed through difficult choices between alternatives. The overriding problem of course is that the available alternatives are more often than not politically aligned. It would seem that whoever can best mobilize the electorate gets to choose the alternative. Consider the latest example in Australia. Most readers will know that Australia has a democratically elected two-house parliamentary system. As with any democracy, Australian Federal governments change from time to time and this invariably means the appointment of an Education Minister with a reform agenda, especially if the party in power has changed (and sometimes even if it hasn't). Inevitably, the 'reform' agenda is based on 'righting' the errors of the previous administration around curriculum making and curriculum design.[3] Hence the Australian (National) Curriculum[4] is a broad curriculum initiative in core school subject areas that aims to have all children across a nation of federated states study roughly the same thing – the idea will not be lost on readers from the UK who would know that their education system went through such a process in the late 1980s and early 1990s.

The Australian Curriculum, then, several years in the making, informed by a wide-ranging evidence base, the subject of numerous working parties, submissions (in their thousands) and consultative meetings, becomes the subject *of* reform by virtue of a change in government. In a sense the political colour of the party in power is almost irrelevant – the message here is that the intense politicization of education continues unabated. Meanwhile, the universities and colleges mostly (though it should be said not exclusively) responsible for teacher education wait in the wings, second-guessing ministerial decisions anxious to bed down some policy related to teacher education. We are sure many readers will find this example very familiar. Health and Physical Education (the full name of the school subject area in Australia), far from being immune from this type of agenda, is generally caught up in such reform as a consequence of its contested subject matter.

Motivations for reform

Motivations for reform are invariably immersed in the language of failure (Mayer *et al.*, 2008). Cochran-Smith and Fries (2005, p. 75), for example, show how the launch of Sputnik in 1957 (which put the former Soviet Union into space ahead of the Americans) sent the USA into a frenzy (they use the term 'public hysteria' from Lagemann, 2000) where the perceived failure of the nation's schools to prepare future citizens for a technological world was matched only by the derision aimed at the nation's teacher educators and the programmes they ran in universities. We are sure this will have an all-too-familiar ring to it. It was only a few years after Sputnik that Koerner (1963) declared that American teachers were being 'mis-educated'. Today, the near hysteria, though largely media driven, points to the failure of teachers to prepare the children in their charge to compete in international comparative testing regimes as being the central problem in education. There are plenty of believers in Australia who similarly consider pre-service teachers in Australia to be mis-educated (see, e.g. Donnelly, 2004). Of course it is not only those in high office who have something to say about teacher education. Many pre-service teachers, for example, often assume that the most significant part of their course will be the practicum. As we found, for some the story is a little different once they have been in schools. However, we should not be at all surprised by this initial enthusiasm for the practicum. In appearance at least, it must seem like the opportunity to really try out this thing called teaching … the very reason for being in the course in the first place. When it becomes apparent that the experience may be constrained by convention, tradition and compliance needs, is unnecessarily stressful and for the most part artificial, the practicum poses a rather more significant philosophical challenge. For others however, this seems not to matter. The fact is that time in schools learning how to be a teacher is regarded as so obviously the place where the most important learning takes place that to argue otherwise would place one on the fringes of insanity.

However, as Phelan and Sumison (2008) suggest, 'practice' is generally regarded as a one-size-fits-all procedure governed by pedagogical rules and a set of generalizable principles. Theory, they claim, is eschewed because of its irrelevance to the job at hand. It seems not to matter what theory either, by the way; whether it is the musings of a dead American behaviourist or a dead French historian, any theory it seems is despised in equal measure. As Phelan and Sumison continue, the sustained attempts to use reductionist approaches to generalizable knowledge that renders being a teacher more procedural than pedagogical are virtually universal. Phelan (2005) says the push to return teacher education simply into the realm of the practical has been overwhelming and Levine's report in 2006 is a prime example of this. Levine, in a staggeringly instrumentalist view of teacher education, proclaimed that programmes of teacher education in the USA were failing to prepare teachers for the standards-based accountability-driven classroom where the only real measure of success (and, one assumes, therefore excellence) is student achievement. We are sure that if Levine were in close enough proximity, the various elected Minsters or Secretaries of Education around the world bent on 'reform' would be heartily slapping him on the back. All this serves to underline the idea that teacher education is for the most part under siege largely from particular public interest groups (it has to be said predominantly groups that sit on the right of the political spectrum) who find nothing of any merit in university-based teacher education and who seek to remove as many barriers to becoming a teacher as possible, and this includes bypassing university-based teacher education altogether (Mayer *et al.*, 2008). One could be forgiven for assuming that this is a right-wing conspiracy. However, much of the teacher education reform in the United Kingdom has occurred recently and under a Labour administration. In Australia, similar education (and higher education) policies were initiated under the Australian Labor Party and in the USA Barack Obama's administration has retained some of the most contentious and divisive education policies. This demonstrates perhaps that the neo-liberal imaginary has indeed secured an embedded reach in the psyche of all politicians, regardless of their political banner.

What makes this all the more contentious is that arguments about how teacher education should be organized and structured (more years, less years, university or non-university based, apprenticeship or practicum models, etc.) are seldom based on any evidence. There is good reason for this, as Zeichner and Conklin (2005) clearly identify in an extensive meta-analysis of teacher education in the USA. The evidence is clearly mixed, with few if any definitive answers about how best to educate teachers for working in classrooms of the twenty-first century. This is hardly a great a surprise given the wide variety of methods used to research teacher education in the United States (and elsewhere for that matter). As a consequence Zeichner and Conklin (2005) claim that it is extraordinarily difficult to say anything definitive about teacher education (in the USA at least), in terms of its efficacy, value for money, effectiveness, capacity to build a committed workforce and so on. They are able to point to some trend data which suggest that teachers from traditional programmes (e.g. a four-year undergraduate programme) regard themselves as better prepared as teachers than those from highly truncated programmes such as the Teach for America programme. In addition, those from five-year programmes were more likely to stay in teaching for longer than those from a shorter programme, including graduate entry programmes. However, the limited usefulness of the data across many studies often stemmed from methodological limitations. They do not suggest that the research has been sloppy; rather that identifying variables to isolate and then test is extremely difficult and few studies identify what the prospective teachers themselves take in to the teacher education programmes to begin with. A more recent review of US teacher preparation (Greenberg *et al.*, 2013, p. 94), an exercise that has ranked 608 institutions' teacher education programmes, recently concluded:

> Teacher education is at a turning point. With the publication of the *Teacher Prep Review*, the consumers of teacher preparation – aspiring teachers and districts – at last have the information they need to choose what programs to patronize. Collectively, their choices will shift the market toward programs that make training a priority. Policymakers, too, will raise their expectations of teacher preparation in the wake of the *Teacher Prep Review*, and will implement new accountability mechanisms to ensure that more new teachers get what they need to help their students succeed. By productively engaging with these developments, teacher educators can help propel the country to the top of the global ranks of educational achievement.

Again, the language in this paragraph is instructive – 'consumers', 'choose', 'market', 'training', 'accountability', 'succeed', and 'global ranks' – and potentially foreshadows a shift in US policy and practices reflective of an explicit neo-liberal discourse (see Macdonald, 2014).

Given the neo-liberal times in which we live, the alleged 'failure' of teacher education programmes to train high-quality teachers capable of producing educated citizens who can complete on a global stage make those programmes easy targets for derision (Ball, 2006). It is not difficult to recognize that what is meant by 'high-quality teacher' is frequently tied to compliance and measurement techniques that have the most extraordinary 'narrowing' effect on how teachers' work is perceived (see Ball, 2003; Zeichner, 2010). And, by the way, this narrowing is not confined to politicians. The media's scope to 'take the population along' with the deficit view of teachers is mind-boggling. In the United Kingdom, a simple blog-line following the comments by an Education Secretary of the time about lengthening the school day, shortening the summer holiday (because it was born out of an agricultural need and no longer relevant) and starting children at school earlier was well supported, with blog commentary praising the Minster and his moves to de-unionize and professionalize the teacher profession and how this would mirror the Asian miracle in education. It is a position that has currency in Australia where various commentators frequently point to how countries in Asia are always close to the top of ranking tables of pupil performance. The success of Scandinavian schools in producing high-performing pupils by using quite different and far less draconian approaches is often forgotten or more likely dismissed. It is a line commentators generally peddle as part of the 'systematic attack waged on schools of education, teacher educators and researchers' (Mayer *et al.*, 2008, p. 83) that Mayer and colleagues suggest has been conducted by Newscorp in Australia in particular but on a global scale given the reach of the multinational.

The corollary of all this is the way in which such educational commentary shapes education, policy, teacher education policy and the practice of both. Increasingly in the developed world this seems to equate to the foregrounding of subject matter knowledge – allegedly best acquired *away* from schools of education or their equivalent while the 'rest' (the learning to be a teacher bit) can be simply learned on the job. There is a groundswell of support for 'training on the job model' across the developed world (see Phelan and Sumison, 2008) and what appears to stand for 'quality', a question we were grappling with earlier, appears to be reducible to the efficient delivery of a state-sanctioned syllabus across the mandated years of compulsory education. In Australia there are attempts to limit the impact of such reductionism through a discussion of professional standards that account for a lot more than the delivery of 'content'. However, such a solution is far from perfect and a glance at the Australian Institute for Teaching and School Leadership national standards reveals an intimidating list of standards and levels of performance by which teachers may be 'judged'. It may seem a statement of the obvious but in Australia, teacher education programmes (wherever they may be located) are required to prepare teachers who meet the professional entry-level standards. We do not suggest that this is inappropriate. It is nonetheless another example of the audit culture (see Ball, 2006) with which we now live and in which we must function.

The place of the 'practicum' in teacher education reform

We indicated earlier that the word 'practicum' may be quite meaningless to some readers, so we should begin this section by ensuring a broad understanding of what we are talking about. The 'practicum' is a term that applies to the work-integrated learning aspects of (most commonly) professional programmes of study. The word practicum has broad application in that it tends to mean the same thing, for example, in nursing as it does in teacher education. That is, it is a common term for the part of the 'training' that is done in the 'real world' situation. In teaching, were you from another era or jurisdiction you might recognize this better as 'teaching practice' or the 'teaching rounds'. The reason to raise this now is that for some authorities this idea is increasingly an anachronism. The reason for this, as we alluded to above, is that increasingly teacher education is something that in some places is no longer regarded as the *exclusive* domain of higher education where selective periods of time are spent in schools. Rather there are designs for teacher education that move towards a model where learning to be a teacher *is* the experience in schools. We do not necessarily refer here to the truncated forms of teacher education mentioned earlier (such as Teach for America, its Australian counterpart Teach for Australia and the UK model TeachFirst). Rather we are referring here to the wholesale movement of the responsibility for educating teachers to the school sector. As Furlong (2013) describes, in 2012 in the UK the Secretary of State for Education set out a goal to award over 50 per cent of all teacher 'training' places to schools within the life of that Parliament. The funding to support this was to follow the students into schools, and schools were at liberty to *buy* the support services they needed from a university of its choice or another accredited service provider – hence creating a teacher education support service market. As Furlong (2013) continues, there is something of a paradox here. The school systems to which policy-makers most frequently turn to identify high-performing school students, as we alluded to earlier, are Finland, Singapore and Hong Kong which, as it turns out, 'have forms of teacher education that place strong emphasis on the practicalities of teaching in schools but also retain a commitment to university-based provision' (Furlong, 2013, p. 5). The paradox then should be obvious. We exalt high-performing school systems yet ignore the teacher education programmes that serve the system. We appreciate that the relationship between these is not as linear as we are describing here; nonetheless, it seems somewhat gratuitous that no credit may be ascribed to the very system that supplies what one assumes are highly qualified and highly respected teachers.

So, as Furlong (2013) suggests, high-performing school systems are supported by highly effective university-based teacher education programmes which have as part of their programme dedicated and well-supported 'in-school' experiences (practicum) that support the on-campus learning. This is a model common to the research team on this project even where for some of them their teacher education was over 30 years ago. However, it is important to note that Furlong (2013) does not support the dinosaur approach to these matters. He argues that to remain the driver of educational practice for the twenty-first century, universities must continue to change and grow to suit these needs, and developments in pedagogical and curriculum research must inform teacher education research and educational practice more broadly. In a sense this endorses the role of universities and eschews the ' "craft" oriented view of teaching' (see Whitty, 2013). For both Furlong and Whitty, the university retains its importance in teacher education. While the policy imperative (in the UK in particular and in some US states) may sideline this view, for those who support the role of the university in teacher education, the practicum similarly retains its importance. The question surrounding the practicum however has always related to what this experience looks like.

Regardless of the structure of a university-based teacher education program (graduate entry, undergraduate programmes, etc.), the practicum components are invariably constructed around visits to schools, followed by consolidated time and then extended time in schools. As Whitty (2013) points out, even the House of Commons Select Committee on Education acknowledged that there were serious risks to reducing the roles of universities in teacher education and that the retention of theoretical and research elements to support significant 'in-school' experiences were crucial.

Physical Education Teacher Education (PETE)

How PETE has morphed and developed, and indeed been compelled to change over the past 40 years, has been written about widely and needs no great detail here (see Macdonald *et al.*, 1999; Kirk and Macdonald, 2001). Suffice it to say that the scientization of physical education teacher education has led to changes in the status and structure of programmes (Kirk *et al.*, 1997; see also Macdonald (2014) for a more recent analysis based on the neo-liberal imaginary). In some programmes socio-cultural aspects have been denuded or removed altogether and in others they have led to new types of programmes related to sport and physical activity. In the United States a change of name (and some would argue identity) to Kinesiology was clearly significant. In most programmes the practical courses (in games or gymnastics or swimming, etc.) that once dominated PETE programmes (especially in the Certificate or Diploma days) have all but disappeared in favour of academic course work. In some respects this been reflected in the development of research programmes into curriculum, pedagogy and learning and, more recently, assessment in physical education. Thus, though there have been changes to programmes since the claim of disciplinary status for physical education by Franklin Henry in the mid-1960s (a cause given impetus earlier by Eleanor Metheny), the requirement of those wishing to become physical education teachers to spend time in school 'working' as teachers has been retained, legislated for, and minimum time standards (i.e. number of days) established.

At the same time there has been significant work undertaken about how those interested in teaching physical education are socialized into it (see Templin and Schemmp, 1989) and work conducted by Lawson in the 1980s (see Lawson, 1983, 1986, 1988; Dewar and Lawson, 1984) discussed the idea of the 'subjective' warrant, something to which we return later in the book. At this point suffice it to say that the dispositions, desires and interests (usually in sport) that take people into PETE were identifiable through this research. Later, this work was conceptualized using the tools of Bourdieu (1997) and some of the earlier work associated with this project (see Sirna *et al.*, 2008, 2010) is an example of this. Hence those who go into PETE programmes have been clearly identified, and the identifiable features for this have been cemented even further through more recent research and include sport loving, body conscious, mesomorphic, and the relationships among these features tend to be unproblematic for the candidates (see McCullick *et al.*, 2012; Wrench and Garrett, 2012). PETE students are also invariably high performing and increasing in recent years; this means academically as well as in sport as the university entrance requirements have edged upward.

Perhaps the ongoing challenge for PETE has been the discourse of 'crisis' that has surrounded physical education more broadly. As Swabey and Penney (2011) describe, the crisis discourse has flowed across international boundaries since the late 1980s. The language of crisis may be more tied up with discourse alliances between various vested interest groups. Here Swabey and Penny (2011) point to Thorpe's (2000) analysis of crisis in which it is argued that much of the contention around physical education (internationally) has been around purpose and relevance in children's lives, and as a profession we continue to grapple with this well into the twenty-first century.

More recently, entangled among the competing interests seeking to influence PETE are sport and physical activity as a health intervention, the place of fundamental motors skills (FMS) education, status and curriculum time in schools, and what these interests might mean for the preparation of teachers. In some cases the actual name of the school subject area (for example, in Australia in 1992, physical education was subsumed for a time under the broader banner of

'Health') is an important concern. It needs to be acknowledged that in Australia, the severity (or even the existence of) some of the axes of crisis, for example, the deterioration of FMS, drop-out rates (seemingly associated with low motor competence) were equivocal, and yet these discourses persisted (see Swabey, 2006; Swabey and Penney, 2011) and still do today. Swabey and Penney (2011) have maintained that Health and Physical Education remains in a precarious position and that the language of crisis remains. The contemporary crises surrounding HPE are now framed by its role in combating obesity, inactivity, excessive sitting and screen time, diet and nutrition. These factors are considered to be crises on a global scale and school physical education (with its variations on health orientations) is offered up as the solution (see Dowda *et al.*, 2005; Trost, 2004; McKenzie and Lounsbery, 2009).

The challenge for PETE then is how to prepare teachers to enter this contested space for being able to critically analyse competing policy texts and make sound educational decisions related to curriculum, pedagogy and assessment, and increasingly, public health policy. As Metzler explained (2009), using his own university as a descriptor, this process invariably requires programmes to ensure that prospective teachers 'get enough field experiences with diverse student groups and across several grade levels', and to 'be provided quality supervision and support' (p. 305). He then goes on to say that this must be experienced (in the case of PETE) in a second teaching area – a common theme for most of us in teacher education. What is interesting however about Metzler's (2009) analysis of the crisis of teacher education and of reform upon reform upon reform (Metzler's description of almost 100 years of reform is comprehensive) is that HPE may become positioned (and its existence justified), as we suggested above, as an antidote to the crises of obesity and underactivity. The kind of 'practice' this may require in the field may be distilled down to the capacity to reduce (and measure) pupils' BMI. There are some who would endorse a HPE programme founded on these and associated principles (Trost, 2004; McKenzie and Lounsbery, 2009). Thankfully, current practice in HPE is not so constrained, and indeed the new Australian curriculum for HPE has at its core the 'educative' role of HPE (see Macdonald, 2013); therefore learning in the field or the 'workplace' remains an important facet for both pre-service and beginning teachers in coming to grips with the wide-ranging complexities of HPE.

Our research

Our research interests associated with the 'workplace' were very specific. Our focus was fairly and squarely on what is known locally as the departmental office or staffroom. To introduce this we have included a short narrative that follows. We are sure that the motivations for the research will become abundantly clear.

> As tends to happen in many teacher education contexts, pre-service teachers placed close enough to the university often visit the campus during their practicum. This may be to catch up with others in the same

programme or to gather resources or equipment. For us as teacher educators this is an opportunity to say 'Hi' and to ask them how things are going on their practicum experience. And so it was when one of us encountered a student back on campus after the school day had finished. Fully expecting the usual 'yeah everything is great' response (the anticipated response regardless of the situation), the student was asked what to many must be an irksome question: 'How is it going?' On this occasion the student could not contain himself.

He proceeded to tell a tale that was a litany of events that would have challenged the most thick-skinned of students. He told how he was introduced to staffroom cricket in the first week of his practicum. This game involved the use of a cricket ball (for those not familiar with the game this is a very hard, leather-bound ball with a seam involving six lines of stitching that usually divides the ball into halves; the ball is a little larger than a tennis ball or a baseball). In the situation described to us, the ball was thrown around in the staffroom and it had to be fended away by the 'batter' using a shortened – in other words, sawn-off – cricket bat. Not being entirely sure how to conduct himself, the pre-service teacher noncommittedly sat watching the game at his designated desk and was subsequently struck on the head with the ball. As if this were not humiliating enough, his 'incompetence' was met with howls of derision, name-calling and questions about his sexuality.

Picture the scene back on campus, the story being related to a senior member of the academic staff who starts to fume at the ears as the story unfolds. This reaction is hardly surprising, since as it turns out he has some equally troubling stories of his own to tell from his visits to schools. A few days later other staff members had got to hear about this over coffee. This and other stories that had been sent back from a range of practicum school settings started to paint a fuller picture. In among the stories of enjoyment, fulfilment and success were tales of hyper-masculinity, rampant sexism, xenophobic attitudes, blatant disregard for the role of mentor or adviser, dismissal of campus-based knowledge, commentary on pre-service teachers' personal size, shape, weight, sexual orientation and other belittling observations all of which appeared to emanate from within the departmental staffroom or office.

This idea of a departmental staffroom probably warrants some explanation. In Australia, like many schooling systems around the world, it is not uncommon in secondary (high) schools for each subject department such as Mathematics or Science or HPE to have its own staffroom for teachers from the same specialization, or to have their home desks clustered together in a particular space. Such environments take many guises. For example, they are sometimes shared with another department, or in small schools clustered within a whole-staff area. Indeed, we witnessed a plethora of such spatial arrangements in this project. In other schools of course, departments may be located in designated rooms that are close to the suite of teaching rooms that the department most often uses. An obvious example of this might be a science department staffroom next to the science labs. What is common to all of the departmental 'places' is that they are likely to sit apart from the main 'common' room where, for example, 'whole-school' staff meetings, lunch, social gatherings or briefings may be held. For one of us whose school teaching career was in England, this was less common except for the HPE department and there were three reasons for this: location, location, location! The likely location of the HPE base tends to be governed by close access to playing fields (called ovals in Australia), to gyms and sports halls, and to equipment-storage facilities. Hence the idea of a HPE department staffroom or office probably transfers across similar cultures. The full complement of the research team could each tell different stories about the locations of the various departments of which they have been a part.

For those of us who experienced teaching Physical Education (PE) in England, such a place was often little more than a small room between the gym and the changing (or locker) rooms and showers where one could sit and gulp a cup of tea or coffee in the break before the next lesson. For one of us who taught in Scotland it was a small room where the six HPE teachers barely fitted around the table and was above the gym. For two of us who have spent most of their time teaching in Australia it could have been any of the following: a noisy cordoned-off section of the Manual Arts[5] construction area next to courts, ovals/playing fields and equipment sheds, or sharing with affiliated science teachers next to their labs at the opposite end to the HPE teaching areas; in a designated HPE staffroom attached to a new sports hall and playing fields; or in a tiny, dark, shared space next to the equipment shed with two other HPE teachers.

In Aotearoa/New Zealand one of us had witnessed a state-of-the-art multi-purpose hall with breakout classrooms, coaching suite and a staffroom equipped with the latest technology, to all the HPE teachers crammed into a mezzanine room-cum-equipment room above the gym. In Japan one of us witnessed a large room with teachers' desks, many books and movement equipment, a refrigerator, and examples of student work. We have seen similar examples of all of these forms of staffrooms in other countries around the world, such as Canada, the USA, Eire, Spain, Singapore and Hong Kong.

The staffroom, as a place, may well be more than a 'room'. It will be where the HPE staff gather, where there are computers and workstations, telephones, a repository for resources and so on. Needless to say it is a place where HPE pre-service and beginning teachers can potentially spend much of their non-teaching time. As a consequence we considered that such a place could be a significant site of professional learning and one that we came to realize, through a series of events, narratives and in some cases horror stories, was worthy of study.

In this book we draw on samples of the datasets, which we prefer to call constructed field texts, and we represent them in the form of thematic accounts. However, we also make use of stories and narrative and we do this for several reasons. First, narrative was an important research method that we employed, along with others, across time. There seemed to be great power in narrative to represent not only the participants in the study but also the study itself. Second, we managed to follow a number of the participants into the field as they became beginning teachers and their individual stories of development contributed to the broader research narrative. At this point our purpose is to invite you, the reader, to delve more deeply into understandings of why professional workplace learning is a topical but also a shifting object of research and practice.

Illeris (2011) suggests that 'workplace learning' has become a popularized 'slogan' (his choice of word) over the past 20 to 30 years and perhaps reflects the increased degree of vocationalism that has crept into university coursework. Irrespective of the value of this evolutionary shift, it is hard to argue against Illeris. Moreover, there is an increasing expectation from employers that they want their recruits to be work ready, competent, even though these might be ill-defined, and once in the workforce to demonstrate a high capacity to learn through the performance of work. Of course this has always been the case in professionally oriented programmes like teaching and nursing. As we have indicated already, these types of programmes have always had a professional placement component to a lesser or greater degree. In this study we subsequently realized that there is no *one* professional space within a placement; there are many. There may be a small number where teachers, pre-service teachers and beginning teachers spend most of their time, but they are not the only places where school personnel venture.

Perhaps what is more important is the idea that what goes on in those spaces is of profound importance to becoming a professional in any given field. Thus, in the case of teaching, the very idea that a pre-service teacher will go into a school to learn how to teach as a consequence of being there is far too simplistic. A pre-service teacher will go into a school and find that learning to be a teacher occurs in many spaces within the school and most likely in many spaces within a department. Some of these spaces are likely to be more effective than others in the process of learning to be a teacher. The very idea that the school is a simple, homogeneous learning space is misleading. This position merely reifies school as the context of learning to become a teacher, where professional learning is always relevant and always positive, and allegedly always important.

Of even greater concern, in this study and as we will report throughout the book, we found that some spaces in some schools were actually detrimental, even counter-productive to becoming a teacher. In the case of HPE, the focus of this book, those spaces were often inextricably bound up with the precise focus of the research: the departmental office or staffroom. We want to stress that not every experience for every pre-service teacher, or beginning teacher for that matter, in every school was negative. However, at the end of the project we were left with the view that professional learning in in the departmental staffroom, both pre- and post-certification, is something that could be done a great deal better. Later in the book we explore why we take this view and what it may mean for mentoring, for policies surrounding the practicum and for teacher education more broadly.

What you will find in this book

This book is about teacher workplaces as sites of professional learning. Using shortened narratives and other field text samples, such as that above from the experiences of pre-service and beginning teachers, we explore how, where and why professional knowledge is developed. In Part I, we investigate the notions of *professional, workplace learning*, and the literature associated with *teacher 'practicum', 'fieldwork'* or *'school experience'* (Chapter 2). We then describe the research methodology which guided the study (Chapter 3) and offer five significant dimensions of workplace learning which we consider would be useful in making sense of our research findings (Chapter 4). We then try to convey what the data told us using these significant dimensions in Part II (Chapters 5 to 9). These dimensions are:

- Social tasks.
- Performance and practice.
- Identity/subjectivities.
- Space and place.
- Micropolitics.

We use a variety of pre-service teacher and beginning teacher research findings to illustrate these significant dimensions of workplace learning and draw on a variety of theoretical positions to understand what might be going on. Not all of the data we collected have been used in this book and indeed some are already in the public domain, as indicated in the Acknowledgements. In Part III, we consider the issue of policy as a central concern and try to re-engage a discussion about the role of the workplace in professional learning and how this plays out against policy discourse in education, teacher education and curriculum policy-making. In doing so we discuss the policy implications of teacher education and beginning teacher induction and juxtapose this with what we learned from this study, particularly with respect to the idea of a 'safe' (see Illeris, 2011), 'healthy' (see lisahunter, 2010) and educational/professional workplace. In concluding the book we reflect on the potential contribution of understanding workplace learning through the interrelated dimensions we have identified. We further consider, as we do throughout the book, the evolving challenges that lie ahead at a time of educational reform, rhetorical or otherwise, and of equal significance we take a futures orientation to consider just what a HPE teacher of the future will need to look like.

Notes

1 This is the common term for in-school experience in Queensland, Australia, also referred to as 'prac'. Elsewhere it is known as teaching rounds, teaching practice, section, and other, similar terms.
2 This is the formal name of the school subject in Australia. We acknowledge that in other countries health is not necessarily linked to physical education in the same way.

For the purposes of this book Health and Physical Education may be read as Physical Education. However, to stay true to the research project we will use the Australian nomenclature and its acronym throughout.

3 It may seem cynical to suggest it but it often seems as if education is where people try to make their name before they are moved to more serious portfolios like Defence, The Treasury, Foreign Affairs, etc. In other words, education is an easy target for reform.

4 The word 'national' is not ordinarily used in the Australian context – here it is to purvey intent.

5 It is difficult to translate this subject across to other cultures, though it is probably self-explanatory. In Britain this may have approximated to Craft Design and Technology (CDT) before the advent of the National Curriculum in 1989. CDT included subjects such as woodwork and metalwork, but also included in some schools home economics (or cookery). In the USA, the subject 'Shop' (workshop) may have at one time been equivalent to Manual Arts. Such subject areas, once the sole avenue for children on a non-academic route through school, are in a constant state of change as a consequence of advancing technology. Different students on a range of pathways now take subjects such as this and will often complement studies in Information Technology, Engineering and Science.

2 Defining the subject

The profession/al, and workplace learning

Introduction: work ... a small word in a neo-liberal world

It is almost a cliché to suggest that the world of work has changed in the post-industrial world. Under the auspices of advanced capitalism manufacturing, once the central plank of an advanced economy, is now increasingly located in the developing world where labour and land are both cheaper and easier to control in the absence or relative weakness of worker organizations. Most financial services are global, market economics on a global scale being the accepted orthodoxy, part of this orthodoxy being to scale back the role and more importantly the intervention of government, and often this is achieved through the networking of governance mechanisms, whereby *governance* is distributed beyond the direct involvement of government (see Ball (2012) for more on this). We pick this up later in the final section of the book. Much of this can be traced back to the influence of (among others) the likes of Friedrich Hayek (2007) and Milton Friedman (2002) and is what is generally referred to as the 'Washington Consensus' or neo-liberalism (Harvey, 2005) whose DNA is often traced back to classical liberalism. Krugman (2007) argues that this is the dominant economic discourse within most advanced economies (or sometimes called first economies), though what led to it being embraced so completely remains unclear. There are many texts[1] that deal thoroughly with such issues and they are not for discussion here. The consequences of this dislocation of labour and services is that, for most people working in the advanced economies of world, change is a common feature. That said, what seems to have persisted in the developed world in spite of the general shift to less economic regulation and a greater dispersal of the provision of services and the manufacture of goods is, as we suggested in Chapter 1, the way in which a novice is socialized into a profession or even a trade, and the degree to which this process of training and point of transition is heavily regulated.

While the nature of what actually happens when one is *in* the workplace may have changed dramatically mainly through ongoing technological advancement, measures of accountability and performance audits, the process of moving *into* a range of professions and trades has plenty of commonalities across the spectrum of different types of work. As we said in the previous chapter, there are multiple pathways and combinations of work/study/practice that provide the access point to a particular line of work. This is then followed by a period of time (it is sometimes a formal process) loosely described as 'induction' – in other words, the very early period in a trade or profession (or even a job) where there is a degree of monitoring, mentoring and guidance. Within the contexts of trades or professions this process may also have an associated time requirement. This might be represented by a period of probation (as is common in teaching), for example, or it might be a very short time frame, barely enough to cover occupational health and safety and a tick-box approach of demonstrated skills and techniques, as is often the case in highly casualized labour, or it might be a lengthier, more protracted time frame. Finally there is the acceptance as a 'beginner', whether it is teaching, law, nursing, engineering, the building trades, hairdressing, medicine, etc. While we acknowledge that not all types of work involve *all* of the described expectations, most work will require *some* of them. We would argue that all work, even casualized labour, is likely to have an induction period of some kind. A professional proceeds from this point to 'becoming experienced' or even an 'expert' over a period of time (often protracted), and this might involve some learning interventions such as professional development programmes, in addition to extensive 'learning on the job'.

In 1989, Wallace argued that work and specifically workplaces would become 'high-flex'. By this he meant that standardized modes of work (for example, of production lines or work based on predetermined plans) would become obsolete in a fast-changing globalized economy. If we can say anything about Wallace's predictions, it is that they perhaps underestimated the rate of change in the nature of work we would encounter. In essence he suggested that work would become increasingly 'customized' to suit work requirements or (as it turned out) the vagaries and almost capricious nature of markets. One of the likely effects Wallace (1989) predicted was the idea of up-skilling and down-skilling. In other words, some aspects of what was then understood as work would be reduced, or changed, in terms of their skills or knowledge requirements (contemporary examples might be factory-made roof trusses in the building industry – even flying bomber and missile attacks into hostile enemy territory). Other aspects of work, however, were likely to require ongoing knowledge and skill development (we can use the same example of flying an attack drone using a computer screen and controls!). Wallace's point was that learning through work was going to become an ever-increasingly important part of the work itself. As Wallace said, the 'New Economy' (p. 373) would be characterized by what he termed 'skill disruption' (p. 373) requiring learning, re-learning and unlearning the requirements associated with particular work. As he said, learning, training and skill upgrades were likely to be part of '*the subjective experience of workers*' (p. 373, italics in original). Wallace (1989) further comments that employers were likely to seek employees who knew how to learn. It is not unreasonable to suggest that much of what Wallace foresaw through his research has come to pass, even if he misread the intensity with which it might happen. Work, then, is not about simply moving into a 'job' or 'profession', or even performing the roles within them. As a consequence work, career, profession or simply a job cannot be regarded as a destination or even in some cases a 'lifetime state' (see Shutt, 2010). Rather, it is part of the state of reflexive becoming. That state is in part maintained through the processes of work and these processes involve extensive learning over a working lifetime.

The brave new world of work

Ulrich Beck (2000) coined the phrase 'the brave new world of work' in his book of that name to describe advanced capitalism and what he suggested is the Brazilianization of the West. By this he was suggesting that the surge in low-paid part-time contracted work is part of a modern orthodoxy related to first economies and then, by implication, the work that fuels those economies. While Beck's analysis is a more Europeanized account, and indeed a critique of the neo-liberal world in which we now live, it is worth drawing a little more from him.

First, it is useful to acknowledge Beck's idea that the notion of work is so omnipotent that any critique of it is 'open to the accusation of cynicism' (p. 10). He continues by suggesting that, in contrast to freedom in Ancient Greek and Roman terms being constructed through not having to work, modernity is defined by the freedom that flows from being in and having paid work. More recently Charlton (2011), in a detailed analysis of the economies of global development, suggests that freedom from chronic poverty in the underdeveloped world is most likely to be brought about through the employment created by industrialization. In addition, spokespersons for marginalized communities and groups argue that 'work' is a route to economic freedom and self-determination (see Steele, 2006; Pearson, 2009). More increasingly, then, 'work' is part of what defines 'being human' and 'being a citizen', and much more recently has come to define human beings politically. Notwithstanding the complexity surrounding those terms, one can see how through time, 'work' has become a central human value that shapes and reshapes a nation's citizenry. Paradoxically, according to Beck, we had arrived at a time where 'work', such a central pillar of human existence, is being reduced in order to increase productivity and in the process profitability (see Shutt (2010) for a more recent account on this subject). Beck's somewhat optimistic thesis is that such a situation should not be viewed with doom and gloom. Rather it is the dawning of a new work order where paid labour sits alongside leisure, unpaid work, family time and education in a seamless living of life where the demarcation between these facets of life is barely discernible. As one might imagine, Charlton's (2011) more critical global economic analysis varies significantly from Beck's position. For Beck however, this was the coming of a 'second modernity' which he saw as a less certain form of civil life where ecological crises, globalization, individualization and the absence of 'full' employment were likely to be the watchwords replacing certainty, collectivism, and the sovereignty of the nation state. In this, there is agreement with Charlton's analysis and according to Beck this is what increasingly defines a 'risk society' (1992).

Within the work context, we are focusing more specifically on those deemed as professional, and more specifically as part of the profession of teaching. It is useful to pause for a moment to try to get a tighter sense of what a professional actually is. For example, Brown (1992, p. 19) suggested that professionals are:

> workers whose qualities of detachment, autonomy, and group allegiance are more extensive than those found among other groups ... their attributes include a high degree of systematic knowledge; strong community orientation and loyalty; self-regulation; and a system of rewards defined and administered by the community of workers.

Historically, the three occupations identified as professions were medicine, divinity and law (see Larson 1978). By the late nineteenth century professions such as teaching, pharmacy and nursing were established (Bullock and Trombley, 1999), with trades and occupations becoming professions through 'the development of formal qualifications based upon education, apprenticeship, and examinations, the emergence of regulatory bodies with powers to admit and discipline members, and some degree of monopoly rights' (p. 689). Larson (1978) argues that in the USA (following its lead from Britain) between 1840 and 1887 the number of occupations considered to be professions rose to 11, indicating that entry into the professions for so long a birthright was now about talent and work. What may also be said about professions in Europe and the 'New World' is that the rise in their number is commensurate with the rise of industrial capitalism, and this progression has continued into the more advanced style of capitalism and its corporate form. On a more contemporary note, Jackson (2010, pp. 23–24) suggests that a profession is:

> a special type of occupation ... (possessing) corporate solidarity ... prolonged specialized training in a body of abstract knowledge, and a collectivity or service orientation ... a vocational sub-culture which comprises implicit codes of behaviour, generates an esprit de corps among members of the same profession, and ensures them certain occupational advantages ... (also) bureaucratic structures and monopolistic privileges to perform certain types of work ... professional literature, legislation, etc.

A professional therefore is one who subscribes to a profession, embodying many of the qualities of a profession as well as the more specific nature prescribed by the type of profession such as teaching. But the word 'professional' is both a noun and an adjective, a point made throughout the book. This has implications for how one is and should be as well as what practices and spaces are legitimized or not, including those practices reinforced in education, credentialing processes, and the shaping of the profession/al for and by its members.

It is reasonable to ask what connection there is between the sections above and teaching, learning to teach, and workplace learning in teacher education and induction. In the legitimation of membership and practices within pre-service teacher education, in workplace experience in schools, and beginning teacher induction and mentoring, the connections are robust, and this will become increasingly apparent. Suffice it to say at this point that education in the market ideology may be thought of as either an industry, to use a word from first modernity, or as a profession, and is hardly immune from the forces mentioned above. Hill (2008), confirming our earlier analysis, suggests that reforms around and within teacher education 'have been imbued with the dominant ideology of the market' (p. 210). Ball (2012), however, is perhaps more specific, suggesting that new public management mimics business practices in almost every way it can, and that we exist in a neo-liberal 'imaginary'.

Although we discussed teacher education in the USA earlier, Zeichner's (2010) position is worthy of further attention. He offers more detail regarding market ideology and perhaps with a greater sense of foreboding. While not necessarily reflective of *all* teacher education policies in *all* developed nations, Zeichner clearly identifies a trend of deregulation, marketization and alternative pathways into teaching. Ordinarily, diverse career pathways are not necessarily bad options. However, as Zeicher describes, the redistribution of funding to suppliers with relatively low accountability, modest standards, but who can show a sound business plan to investors including predicted profit margins, is creating a form of educational apartheid (Kozol, 2005). It is in this climate that children who live in the poorest and most impoverished areas of the country are more likely to be taught by teachers with the least amount of – and in some cases no – preparation. Hence the recruitment and 'training' of teachers is no longer exclusively the terrain of higher education but is open to other suppliers.

At this stage, the connection of this to our project may appear unclear. However, if we are in an audit society, as Ball (2003) suggests and we exist within the context of networked suppliers (Ball, 2012), then the preparation of new teachers is as much under scrutiny (and indeed open to competition) as anything else. Therefore, so too are the environments where that preparation is meant to take place. The pre-service teachers in this study (and then the teachers they became as they formally entered the profession) were required to learn in a community itself under pressure from the burden of expectation such as success at school sport, high scores and grades by students in the high-stakes senior programme, and minimization of costs associated with running a HPE department which traditionally has been expensive. Much of this expectation is driven by a marketized school system where the economic imprimatur of high enrolment numbers is of significant importance. As Zeichner (2010) suggests, in an audit society the work of a teacher is more about the performative than the substantive (see also Ball, 2003). In other words, for reasons of compliance to imposed standards and declining sovereignty over one's professionalism, teachers do 'what needs to be done' to be seen as conforming to a system. These are hardly the best conditions in which to learn about one's chosen occupation, let alone resist such practices.

It is into this context that we thrust pre-service and beginning teachers, fully expecting them to learn through professional engagement, mentoring programmes and mechanisms of so-called support. It is reasonable to suggest that such plans and schemes vary extensively from school to school in their intensity, content, depth and all-round organization. However, it is here and specifically in this study within the context of the departmental staffroom that we expect the routines, discourses and practices of good HPE teaching to be somehow absorbed as if by osmosis.

Learning as ongoing

As Boud and Garrick (1999) suggest, 'There are few places left for employees at any level who do not continue to learn and improve their effectiveness throughout their working lives' (p. 1). For Boud and Garrick, the learning possibilities through work are all encompassing and much of what gets learned spills into other facets of people's lives such as technological skills (particularly IT skills), communication and collaboration skills, and often problem-solving skills. This phenomenon has really only been recognized over the past 20 years. Prior to this, work and learning were considered separately largely due to the industrial mindset that dominated the twentieth century in highly developed economies. This mindset saw learning as being something to do with the processes of institutionalized education, situated in pre-service training or education, in workplace observations or partial workplace experience with an education focus such as the practicum, or in quarantined time under the auspices of 'professional development'.

Work, on the other hand, was to do with the process of production which one did invariably to earn a living (i.e. receive a wage in exchange for labour). In this context, whatever needed to be 'picked up' was done by watching and copying colleagues, asking questions of more experienced workers, or going to the supervisor or line manager and asking for help. This edifice of modernity simply does not exist any longer. There are a number of reasons as to why this is so but we would argue that chief among them is that the performance of work is no longer separated from learning how to do that work.

It is also something of a misconception to suggest that this type of learning is haphazard or somehow informal. It may not be institutional (or even institutionalized) but often it is legitimized and formalized through the performance of accepted routines that build and develop a repertoire of skills and knowledge leading to improved performance, competence, and possibly even expertise. In addition, this type of learning is not the same everywhere. In other words workplace learning is distinctive by its diversity both across and within professions and trades.

Billett (2001), drawing on Lave and Wenger's (1991) conception of communities of practice, provides an excellent description of how the experiences of hairdressing apprentices vary from salon to salon – a phenomenon that even at this early stage of the book we can say we observed (and about which we comment much later). Learning is still structured and formal in that there are accepted routines for learning that are well established. They just happen to be different in different contexts, a significant point we make throughout the book. Contrast this to how children are continually pushed through the same curriculum in institutional forms of learning, doing the same tests at the same time – a process that will become ever more standardized as the curriculum is increasingly corporatized. It is a process that Marsh (1987) describes as 'batch processing'. In the workplace, the performance of work today is a product of continual diverse learning about how to do it better and it does not matter whether one is talking about manufacturing, teaching, nursing, law enforcement or hairdressing; the principle of learning through the performance of work holds.

Referring to a work task as routine may sound rather pejorative. Again, Billett (2001) is clear on this. Workplace routines are a way that learners are able to learn, understand and then automate various job-related activities. Arguably, as in any learning environment, unfamiliarity on the part of the learner requires a number of stages to master the techniques/skills or procedures. Irrespective of how seemingly dull the work (in other words, the routine) becomes, it still provides a context for learning about the nature of the work to be performed. In addition and perhaps more importantly such routines provide the basis for dealing with non-routine tasks that tend to demand higher attention, possibly need a creative (i.e. novel) response and may well draw on analytical skills. It is highly inefficient to have to think about routine tasks when faced with this kind of challenge. The key is to ensure that workers face degrees of change and challenge on a regular basis. This is of course a break with the rituals of modernity where mechanization forced the repetitive routine or Fordist approach to assembly-line work. Billett (2001) argues that the expectation of, and the need for, change and adaptability requires a constant reappraisal of previously acquired skills and knowledge, and for them to be applied to modestly novel circumstances. This, Billett (2001) would suggest, is the worker constructing new knowledge, a process that extends and transforms a worker's knowledge of the job, and, one assumes, their capacity to perform it better.

It would be foolhardy to suggest that this is all there is to learning in the workplace. However, one can see that there are familiar patterns of learning that exist in the workplace as exist anywhere. As members of a community of practice (Wenger, 1998), teachers gain experience through environments that offer guidance, but more importantly the opportunity to practise, and for that practise to have variable elements within it. As practises become routinized through repetition, a capacity is developed to take on novel situations that are likely to be much more contextually specific. Not all novel tasks can be resolved satisfactorily. In other words, the transfer of one's knowledge may not extend far enough to accommodate the new task (it may be new software, a new machine or a new technique, etc.). What tends to happen is that workers seek advice or guidance from other workers, some of whom might be more experienced, but not always! Often, a small cluster of people is drawn into solving the problem. From the collective the solution 'emerges'. The learning that takes place here includes not a single worker but a number of workers. The following vignette from one author's experience might make the point more easily.

A vignette

A professor at a university is trying to embed a film clip into his PowerPoint display for his class later that week. He is trying to make use of a clip which emphasizes the exact point he wants to get across to the students. He finds that when he attempts to place the clip into the slide it does not play. The computer message says that the particular format of the clip is not supported. The professor finds this very frustrating. However, he perseveres and tries to figure out what to do. Eventually he realizes he cannot do it so he wanders down the hall to ask a colleague. The colleague considers the problem but then says that someone else makes greater use of film clip material. Now both staff members proceed to the third colleague's office and explain the problem. He believes that conversion software is required and suggests where it may be found. Now all three members of staff head back to the professor's office so that the problem can be solved on his computer. After a number of false starts and suggestions from everyone the problem is resolved. All three members of staff return to their offices having learned something.

There are competing theories as to how this learning came about. Some would claim it as constructivist (see, e.g. Billett (2001) drawing on Vygotsky), others prefer to go further and suggest it is complexity learning as the learning has 'emerged' as a consequence of collaboration, reflection and the nested nature of knowledge (Davis and Sumara, 2000), and Wenger (1998) would suggest that the learning has come about through participation in a community of practice. The membrane between these theories may possibly be pretty thin but really that is not the point. What is important here is that by engaging in a particular work task, the professor learned something new and his colleagues learned something as well. The very factor that co-joined this effort was work. In this sense then, *opportunities* to learn from others through work would seem to be an important if not prime condition for learning in the workplace.

Required conditions for learning in the workplace

It would be a mistake to assume that learning in any workplace much less in schools simply happens through absorption. Learning in the context of work emerges through various states of practice and social arrangements and, as we saw from Billett (2001) earlier, there are many routines, subroutines, processes and experiences that are acquired through the process of 'working'. As he suggests, much of this is not organized in an institutional sense. It is what Moon (2004) might call unmediated learning. However, there are workplaces where a more structured approach is taken in the form of organized mentoring, assessment of task performance, competency and skills inventories, and so on. Learning to become a teacher involves a combination of mediated and unmediated learning but as always 'it depends' on the context and, as we will show through the book, on the nature of the experience both during pre-service and post-qualification. As the material we share later will illustrate, these were far from uniform within our cohort of participants.

LIVERPOOL JOHN MOORES UNIVERSITY
LEARNING SERVICES

Groundwater-Smith *et al.* (1996) suggest that adult learning is a continuous reorganizing of experience brought about by assessing the essence of such experiences so that we extend our understanding of the world we occupy. This accumulation of experience enables us to better interpret the world and the novel experiences we encounter, such that we are able to make better decisions. There is no hierarchy attached to our interpretations, as each or all are likely to be valid in some way. In the world of work, the experience of the practice of work provides the basis for improvement through either formal or less formal situations (Billett, 2001). What Groundwater-Smith and her colleagues go on to say is that for teachers, ongoing professional improvement and development is contingent upon the 'degree to which the school itself is a dynamic site, generative of serious intellectual questions about the nature of teaching and learning' (p. 30). Groundwater-Smith *et al.* point to a study by the National Board of Employment, Education and Training (National Board of Employment, 1994, p. 31), and it is worth citing their analysis at length:

> It argued, *inter alia*, that facilitating conditions emphasised [*sic*] a personal communal ethos in the workplace; problematic approaches to reform; a recognition of the relationship between differentiated personal and professional dimensions in teachers lives; and a view of the school as an educative workplace bent upon improvement. By comparison inhibiting conditions were ones where the ethos was bureaucratic; only students were viewed as learners in the school; professional development was fragmentary; and teachers were isolated in their classrooms.

What is striking about this is the relational nature of the facilitating conditions. In other words, there is no one set of circumstances or conditions whereby workplace learning and improvement is brought about. It tends to be connected to the interdependence of all of the facilitating factors. By contrast, there appears to be little relationship between the inhibiting factors; they are for all intents and purposes isolating and divisive features of workplaces. While we would like to assume that schools and school department offices are characterized by the facilitating features listed, first, we will be able to show that this is not always the case, and second, schools tend to be 'balkanized' environments (Hargreaves, 1994); that is, the culture of a school is often made up of competing sections or groups which have at best only loose connections and are more likely to be akin to 'antagonistic city states' (Groundwater-Smith *et al.*, 1996, p. 31). And yet it is widely accepted that collegial approaches to professional learning and development are the most effective (Little, 1990; Hargreaves, 1994).

The importance of a safe context for learning cannot be overstated. As Illeris (2011) suggests, for at least the past 20 years the quality of the workplace learning environment 'is directly decisive for the everyday learning and thereby also indirectly has a strong influence on more specific and goal-directed learning initiatives' (p. 131). Given this level of importance in both economic and healthy workplace terms (Ellström 2001), Illeris (2011) suggests that the single most important factor for a workplace to be conducive to good learning is that it is 'experienced as essentially confident and safe' (p. 131). What Illeris means here is that in general terms rather than for specific situations, the nature and everyday atmosphere – what some refer to as workplace climate – must be conducive to learning. He continues by saying that what this really comes down to is a feeling of security, security in terms of intellectual risk-taking, creativity, experimentation and freedom from admonishment or ridicule if things do not go as planned or attempted. We too have suggested elsewhere that for learning to be facilitated in the practicum and beginning teacher contexts the workplace needs to be a healthy space. By this we refer to the social, emotional, spiritual, relational and physical spaces within which one practices the work of a teacher (lisahunter *et al.*, 2010, 2011; lisahunter, 2010). While Illeris' analysis is at a general level there are ample examples within specific work sites where his advocacy is born out. For example, in a study of medical residents – that is, postgraduate medical education based within the practicum context of hospitals in Holland – Stok-Koch and colleagues (2007) found exactly the same thing. Their analysis of a wide-ranging textual dataset extracted over 50 factors of importance for meaningful workplace learning to occur within medical training. However, chief among them was the importance of social integration, which when more tightly defined referred to a sense of belonging and a good atmosphere. It is reasonable to suggest that in the study we undertook, such conditions were not always present and some of the narratives and field text samples we share later will demonstrate this, with, on occasions, devastating effect. Needless to say, Illeris (2011) describes the counterpoint which is that any work environment that is doubtful or uncertain will likely provide opportunities to learn that are defensive or evasive. The result, Illeris suggests, is that 'learning that takes place under such conditions will tend to be weaker, less significant, easier to forget and more difficult to recall (p. 131).

Learning to be a teacher in schools

As we indicated earlier, induction into a profession involves certain stages between being educating for, gaining entry to, being accepted as a professional, albeit as a beginner, and then the relatively slow progress towards becoming an experienced worker and perhaps even an expert. In school-based teacher education, the formative years of becoming a teacher are dominated by two particular phases of significance: the pre-service teacher education major practicum, and the induction year or first year of teaching following graduation. As we identified in Chapter 1, in both phases, learning to be a teacher occurs not just in the formal classroom context but also in the staffroom, on playground duty, in staff meetings, in parent–teacher meetings and a host of other incidental sites of importance. For our research project one of the key sites was the subject department office. These are all workplaces or subsections of the larger workplace of school and the profession of teaching. As such, they are all potential spaces for learning to be a teacher. As far as we could see, next to the formal classroom context, it was participation in the subject department culture that occupied most of the in-school time for pre-service and beginning teachers. Thus, although locations within and beyond schools have been found to function as sites for experienced teachers' workplace learning (McGregor, 2003), little is known about how the subject department functions as a professional learning community and how this affects the process of becoming a teacher or learning to teach. Hence our focus on this particular site, but not our exclusive attention – as the story of this book will show, this enabled a close examination of the ways in which social, physical, political and cultural dynamics of teachers within a community influence professional learning.

As we mentioned in Chapter 1, teacher education regularly comes in for considerable debate (if not outright criticism and hostility) at an international and local level. Government reports and inquiries into teacher education have also been numerous across the globe, and in Australia one of the most recent was the House of Representatives' (the 'lower house' of governance) *Inquiry into Teacher Education* in 2005. What is perhaps alarming is that the 2005 Inquiry reported that not much had changed since a 1998 Senate (the 'upper house' of governance) inquiry and that the same issues were still apparent.

The 1998 Senate *Inquiry into the Status of the Teaching Profession* reported that: 'The most trenchant criticism of teacher training related to its practical component' (1998, p. 183) most typically referred to as the practicum or teaching practice. While the value of university-based teacher education has been defended (e.g. Australian Council of Deans of Education, 1998), arguments for more time in schools (practicum) and less university theory has been a persistent criticism, as we have already indicated. The Senate *Inquiry* (1998) also reported that while the induction year was generally a worthwhile professional development experience for many teachers, there were many other teachers who experienced little or no support and had struggled to survive their first year. Further, given that many teachers are assessed for continuing or contract positions at the end of their first (probation) year of teaching, the ad hoc nature of the induction year (Senate *Inquiry*, 1998, p. 209) results in differential dis/advantages.

In both the teacher education major practicum and the induction year following graduation, the subject department culture is a key factor in facilitating a positive and productive professional development experience (NBEET, 1994). Subject departments that afford sustained professional contact between teachers (i.e. shared norms and values; focus on student learning; reflective dialogue) correlate with the quality of teachers' school life, curricular collaboration (Hodkinson and Hodkinson, 2004), and teachers' sense of responsibility for students' learning (Louis *et al.*, 1996). Moreover, while these outcomes seem to impact positively upon student learning, there is considerable variability across schools in how subject departments sustain these dynamics (Talbert and McLaughlin, 2002; Hayes *et al.*, 2006).

In the small pilot project to which we briefly referred in Chapter 1, conducted in 2006[2] with a cohort of HPE/Science[3] pre-service teachers, the data revealed that, while some students experienced very positive subject department cultures (in both HPE and science), others found one or both department cultures to be far less supportive and in some cases of very questionable worth or abuse. For instance, some language and practices ridiculed women and individuals because of their body shape and/or their sexuality. The HPE context often emphasized a discourse of competitive hyper-heterosexist male sport and encouraged techno-cratic perspectives of teaching. Within these environments, student teachers reported feeling pressure to 'play the game' of that social environment in order to be accepted in the subject department. While such game-playing is not new (see Tinning and Siedentop, 1985), its significance, and the power of the subject department as a site for learning and developing a professional selfhood as a teacher, had not been rigorously studied.

Subject department culture is the product of numerous factors, including the personal and professional identities of the teachers themselves. Several studies have attempted to understand the 'nature' of the PE teacher (e.g. Dewar, 1989; Templin and Schempp, 1989; Tinning *et al.*, 2001). To reiterate: PE teachers have been found to have relatively similar discursive histories with respect to the central place that physical activity, sport and the body plays in their identity construction (Macdonald and Tinning, 1995). They have been described as insensitive to social issues, elitist, sexist, anti-intellectual, and full of 'pragmatic sceptics'. How such characteristics might influence the culture of the subject department as a com-munity of practice and workplace learning environment was of great interest to us.

Some have argued that the identities or subjectivities[4] (both personal and profes-sional) of pre-service and beginning teachers are 'in process' as they become PE teachers (O'Connor and Macdonald, 2002). According to Nias (1991), personal and professional identities become fused in the process of becoming a teacher. Importantly, teacher identity development can be undermined by negative experi-ences (Macdonald, 1995), with poor consequences for student learning and teacher attrition. This is particularly significant, as the human and financial costs of begin-ning teacher attrition are considerable. As reported in the Commonwealth Review of Teaching and Teacher Education (DEST, 2003), the rate of teachers leaving the profession after fewer than five years working as a teacher may be as high as 25 per cent. Data from PE cohorts have previously suggested even higher rates: up to 50 per cent (Macdonald *et al.*, 1994), with reasons cited including alienating school culture, boredom and harassment. While these data might be considered old, there is little to suggest that much has changed, in Australia at least. In our study HPE teachers were also teachers of junior science; hence this loss to both discipline areas currently represents a serious issue given current societal concerns regarding issues of citizens' health and physical activity, and the difficulty of recruiting quality science teachers.

Learning as situated within a workplace

At the start of this project we considered pre-service and beginning teachers' learning in the workplace, to be mediated through social participation in the form of 'communities of practice' (Lave and Wenger, 1991). Lave and Wenger (1991) indicate that, through interactions, individuals engage in a 'process of being active participants in the practices of social communities and construct identities in relation to these communities' (p. 4). Such practices are both explicit and implicit, and the negotiations between individuals of those practices leads to the construction of meaning (Hodkinson and Hodkinson, 2005). Communities of practice share not only a domain of interest, the pursuit of the interest, and engage as practitioners of that interest, they also share ways of interacting (Lave and Wenger, 1991; Wenger, 1998). The last point refers to a repertoire of: gestures, words, actions and behaviours that reflect negotiated and shared meanings.

Generally speaking, members in communities interact with one another, share information and build relationships that support their learning from one another – we described this process above in the narrative of the university professor. Furthermore, through their engagement with others and their interests, members share experiences and resources, working towards a deepened understanding of shared interests (Wenger, 1998). As we have previously described, Billett (2001) has explored the concept of communities of practice within the workplace context as a way to make sense of learning as a social process of participation. Billett argues that the ways in which workplaces support or inhibit individuals' engagements in activities are important in shaping the learning that takes place. In this way, communities are contested social spaces where individuals are invited or afforded different modes of participation based on power dynamics, capitals, positioning and perceptions. There is a dynamic of negotiation at play between participants (Lave and Wenger, 1991; Wenger, 1998) and these are influenced by values, knowledge, conceptions and personal history (Billett, 2001). The interconnection between the individual and the workspace is under constant negotiation. It is a 'space of culture' (Somerville, 2005, p. 8) infused with negotiated symbolic meanings as well as perceptions of gender, race, class, competency and identity.

According to Wenger (1998), individuals may be peripheral rather than full members of a community of practice, though over time they may become more fully recognized. For our purposes we considered pre-service teachers in the workplace-learning situation to be peripheral participants actively working towards acceptance as full members of the HPE teachers' community of practice. For beginning teachers, while they are full members of a work community nominally, we considered that in spite of their differentiated status (i.e. qualified and accredited) they also start as peripheral participants. However, the processes and learning that they go through to become more active members of a community of practice are of different characteristics and intensities (i.e. cognitive, conceptual leaps, effort required, experience and personal trauma of change) and function across different time frames.

Where learning about work gets done

In current first world capitalist systems for most employed workers, learning as a member of the workforce will occupy a far greater proportion of one's life than any institutionalized form of 'schooling' or compulsory education. Clearly greater attention to this phenomenon is warranted. However, we contend that the spaces where such learning happens have not been the subject of intense scrutiny. In this study, as we indicated in Chapter 1, we started with the subject department office or staffroom as the site of learning to be a (HPE) teacher. We soon realized that this site, though highly important within the context of this study, was one among many where learning was sought or occurred. It was also a multidimensional place encompassing physical space, social space, symbolic space, conceptual space and professional space. We will explore these places and spaces further in Part II.

Notes

1 The texts referred to in this section are particularly compelling (Harvey, 2005; Krugman, 2007); however, for an account of the devastating effect this has had on certain segments of the British workforce over the past 30 years see Owen Jones' book entitled *Chavs* (2012).
2 The *pilot study* focused on the experiences of HPE/science pre-service teachers based in the Southeast section of the Australian State of Queensland as they participated in their ten-week major teaching practicum. This was then replicated in the major study.
3 Many (though importantly not all) HPE teachers in the State of Queensland qualify as junior science teachers as their second teaching subject.
4 In Chapter 9 we discuss how these terms might be considered similar but also how perhaps they are better separated according to how they are used in social theory literature.

3 An evolutionary and reflexive process in researching professional learning

Gathering field texts, making sense, and the telling and retelling of tales

Introduction

We have already told the story of how this study was set in motion. Given the commitment all of us have to issues associated with social justice, the toxic jock idea was almost too easy a target. However, it did provide a necessary catalyst which took us into a project that clearly had not been done before. As always we had to make research-based decisions, particularly as it was apparent that the research could be sensitive in nature. This may sound somewhat pompous; however, across the life of the research programme we were going to be asking students about the nature of their experiences in environments that seemed to us to range from highly supportive and committed to the task and roles of teacher education to the outright hostile. Amidst this, at least in the early phases when the pre-service teachers were in their final year of the teacher education programme, the stakes were high. This was because their performance in the school and the judgements made of the pre-service teachers would have considerable bearing on their 'teacher suitability rating', known locally as their 'S' rating. A pre-service teacher with an S rating of one (1) is the highest sought-after graduate in school employment, the sliding scale continuing to a rating of four (4), which would render individuals virtually unemployable other than in private sectors not governed by the scheme. This potentially acted as a constraint to the research process, since adverse comment from the participants, in spite of promises of anonymity, about the practicum schools they were in and departments (of which they were temporary or new members) could potentially lead to a detrimental appraisal by their teacher mentors. In addition to this, our research participants would be placed in schools used by the university for practicum experience year after year. Airing less than complimentary tales, or even horror stories from practicum experiences would not bode well for the university's future relationship with such schools. Once in the system as beginning teachers, the situation would be similar. As a consequence the mantra of 'proceed with caution' was always going to be important.

Early decisions

As is most common, we were driven to some extent by convention. We agreed that we were likely to recruit a reasonable number of participants but not a number where statistical data might be useful or even warranted. We therefore decided on a more qualitative approach. While this was in keeping with our expertise we were not opposed to quantitative methods. However, the original idea for the study had been sparked by a story from the field and it made sense therefore to create field texts (Clandinin and Connelly, 2000), varying forms of data from which case study narratives could represent the evolving research.

Going with cases

Case study approaches are considered to create nuanced, rich portrayals of life in schools, recognizing that human systems have 'integrity' or a wholeness of their own (Sturman, 1999). This uniqueness of context is what made case study methods so attractive to the research team given their power to capture nuance (Cohen *et al.*, 2007). However, case study methods remain contentious and their approach is often misunderstood (Flyvbjerg, 2004; Merriam, 1998). Part of the confusion, Merriam (1998) suggests, is the conflation of the case itself and the products of the investigation. However, for Flyvbjerg (2004) the confusion lies in the deep mistrust of case studies to be meaningful beyond the case itself (see also Yin (1994) for a discussion of concerns relating to rigour and generalizability). Merriam (1998) goes on to suggest that the defining characteristic of case study research is the process of delimiting the object of study. In other words, what is being studied should be 'bounded' by the contextual parameters of the phenomenon itself (see also Miles and Huberman, 1994). It occurred to us that while we did not want to restrict the research by boundaries, and this became ever more evident when we drew upon theories of spatiality, the research was bounded by research sites themselves. Thus, while we were cautious not to impose boundaries within the sites, the research was bounded through the use of different school sites. This situatedness may be regarded positively however, and is argued as necessary by scholars such as McGregor (2004a) and Massey (2005). Those ascribing to the 'spatial turn' (see, e.g. Massey, 2005; McGregor, 2004b; Morgan, 2000) argue for the importance of recognizing emplacement as a serious influence on any research whether based on cases or on other forms of study.

One of the more widely recognized advantages of case study research is that it gets the researcher as close to the subject of study as possible through direct observations often in naturalistc settings, through access to the more subjective concerns such as thoughts and feelings in interviews and other narrative forms, and through access to documentation and records relevant to the context. In this sense case study research has a particularly heuristic quality. It is reasonable to suggest that there were limits to the amount of time we spent in schools. Due to the sensitive nature of the project this was necessary. Early on in the research process we made the decision not to physically enter the pre-service and beginning teachers' schools and staffrooms in the capacity of researcher. While some of us visited schools in our roles as tutor, lecturer and mentor, this decision was based on developing a sensitive, supportive and trusting relationship with each participant. Given the sensitive and relational nature of pre-service and begin-ning teachers' situations, we wanted to allow each participant to tell his or her story without concern for negative consequences within the staffroom and school. For us, getting close to the subjects of the study came through develop-ing relationships through intense interviews and over time, in some cases several years.

Case study research lays no particular claim to specific methods (Yin, 2003). Far from being unstructured, this provides the researcher/s with the opportunity to draw upon methods likely to be most effective and suitable for gathering field texts aimed at answering the research questions. In this study, the case studies were cases within cases where interview was the prime method of field text cre-ation but supported through photo elicitation, focus groups and ongoing corres-pondence. It is generally agreed that interviews vary in their purpose, structure and intensity (Padgett, 2008). Since the warrant for interviewing in the first place is goal directed the focus for the interviews was the nature of work and the work-related learning in the day-to-day lives of our participants in schools.

We were then faced with deciding whether we were researching school HPE departments (our view was that we were), or were we researching emerging teachers' learning in work-integrated contexts? It was really a non-issue; by researching emerging teachers' learning within the confines of a department we were creating 'cases' of those departments that the pre-service teachers, and then later the beginning teachers, were in. Admittedly, we initially took a narrow per-spective of each case but this was guided by our research questions. In this sense, some might argue that it is a stretch to call what we did case studies. Hence, as we described earlier, the participants in this study were cases within cases. In other words, each participant was a case in the process of work-integrated learning either through a formal curriculum of teacher education (represented by the practicum) or learning through workplace participation once they had graduated and were employed within a school as a credentialed teacher. These arrangements also painted a picture of the way such learning was experi-enced through the way the workplace (specifically, the department) functioned, within the larger organization of the school. Thus, though these were not *classic* case studies per se characterized by *x*, *y* and *z*, the field texts (Clandinin and Connelly, 2000) gathered across a four-year period (including the pilot study) enabled us to craft a picture of case-based workplace learning. Thus, even though there were limits to the idea of a case, we considered the participant voices to be representing not only *their* case but, in addition, the case of the staffroom as a learning organization.

Representing the cases through narratives

As we indicated earlier, this entire project was motivated by stories coming back to us from the field. Narratives seemed to be an appropriate way to represent not only the findings but also the participants and the story of the unfolding project. More-over, we regarded narratives to have explanatory power and to be engaging for audiences as we disseminated the field texts through varying forms of research texts (Clandinin and Connelly, 2000), such as conference papers and journal publications. This proved particularly effective in the former and less so in the latter, mainly because the time from writing to publication seems now to be especially long. As a consequence our early research texts in the project were presented in broad thematic form. However, our field texts still relied on pre-service and beginning teachers sharing their stories from their in-school experiences.

Using narrative as a way of representing participants' experiences might be regarded by some as a narrow use of narrative research. For example, in a commentary article Clandinin and Murphy (2009) argue that narrative itself is a research method and not just a form of storied knowledge. To be fair, their critique of a paper (Coulter and Smith, 2009) advocating narrative as representational seems harsh given that the authors state the premise of the paper up front. Indeed, these authors cite other work by Clandinin with other colleagues (2009) when suggesting that stories 'emerge as data are collected and then framed and rendered through an analytical process that is artistic as well as rigorous' (p. 577). In doing so Coulter and Smith emphasize that the position of the paper is concerned largely with narrative *construction* rather than with narrative *inquiry*. We will not enter into a debate here as to whether these are inseparable or otherwise. Simply we acknowledge that for some, talking about narrative construction is reductionist and fails to grasp the centrality of ontological and epistemological underpinnings of narrative work (you will notice that we have avoided the words construction and inquiry!). That said, we find there is much to support in Barone's (2001) notion of narrative as an interpretive space. Indeed, this was what to us as researchers became increasingly appealing. The capacity to bring the emotion of human experience to life through narrative (even when partially fictionalized), particularly for 'telling' within a conference context, was highly attractive. We were mindful that such ventures might not be so well received by editors and manuscript reviewers of scholarly journals. However, we took a similar position to the likes of Barone (2001) and Sparkes (1995, 2000) and asked 'Why not'? Inevitably, we experienced such prejudice with a reviewer of one of our papers asking why a reader should invest in a fictional tale (a composite character we developed drawn from the field texts of three people). We were not sure what to make of such feedback other than to send the manuscript to an alternative journal where it was received with far greater enthusiasm.

Hence we remained undeterred and set about writing themed accounts and, increasingly, narratives from the field texts to emphasize the nuances and processes in the lived experiences of the pre-service teachers in their final practicum and then when they were transitioning into certified teaching spaces. We were convinced by the argument that the narrative genre of research produced and represented situated knowledge rather than universals, capturing the detail of social life, for example, through 'slice of life' accounts (Denzin and Lincoln, 2005) rather than abstracting from this detail to produce reductive models. Through narratives (Clandinin *et al.*, 2009) we explored how pre-service and beginning teacher subjectivities might become constructed through workplace relations within the context of the departmental staffroom. These narratives, to be found throughout the book, were developed to illustrate the main plot lines (Clandinin and Connelly, 1996) or narrative threads (Thomas *et al.*, 2009) of our participants' experiences.

We use a range of different techniques to represent the stories we have included in this book such as fictional tales and realist tales. The fictional tales were informed by techniques used by Rossi *et al.* (2007) and by Ryan (2005), while realist tales are developed from the work by Sparkes (2002). Most often we do not use temporal scales for any of the narratives, as they were not told to us in this way. In our view the 'whole' of the story in each case is more than the sum of the episodes, and in telling their stories as a form of response to our prompts the participants often used flashback memory techniques. Thus, rather than reorder the stories to suit a conventional temporal reconstruction we have attempted, where possible and where it aids the flow of the book, to maintain the fidelity of the stories as they were revealed to us.

What we actually did

This study traced the experiences of a cohort of final-year students during their final practicum experience as a teacher in a school. We then followed the same cohort, or at least as many as we could and as many as were prepared to stay with the project, into their first year of teaching. We were interested to understand the *where*, *how* and *with whom* professional learning took place and how professional teacher subject positions were constructed and taken up, with an emphasis on the place of the staffroom.

Pre-service teachers in their final semester of a teacher education undergraduate degree at an Australian university were asked to participate in the study as interview participants. Semi-structured interviews with the 18 participants who volunteered were recorded, transcribed and analysed initially by themes and storylines. These interviews were conducted at various points between the final semester as pre-service teachers and the subsequent first year as an employed teacher. These included the following:

- the first interview at post-practicum and pre-graduation;
- immediately prior to the school year beginning as an employed teacher;
- within the first few weeks of teaching;
- towards the end of their first term (in Australia there are four school terms; this point is the lead-up to the break classified and gazetted as Easter);
- midway through the year, just after the start of the second semester;
- at the end of the first year of teaching.

Questions were directed towards their feelings and experiences of teaching and in relation to the various spaces in which they were a teacher, including their staffroom. They were asked to photograph these teacher spaces to use for photo elicitation in interviews.

In addition, in the pre-service practicum phase during the final year of university, periodic emails were requested from the participants using a particular template. These related to teaching, staffroom presence, enjoyment, learning, personnel and a general sense of what it meant to be at that school. These were not particularly successful for a range of reasons, principal among them the participants' irregular commitment to the process. We discovered later during interviews that the problems of privacy – that is, a lack of privacy when using email within schools – made sending personal experiences in emails difficult. Therefore, rather than be used to contribute to our understanding of the emerging narratives related to the workplace experience, emails were used as a modest cross-check of the stories and as a way to 'feed back' the emerging narratives as a form of member checking. Upon the conclusion of the school workplace experience (ten weeks), the students re-formed as a class at the university. At one of these sessions the entire research team was granted access to the students and two focus group discussions associated with our research project were conducted. During the beginning teachers' induction year, a more flexible approach was taken to follow and interact with the participants. At one level this was entirely pragmatic. Keeping track of and in connection with busy first-year teachers was not easy. We were guided by their privileging of social media, namely a closed Facebook site as their primary communicative tool. Thus, though pragmatic, it became an innovative data-gathering tool. These types of less formal field texts served as additional cross-check material against the more formal interview and focus group field texts in the creation of the emerging narratives. The use of social media as an approach to research is in its infancy; however, there are an increasing number of examples available in the literature (see, e.g. Olive 2013).

All interviews and focus group discussions throughout the entire project were recorded and subsequently transcribed by an external service provider. The transcriptions were read and listened to by two members of the research team and the written text checked against the digital recording. The same researchers then analysed the transcripts for key incidents, observations, regular and constant themes and reflections in order to hear storylines or narrative threads (Thomas *et al.*, 2009) or story maps (Richmond, 2002). This was done in various ways but by way of an example, the transcribed text was placed into the left-hand column of a two-column, one-row table. Emerging storylines were then constructed in the right-hand column using the text from the left-hand column. This, like most of our scholarly processes, was inevitably reductionist to some extent, in spite of our intentions not to be reductionist. However, it enabled what was considered to be surplus text to be edited out, leaving units of text from which to construct meaning. As the interviews were not temporal in nature the stories were not necessarily serialized or sequential: a feature of narratives generally considered important. In this case however, the narratives that emerged told a story of the whole experience based on sedimented memory, recall and reconstruction. As might be expected, the stories were inevitably structured around the questions and prompts that were used. The questions were far from random and were inspired by our experiences in the pilot study, the relevant literature, and by the emerging field texts and narratives developing as the project progressed.

Reflexive telling and retelling

The necessity for this project to be a reflexive endeavour was apparent from the start. We should be clear at this point about the researcher–participant relationships. In the first field text construction phase the participants in the study were students within the university section where we all worked. However, none of us taught the students during this time. Importantly though, several members of the cohort had been taught by two of the research team across various points in the programme previous to this. Ordinarily, this would not have been a problem except that the researchers in question were able to make links between their responses and other things they knew about or had heard said, often directly, by the students. As a consequence, some of the developing narratives began to take a different shape with different emphases and motivations. Clearly the project did not yield these parts of the narratives but they were, so to speak, 'in the field'. We realized then that narratives might have to be retold along the lines that Nilges (2001) recommends. In her study, the incompleteness of stories once they had been revisited required a retelling. This process is not one in search of certainty; rather it was about achieving the best possible fidelity between what we knew from and about someone and then representing them and their voice. This phenomenon played out in the third year of the project as we were trying to make sense of the cases and the research sites. It cast our field texts not so much as fallible; rather, in some cases it did not tell the fullest possible story that we knew was available. As we crafted the narratives, each successive telling was different from the previous. To be more reflexive with our field texts and the knowledge we considered it to hold, we turned to the work of Pierre Bourdieu, including *The Logic of Practice* (1990a), *The Scholastic Point of View* (1990b), *The Field of Cultural Production* (1993 with Johnson) and *An Invitation to Reflexive Sociology* (1992 with Wacquant).

The work of Bourdieu was understood by the research team members at a variety of levels of sophistication. As a consequence, reflexivity became more of an issue for those closest to the project, specifically two research team members who had worked with the pre-service teachers across the previous three years of their study in various courses and projects. What follows is an account of how we theorized the role of reflexivity in the project in an attempt to come to grips with the unfolding narratives within the intentions of reflexivity.

Reflexivity as method

This project was reflexive at one level as we turned the gaze back on ourselves for the conduct of the work and the nature of the narratives that emerged from it. This may appear somewhat prosaic and more than just a little self-righteous. The project was reflexive at another level as we used the narratives contained within this work to constantly seriously challenge the nature of teacher education know-ledge, its well-practised orthodoxies, and the way we generally understood teacher education. This required us to make every effort to ensure that we were not simply engaged in some kind of confessional, or moralistic wringing of hands, or to shroud our representations of research participants or our reflections as researchers and teacher educators in guilt or apology. We knew though that we were having the 'internal conversations' (Archer, 2007). As Archer suggests, reflexivity is dependent upon the conscious deliberations within internal conver-sations. For us, our concerns largely focused on the very epistemology that pro-duced the representations of persons in the first place and the nature of such knowledge that we were dutifully sharing with the academic field at various con-ferences and in scholarly journals. It is this epistemic reflexivity that seemed to be of significant importance. This presented a challenge, in varying degrees, to the very ontology of the members of the research team but, as one might imagine, one inherently wrapped up with individual ontologies, or perhaps as Giddens (1991) would say, individual ontological security, but more on this later. It seemed to us that the work of and work associated with Bourdieu would be of some assistance in this challenge. It was a long road.

Relativism, reflexivity or what's in a name?

Some prosecute an argument that relativism leads to reflexivity (see, e.g. Lawson, 1985). However, claiming a relativist position can sometimes seem like an argument in self-defeat. Establishing a discourse with an epistemological fidelity as being 'contingent' surely is, itself, contingent. As a way of progress-ing our understanding of the world, notions of contingency seemed both counter-productive and counter-intuitive, not to mention extraordinarily frustrating. Woolgar (1988) seemed to experience similar frustrations with what appears to be an exercise in self-referentialism. However, the limits of science both episte-mologically and methodologically are well rehearsed (Latour and Woolgar, 1979) and we do not need to repeat them here. That said, the sheer discipline of inquiry within the academic/scientific genre has appeal not least because it makes claims to certainty, and with certainty comes assurance. We were mindful that we were in no position to claim certainty.

Trying to be reflexive researchers

Paralleling Bourdieu's invitation to reflexivity (1990a, 1994), Woolgar (1988) suggests that 'we need continually to interrogate and find strange the process of representation as we engage in it' (pp. 28–29). This of course was how the chal-lenge before us took shape. Clifford (1983) talks about research accounts as 'specific inventions' and goes on to suggest that there is a reliance on improvisa-tion and what he calls 'historically contingent fictions', and in this sense he advocates an equal distribution of responsibility for and power within the con-struction of narratives between the researcher and the research. He suggests that in not doing so the researcher will fail to take advantage of the dialogical implications of the relationship.

This was the issue in a nutshell and yet one that appeared to be unsolvable. For example, member checking became increasingly difficult as the pre-service teachers dispersed into a less teacher-focused situation (i.e. they returned to study additional discipline-based knowledge in the exercise and movement sciences) on campus after the period of practicum and disappeared after graduation, in some cases to the four corners of the known world. There were rare occasions during the process when the participants came back, physically or virtually through Skype or the telephone, for subsequent interviews or group discussions. Here, deeper probing could be done but as their lives stretched beyond the intense and focused initial life of the project this became increasingly difficult to do. Progressively, we considered that the best way to do justice to the participants represented in this study was to move away from thematic analysis to tell 'realist tales' (Sparkes, 2002) and instead represent participants' storied experiences (Connelly and Clandinnin, 2000). It seemed that such a device would allow the 'objectivism' of the tale to come to the fore. We developed this further to construct fictional tales based on 'composites' or coalescences of individuals to facilitate the telling of the research story (see Rossi and lisahunter, 2012)

However, when crafting the narratives it was clear that we were drawing on field text information, insights through discussions and more that existed as knowledge outside the formal parameters of the project. This was an epistemological and methodological dilemma. Indeed, some of what we came to understand about our participants we had learned through interviewing them for a different project altogether, through teaching them, through working with some of them on conference organization, and through the Honours supervision of one researcher for two of the participants. Between us on the research team, we had counselled many of the participants on the nature of teaching HPE as a career, a job or, as some of them saw it, a jumping-off point for other things. If we included such material, were we overstepping the bounds of the project, were we going to be accused of fictionalizing our accounts, or if we excluded the extended field texts would we fail to represent the participants fairly?

Virtuous researchers?

It was Maton's (2003) description of the 'virtuous researcher' that made one of us uneasy and it was clear that it would be easy for us to be described in such a way. Through internal conversations and conversations within the research team, by thinking about our research practices and the relationship of our histories and interactions with and to the field texts, there was a certain smugness in the knowledge that the influence of all these things on the research had been duly acknowledged and appropriately 'accounted for' as we prepared the narratives. Of course one among the many reasons for doing this was to be confident in the knowledge that we had conducted this research within the accepted principles of social justice and power sharing (see Pillow, 2003). Maton (2003) argued that this kind of 'enacted reflexivity' is tantamount to an academic guilt trip or, worse still, academic reflexive vanity (Kenway and McLeod, 2004) that rings of little more than narcissism and is often overtly patronizing of the audience or readership.

Our reflexive approach

Woolgar (1988) suggested that the 'conventions of the realist genre encourage the unproblematic and unhesitant singular interpretation of text, the un-reflexive perception of a reported reality (subject/object) and the essentially uninteresting character of the agency involved in the report's generation' (p. 28). Given Woolgar's stinging rebuke of the absence of the researcher within the realist genre, there was urgency in coming to grips with reflexivity and it was this that precipitated the turn to Bourdieu. Although one of the researchers was more familiar with extended works of Bourdieu, others started with the work of Lois Wacquant to provide the portal to Bourdieu's analysis. However, one soon realizes that Wacquant (1989) finds it contemptible that scholars 'use' Bourdieu without a comprehensive reading (and understanding) of most of his work and big ideas as he says 'this work which is so catholic and systematic in both intent and scope has typically been apprehended in "bits and pieces" and incorporated piecemeal' (p. 27). We came to appreciate that were Wacquant looking over our shoulders he may level the same disdain for our interpretations as he did for McLeod (1987) and possibly with the same level of malevolence. However, for the record it provided a starting point.

Wacquant (1992) describes Bourdieu as being obsessed with reflexivity, so much so, Wacquant argues, that it was the key feature of his work that separated Bourdieu from other theorists. Moreover, Bourdieu's term 'epistemic reflexivity' (1994) seeks to move reflexivity beyond the narcissistic and into the realm of the social by arguing that it is the relational position of an actor within a field which is pivotal and not simply his or her life narrative as an individual. If society comprises overlapping but autonomous social fields, then the intellectual capital possessed by us as researchers as a consequence of being a member of a particular field is crucial for how we interpret field texts and tell stories of those who exist in other (yet related) fields. As Kenway and McLeod (2004) suggest, within sociology, fields produce their own intellectual dispositions and it is these, along with the epistemic history of the field, that need to be interrogated rather than the well-intentioned but individualized and autobiographical ramblings of researchers.

Bourdieu (2004) suggests that one cannot talk about an object without 'exposing oneself to a permanent mirror effect' (p. 4). He goes on to say that every utterance about scientific practice, and therefore about the nature of knowledge itself, can be turned back on the person who uttered it in the first place. He is at pains to suggest that the task here is not to discredit scientific knowledge but rather to strengthen it. At the same time he suggests that sociology cannot exempt itself from this process. As with science, the purpose, Bourdieu (2004) argued, is to 'make better sociology' (p. 4). It is significant that Bourdieu lays out a case to suggest that epistemology is simply a discourse in justification of, for example, science, sociology, etc. Moreover, one might readily add to Bourdieu's notion and suggest that epistemology as the term is generally used today might be a discourse in the justification of self, a case of self-positioning to prosecute one's own discourse to be seen both as favourable, but ultimately acceptable. This may sound somewhat uncharitable with more than just a tinge of self-righteousness. It does seem however that unless we challenge our own epistemologies in some humble but critical sense then we are likely to descend into nihilistic relativism, and any claims to reality, objectivity or truth, whatever they may be, are simply wistful. However, as Kenway and Macleod (2004) point out, Bourdieu's very point was to encourage researchers to work from multiple perspectives and to avoid lurching into relativism.

If we were to individualize our life stories or life situation (see Beck, 1992) and place them front and centre of the research process, then arguably we may be positioned as narcissistic if, as Kenway and McLeod (2004) point out, reflexivity seldom gets beyond this point. Of greater importance is undermining what is referred to as the 'scholastic point of view' (Schirato and Webb, 2003), a form of intellectual bias or set of intellectual dispositions produced by one position in the academic field but which serves researchers as a mask of objectivity. To that end we worked this project from a range of frameworks without necessarily privileging any. However, we have always communicated the narratives from within those frameworks and in this sense we have always worked from a 'scholastic point of view'. We are prepared to acknowledge the necessary shortcomings of the research outputs of this project, as should any scholarly work. However, what we do not accept is the charge, as might be levelled by Woolgar (1988), that our texts are neutral as a consequence of their attempted 'realism', thereby exempting them as a 'species of social/cultural activity' (p. 28). Rather, the texts/stories were our attempts at representation. However, early on in the project they perhaps failed to meet our later expectations of epistemic reflexivity. This represented a deeper challenge and we attempt to address this at various points in the book

In closing this chapter we want to reiterate that our methodological backstory is an attempt to make explicit the evolutionary and reflexive nature of this project involving early methodological decisions around cases, narrative and then later the rereading with reflexivity. The book is the woven cloth made up of many threads, not necessarily neatly planned or patterned in its final form. But, unlike the Emperor (from Hans Christian Anderson, 1837, 2008), we do not wish to hide behind an imaginary cloth that we sometimes fashion as participants in an academic field. Instead we wish to expose some of the tensions of the topic, but also the process of the research project. This is to encourage further debate about teacher education, teacher work placement and professional development, but also research and its representation related to these topics.

4 Significant dimensions of workplace learning

Introduction

We indicated in the previous chapters that we prosecuted this research project using a range of theoretical standpoints that we considered would have purchase in explaining the phenomenon of workplace learning in the context of the HPE subject department office. It is beyond the intention and scope of this book to delve deeply into these various theoretical standpoints given the scholarly treatment they have all had elsewhere and, more specifically, within the context of their original conception. In a sense that is why we consider the spatio-temporal term 'dimensions' to be more appropriate. Much like the evolution of methodology, the use of various dimensions to fully understand the workplace in HPE, specifically the departmental office or staffroom, developed 'as we went'. This may sound generative and responsive to some, or somewhat haphazard or sloppy to others depending on one's epistemological perspective, but again, as in the previous chapters, we want to expose the messiness of research often presented as fully conceptualized with textbook enactment and clear theoretical alignments before enactment. However, as we progressed the project, we realized that there were 'dimensions' that not only warranted attention but would also broaden the canvas and tell a more comprehensive though not necessarily complete story. Hence these dimensions became the foci with successive phases of the project.

In what follows, we make the important links back to Chapter 2 where we defined the topic of workplace learning as our starting point. Inevitably the structure and concerns of the research project meant that there was no clear line of demarcation between these complex and interrelated dimensions and it would be foolish to mount a case that there were. However, for the purposes of this chapter it made sense to treat the dimensions separately for the sake of discussion. Like Nespor (2002), we consider there to be interconnection between learning that occurs in various social spaces or sites and across multiple dimensions of the workplace, in this case most closely associated with schools and in particular departmental spaces.

In this chapter then, we lay the foundations for the significant dimensions of workplace learning, namely social tasks, performance and practice, identity/subjectivities, spatiality, and micropolitics. Each dimension is defined and a case made for how the research revealed the importance of each for workplace learning. In addition we show how, for the most part, these dimensions overlap. In doing so, we perhaps strengthen the case for their inclusion and the logic of the sequence in which they are presented. In light of our discussions regarding learning as situated in a workplace, this chapter acts as a jump-off point for Part II of the book.

Social tasks

In the early stages of the project we made strong connections between communities of practices perhaps informed by Billett's (2001) use of this construct and social tasks theory drawn from Doyle's (1977) analysis of the ecological classroom. That is, as pre-service teachers and potentially beginning teachers in particular within the HPE staffroom, certain social tasks, as we will explain later, were of crucial importance in moving from the symbolic periphery to the centre. Therefore, to more closely analyse the ways pre-service and beginning teachers forge understandings of being a teacher and teaching within a contested space such as a subject department office, the linking of social task theory with communities of practice made good sense.

We have already suggested that teachers' work consists of numerous tasks performed in various sites within and beyond the school. We indicated above that such tasks, and how and when they are learned, had been explored generally within the context of classrooms (Doyle, 1977). More specific analysis within the context of HPE classes was undertaken by Tousignant and Siedentop (1983), and later by Hastie and Siedentop (1999). Given our initial focus, we were mindful that the idea of performing tasks needed to be extended since, for a pre-service teacher, the social tasks of learning to become a HPE teacher entail the successful completion of a variety of tasks that extend beyond the classroom. Tinning and Siedentop (1985) extended and adapted Doyle's concept of task systems to account for the duties pre-service teachers must perform in the process of becoming teachers. They proposed that pre-service teachers engage in the three interconnected task systems: the teaching task system, the organization task system, and the social task system. All of these task systems contain related tasks that Doyle (1981) later described as a set of instructions that were either implicit or explicit that must be successfully undertaken in order to cope with given situations. Although the task systems are interconnected, what focused our attention was the specific overlap of the organizational and social task systems within the context of the HPE department office.

The organizational task system comprises tasks associated with preparing and planning related to teaching. These activities include arrangements for the physical place of the teaching lesson as well as planning for the lesson itself. The social task system refers to all tasks aimed at forming or maintaining what Tinning and Siedentop (1985) called 'cordial relations'. Such relations (or relationships) include those with the supervising or cooperating teacher, as well as other teaching and non-teaching staff members. Although seldom used in research pertaining to HPE, we considered that reading the pre-service teachers' practices as part of a system of tasks offered a helpful way to make sense of the complex dynamics of a workplace learning context (see Griffey, 1991).

The simplicity of this dimension should not belie its power. The idea of engaging in a range of tasks that appear to be only superficially related to the work one is supposedly meant to be doing is not exactly revelatory. Many junior workers when they first enter a workplace are called upon to perform or conduct social tasks. Indeed, one of the author team, who in a previous life 'went up' to the City of London to become a shipbroker, spent most of the early part of that (very short) career path making the tea and getting the sandwiches at lunchtime. These were important social tasks. However, the power of orienting the original research proposal around social tasks and communities of practice was that it laid a foundation for all of the other dimensions to be explored. The next dimension to sequentially follow social tasks in the research was perhaps immediately obvious. It was clear very early on that undertaking a range of social tasks required pre-service HPE teachers to perform their role in a certain way. As a consequence, we were soon using the idea of performance and practice to make sense of the field texts.

Performance and practice

Continuing on from the idea of social tasks, specifically cordial relations, we started to ponder the idea of the practicum for pre-service teachers as performance. We also recognized that performance was likely to be important in their first year of teaching. Again, it is not especially new to consider the practicum as a site for performance. At a general level many teacher educators and teachers would acknowledge that this is exactly what it is and in the case of this project this was particularly so given the high stakes of assessment for the suitability rating for teaching that we explained in previous chapters. However, the practicum had never really been *theorized* as performance. Thus not only did this thinking have utility, it was seemingly long overdue.

Although the terms 'performance' and 'performativity' are often conflated, epistemologically they are drawn from different traditions. For our purposes the work of Goffman (1959) on 'fronts' in particular framed our thinking. For Goffman, performance refers to how the self is represented using a repertoire of techniques within a range of contexts or more specifically for given audiences. While this may have the appearance of reducing the notion of performance to theatricality, this was not Goffman's intention. Understandably, this presupposes a self-evident (even potentially fixed) identity with essentialist qualities. Goffman's position then is that there is the pre-existence of a subject or actor able to *do* the performance according to the requirements of the situation. To this end, Goffman's notion of performance is about the negotiation of social contexts such that the actor is able to 'go on' with things (see Giddens, 1991). In this sense, identity for Goffman, to use the words used by Giddens (1991) much later, is reflexive.

Goffman's critics point to his over-commitment to essentialism in terms of a pre-existing masterful self that, as a consequence, suggests that his notion of performance may be regarded as only a façade. Such criticism while understandable is only partially helpful. We say this because at their heart, his ideas around the self and around identity are considered as an incomplete project or, to use the words of Butt *et al.* (1997), identity is processual (by which they mean identity is an ongoing process with no discernible beginning or end). Goffman's ideas are akin to Wexler's (1992) notion of becoming and closely linked to Giddens' sense of the self as a reflexive project, links in fact made by Giddens (1991) himself.

For us, Goffman's position of performance and his notion of 'front' resonate closely with the idea of the subjects/agents (read teachers in preparation) and their place in structures such as HPE departments (schools and school systems). Moreover, the capacity to link the work of Goffman with the identity work of Giddens was for us particularly useful in framing the teacher education process as it is played out in the HPE department office.

We took then the department office/staffroom as a stage upon which the drama that is the practicum is constructed. According to Goffman (1959), we present ourselves in everyday life through a convoluted system of what he terms 'fronts'. This may be more familiar as a mask, though this would be misleading. Goffman chooses the term 'front' rather than 'mask' in an effort to distance the idea of 'front' from the more 'make-believe' sense conjured by the term 'mask'. However, Goffman also suggests that while his concept of front is real (in that it really exists), it does provide a strategy that allows for concealment, much as a mask might. This enables the individual to present him or herself in the most appropriate way as called for by a particular context or for particular audiences. In this sense readers might see a close alignment of the idea of front and the Venetian mask, which allows the wearer to act more freely without fully divulging one's identity or status. However, for Goffman the idea of 'front' is multifaceted and might involve concealment, subterfuge, honesty, exaggeration, minimization and other illusionary tactics that assist an individual to 'go on' with things (Giddens, 1991); in other words, to go about one's business in conditions of security and well-being such that there is a coherent and, in some senses, a cocooned sense of self (Giddens, 1991).

Since Goffman (1959) used the term 'performance' to refer to how the self is represented within a range of contexts, these contexts are likely to include a given audience. While this may serve to emphasize conflating the notion of performance with theatricality (to which we alluded earlier), it is not difficult to see that they are inextricably linked. Goffman's position is that subjects or actors are able to conduct the performance according to the requirements of the situation. To this end, Goffman's notion of performance is about the negotiation of social contexts, which according to Giddens requires routines but not routinized practice in the automatic sense but rather through the maintenance of vigilance and control such that a protective cocoon is created (Giddens, 1991). Such a protective device is not static or stable but allows for creativity and change. In this way an individual's identity and sense of self are constructed through an ongoing reflexive process. As Giddens (1991) says, 'the practical mastery of how to "go on" in the contexts of social life is not inimical to creativity, but presumes it and is presumed by it' (p. 41).

In occupational circles then it seems that there is a tendency to try to idealize the performance in accordance with the professional expectations and the social expectations of the community. There will be some dominant values, for example, within a HPE subject department office to which pre-service and new teachers need to subscribe and show support. Teachers need to show competence through what Goffman (1959) calls the 'rhetoric of training' (p. 55). In other words, they have to demonstrate that they are qualified to be part of the HPE community as a consequence of having been through the rigours of professional education and training. However, teachers, whether under practicum type situations or being inducted into the profession, also have to show how they value and ascribe great worth to the learning experiences within the subject department office. Indeed, they often feel compelled to support this even if it is a misrepresentation.

As the notions of misrepresentation and subterfuge continued to contribute to our understanding of just what was going on in the HPE staffroom, it became increasingly apparent that the dispositional nature of the participants had hitherto received little of our attention. The work of Pierre Bourdieu (1977) therefore was attractive. We were aware that this would potentially challenge Goffman's notion of the self and in particular how he uses the word 'identity'. However, we considered this to be both necessary and important as a way of increasing our depth of understanding of the fieldwork we were undertaking.

Identity/subjectivities

Before we develop this particular dimension, we need to comment on what we consider to be a necessary theoretical caution. Relevant research focusing on 'identity' tends to be informed by a range of theoretical positions that are diverse and sometimes epistemologically incompatible. For example, even within this set of authors, Tony Rossi (1999, and with Tim Hopper (2001)) was heavily influenced by the work of George Kelly (1955), Anthony Giddens (1984, 1991) and, as may be seen above, Erving Goffman (1959, 1974), lisahunter by Pierre Bourdieu (1990a, 1998) and post-structural feminists including Judith Butler (1993, 1999) and Elizabeth Grosz (1994), and Erin Christensen by Jean Clandinin (1986, 2000, and colleagues (2009)). Other writers focusing on HPE teachers' identity draw on other theorists such as Michel Foucault, Paul Ricoeur and Anthony Giddens (see, e.g. O'Connor and Macdonald, 2002; Wrench and Garrett, 2012). This illustrates how writers in the field take up certain theoretical 'alignments', and this is particularly the case when considering identity/identities/subject positions/subjectivities/self. Such academic diversity around similar issues also indicates a preference for linguistic structure and meanings ascribed to such structure. It can lead also to a conflation of language that tends more to confusion than to clarity. In places in this volume we have conflated the terms identity and subjectivity for the purposes of including the literature that speaks to the topic. However, it is important to note that these are sometimes lacking in definition, used quite loosely, or conflated in the literature so that we might be talking past some of the issues central to the negotiation of relationship. To illustrate, some regard identity to be fixed within the individual (see above) while others, using the same word 'identity', refer to a fluid and contextually negotiated self (e.g. Giddens, 1991). Variations include identities, subjectivities, subjectivity, embodied identities and selves. For us, we made a conscious theoretical and a linguistic decision.

First, to give focus to the individual person in the study we increasingly drew upon Pierre Bourdieu's concept of *habitus* because it captured, for us, the interconnected nature of the individual with other concepts of field, practice and capital (1977, 1998, 2000). This progressively became our orienting theoretical position as we moved beyond the Goffmanesque notion of *identity*. In addition, we resonated with the physicality evoked by Elizabeth Grosz's term *embodied subjectivities*, although somewhat clunky to use, and the language of the term *subjectivities* to *identities*. Notwithstanding the work of the likes of Giddens, Foucault and the post-structural feminists, to us the word *identity* increasingly seemed to be bound by durable psychological overtones that we preferred to avoid. By subjectivities we are referring to the idea of 'subject positions' created by contexts as a way of distinguishing between subjectivity and identity. For us then, subjectivity, akin to habitus, is the dialectic between being positioned in certain ways (e.g. novice, student, apprentice) and taking certain positions (e.g. learner, student, novice, professional) that may or may not be embodied as fixed ways of being. For us, subjectivity is neither a given nor is it a blank canvas. It does not reside in the person but rather in the practice or situation that evokes and fills subject positions. It is easy to see here how we might get into a theoretical tangle, especially as in the section above we theorized 'practice' using Goffman. However, in many respects our use of Goffman and the *idea* of practice encouraged us to explore other theoretically fertile ground. Bourdieu seemed a next logical step.

Subjectivity may be considered as the site where competing and complementary influences are played out in the processes of becoming or being, so it is contextual and therefore multiple and shifting. In this sense we would concur with Butler (1993) who suggests that subjectivity is something that is performed, and with Bourdieu (1977) who suggests that it (his term being habitus) is practised. We also take the plural version of the concept, subjectivities rather than subjectivity, to make explicit the multiple positions constituted by and constituting the self, the person in context, through practice. You may also encounter 'identities' as a conceptual move that authors have used (see, e.g. Butler, 1999) to capture the multiple nature of the self. While this is ontologically aligned with how we are working with subjectivities, again, we are avoiding the historical psychological roots of identity and therefore its language, situating ourselves more closely to what is perhaps the most accurately representational term for our work, embodied subjectivities (Grosz, 1994).

To make sense of teachers' understandings of themselves within the HPE staffroom we became increasingly orientated around Bourdieu's concepts within the HPE community of practice in the staffroom (Wenger, 1998). Through participation in communities such as the HPE staffroom, pre-service teachers engage in a 'process of being active participants in the *practices* of social communities and construct *identities* in relation to these communities' (Wenger, 1998, p. 4, emphasis in the original). For Bourdieu (1998), the term *habitus* refers to a set of durable dispositions, tastes, along with ways of thinking, acting and being that are shaped through individuals' experiences in various social settings. Hence though they are durable they are not necessarily permanent. The body is pivotal to habitus because through practice, social and cultural norms become inscribed in the body as gestures, deportment, perspectives, behaviours and tastes. Individuals interact and engage in various overlapping social settings that Bourdieu (1977) describes as fields. Such fields or social spaces are infused with power struggles and organizing structure (Bourdieu and Wacquant, 1992). The relationship between habitus and field is dynamic in that through practice in the social fields individuals both shape their habitus and contribute to shaping the habitus of the field. Through this ongoing experiential process identities are formed. Over time through practice in a field, socially constructed ways of thinking become embodied in individuals and 'naturalized' (Bourdieu and Wacquant, 1992).

We took the social field of the subject department office to be a contested social space where individuals are offered or claim different modes of participation based on power dynamics and perceptions (Billett, 2001). The interactions and social positioning within the department office (social field) are influenced by the relative amounts of valued capital individuals are recognized as embodying (Bourdieu, 1984, 2000). The value or capital granted particular resources is particular to the context and may be cultural, social, physical, symbolic or economic. This was particularly noticeable within the context of spatiality theory and in a sense this provided a prompt to pursue this theoretical framework as being another that articulated with the way in which the project was evolving.

Pre-service teachers enter initial teacher education programmes with embodied understandings and ways of thinking and being regarding HPE. There is research, to which we alluded earlier (see Chapter 2), indicating that many of these pre-service teachers share similar past experiences and dispositions associated with sport, activity and health with practising HPE teachers (Dewar, 1989, 1990; Templin and Schempp, 1989). More recently, Brown (2005) and Brown and Evans (2004) have shown that relationships between teacher supervisors and pre-service teachers may act as 'living links' (Brown, 1999) contributing to (re)producing gender norms. This literature and our perspective of identity formation led to our interest in understanding how the pre-service teachers' participation in the subject department office functioned as a site not only for learning but also for identity formation. We were also beginning to explore the idea of the importance of space as Bourdieu had given us concepts of social space. Given that some of our original concerns were around what went on in the HPE staffroom as a place divided into social spaces we were inevitably drawn to theorize the HPE staffroom using spatiality theory.

Spatiality

As we indicate above, we were drawn to the concepts of space, spaces within space and the notion of place, since they were clearly becoming increasingly important as the research texts grew in volume. We had worked with Bourdieu's idea of social space and peripherally drawn on some of the spatialities of school and the work of Nespor (2002), but the idea of space was playing an increasing role in our thinking. To progress these ideas we set about articulating an epistemological frame of reference informed by spatial theorists, particularly Lefebvre (1991) and Soja (1989, 1996), and later and to a lesser extent Massey (2005). We then connected the framework to the school as a workplace.

It is helpful to consider contemporary conceptualizations of space as a trialectic (or triple dialectic) as constructed by both Lefebvre (1991) and Soja (1996). For both, the real and imagined notions of space developed as part of an ongoing analysis of the 'urban', and for Soja this culminated in his unique analysis of the city of Los Angeles. The relationship of this to our interests in learning in the workplace may not be abundantly clear. However, the trialectic provided a powerful backdrop with which to explain the practical phenomena of a working staffroom and other areas of the school beyond.

Lefebvre's interests were in going beyond the idea that space was just about territory, property, production and, inevitably, the concept of 'ownership', claiming that space was culturally and historically shaped. This is brought about by the interactions of those within spaces, according to their perceptions, to evoke that which can be represented in the form of identities, relationships and practices.

By playing with language a little, we take the position that the shaping of workspaces, as they are identified in this study, is brought about through the practices of the community that inhabits the various spaces involved. This captures Lefebvre's and Bourdieu's sense of socio-cultural and historical shaping of space. Therefore, and as Lefebvre would attest, the relationships across spaces became ever more important. The three moments of the production of space as Lefebvre saw it were perception (or physical), conception (represented) and lived (representational). By this Lefebvre meant that space was experienced in an embodied sense (for further explanations of this see the work of Grosz, 1995, 1999, 2001), meaning that the physical sense of space governed some actions and ways of being. This he argued intersected with conceived space, or how space came to be represented or thought about sometimes in abstract or even in design terms. Even though he was determined to get beyond the idea that space was the context for the means of the production of capital goods and the environment in which the structure of work was commensurate with this, Lefebvre was mindful that town planners, architects and so on, in a world moving inexorably towards mass urbanization, were conceiving spaces where living and working were seamless and where the production and accumulation of capital could occur unfettered.

Soja (1996) acknowledges the ideational principle of the conceived or what he termed 'Secondspace' but goes on to argue that such spaces are not without material reality and that often they become manifest as 'Firstspace' in the form of planned projects which draw upon rational science to see them into reality. In other words, what come to represent 'Secondspace' are the rational solutions to complex Firstspace problems such as overcrowding, relocation of industry and citizens, shifting labour patterns, availability of venture capital, re-zoning and urban renewal, to mention a few. As Soja (1996) says, 'the imagined geography tends to become the "real" geography, with the image or representation coming to define and order reality' (p. 79). The representational, or lived space as Lefebvre called it, is perhaps somewhat more abstract but may be understood as a space of the imagination and resistance. Lefebvre originally ascribed this space to the Avant Garde, the surrealists in particular. For Lefebvre this was the site of counter-discourses and of undermining conventional and conceived spatiality. Soja (1996) prefers to refer to this as the 'Thirdspace' and similarly he regards this as the 'starting point for this re-opening and re-thinking of new possibilities' (p. 81). Moreover, Soja (1996) argues that 'Thirdspace as a concept is not sanctified in and of itself. The critique does not stop at three, to construct a holy trinity, but to build further, to move on, to continuously expand the production knowledge beyond what is presently known' (p. 61). It was unclear to us at the time how the Thirdspace might manifest itself given what we have said about social tasks performance and durable dispositions. As it transpired, 'Thirdspace' or the space of resistance was not as we might have anticipated.

Micropolitics

The final dimension that informed this project was micropolitics. This might appear to sit slightly apart from the other theoretical dimensions. There is a very practical reason for this, which is that micropolitics was the theoretical frame used by Erin Christensen to write the Ph.D. that emerged from the research project. However, at an intellectual level Erin's argument that, no matter how we framed the project any study of a school department, particularly one that tends to be geographically separated form the rest of the school, was a study of micropolitics, was compelling. We have included it last in this chapter not because it is the least important and clearly chronologically it was not the final dimension to be considered as the project evolved. Rather, it is placed here, as it is perhaps the one overarching dimension that connects all of the others.

Micropolitics is a particular perspective used in organizational theory which centres around 'those activities taken within organizations to acquire, develop, and use power and other resources to obtain one's preferred outcomes in a situation in which there is uncertainty or dissent' (Pfeffer, 1981, p. 7). The micropolitical perspective has been used in educational research where schools are viewed as organizations, inherently political:

They are seen as characterized by diverse goals, by interaction and relationships rather than structures, by diffuse borders and unclear areas of influence rather than clear-cut conditions of superordination and delegation, by
continuous, unsystematic, reactive change rather than by longer phases of
stable performance and limited projects of development.

(Altrichter, 2001, p. 13594)

While the field of micropolitics and 'its conceptual boundaries and distinctive
features are elusive and contested' (Malen, 1994, p. 147), there is widespread
and sufficient congruence among researchers to provide effective description and
identification of such a perspective.

The micropolitical perspective is concerned with the examination of internal
processes or politics of the school. Politics have been conceptualized as encompassing a three-sided equation involving management, people and their actions
(Marshall and Scribner, 1991). In this way, the micropolitical perspective
emphasizes how individuals or 'actors' within organizations interact with others
with differing interests, goals, status, power and authority (Ball, 1987; Blase,
1991c; Hoyle, 1982). Accordingly, Ball (1987) describes members of the school
as political actors who employ strategic power to pursue their interests in their
daily work. These power strategies are employed by members of the school in
positions of power and/or by members with particular interest sets in order to
retain or obtain control over resources (Altrichter, 2001; Ball, 1987). School
members may do this as individuals; they may unite in loosely associated interest
sets or use subdivisions of the school such as administration teams, subject
departments and staffrooms as bases of power (Altrichter, 2001).

The use of power is a slippery concept within the micropolitical literature.
However, it is central in understanding the micropolitical context of the school.
Given the abundance of highly disputed social science literature surrounding this
concept, we do not have space to delve into the complex theoretical issues
involved; thus the remarks made here will attempt to summarize and highlight
those issues of power deemed particularly relevant to the micropolitics of the
school. Blase (1991a) describes the array of micropolitical definitions as centring
on the 'strategic' use of power in organizations for two general purposes: influence
(a proactive orientation) and protection (a reactive orientation). Bacharach and
Lawler (1980) differentiate between two types of power: authority (the legal right
to make decisions governing others) and influence (the capacity to shape decisions
by informal, non-authoritative means). This distinction of power manifests within
the school context where complex webs of power relationships are evident among
varying members and groups. The scope of members of the school ranges from
those in traditional administrative or authority-based positions such as school principal, assistant principal and head of department, to those with less official power
such as teacher, sports coordinator, office assistant as well as to those not in designated positions of power such as cleaner and student. Influence differs from authority. It is embedded in the embodied relations among the school members or groups
of school members rather than located in the formal/official structures of the

school. It is situational, dynamic and flexible. All members of the school organization may employ influence; however, it is those not in positions of authority that must rely exclusively on their capacity to make decisions through informal, non-authoritative means, to maintain, defend or advance their interests by using their influence. While micropolitical dimensions are influenced by the formal structures of the school, micropolitical theory generally gives greater importance to the power of influence, derived from an individual's personality, expertise, access (especially to information) and resources (material or symbolic) (Hoyle, 1982). Similarly, Bourdieu talks about material or symbolic capital (1986), that which is valued and acts as the means of exchange within a social space. This capital affords one a more or less influential position within a social space from which to influence or legitimate what gets to count as capital, positioning others strongly or less so. The relative relationships of individuals within a social space and the flow of power make particular practices possible, others impossible, and others unimagined.

The field of micropolitics is not only concerned with ideas of power, interests, authority and influence – or what Hoyle (1982, p. 87) calls 'the dark side of organisational life'. Blase (1991c, p. 11) acknowledged both the cooperative and conflictive actions and processes as part of the micropolitical perspective highlighting that 'any action, consciously or unconsciously motivated, may have political "significance" in a given situation' (p. 11). Further, Kelchtermans and Ballet (2002b) depicted the development of micropolitical literacy as a dynamic, ongoing experience always dependent on individuals' meaningful interactions with the particular context. They suggest that political learning, which they termed *micropolitical literacy*, encapsulates three intertwined aspects: knowledge, instrumental/operational and experiential. Understanding, identification and interpretation of power dynamics, roles and interests at stake in a given micropolitical situation form the knowledge aspect of micropolitical literacy. The instrumental or operational aspect reflects the capacity of a teacher to apply a repertoire of strategies that leverage a situation towards their advantage. Finally, the experiential aspect concerns the degree of (dis)satisfaction the teacher feels about his or her micropolitical literacy. The micropolitical perspective, then, offers not only a utensil for understanding the cooperative and conflictive actions and strategies, both covert and overt in nature, played out in everyday school life (and in the HPE staffroom in particular) but also an understanding of the political learning and experiences of the 'micropolitical reality' (Kelchtermans and Ballet, 2002c) of people within schools, and in this project; of pre-service and beginning teachers. Thus viewing and understanding schools (and staffrooms) as inherently micropolitical, dynamic and contested contexts of interaction offered some 'alternative ways of seeing, interpreting and explaining what goes on' (Willower, 1991, p. 442). As Glatter (1982, p. 161) proposes, the greatest strength of the micropolitical perspective is its 'sheer recognisability' [*sic*] (p. 161); it conveys the essence of reality, the complex relations and interactions experienced by members of the school context. It is the micropolitical dimension of workplace learning that guides the discussions of Chapter 9.

Concluding comment

We are conscious that we could be severely criticized for taking the approach that we did. Other readers may prefer a theoretical purity that rests on fidelity to epistemological practice. We could have written this book framed by any one of the dimensions discussed here. We are convinced that such an approach would have served us well and in many respects may have been safer. However, as an account of the project we present in this book, it would also have been dishonest. Across the life of the project all of these dimensions played a role in extending our understanding. In addition, and equally important, failure to include all of the dimensions would have been unrepresentative of the intellectual effort made by different members (some of whom were temporary) of the research team. In this sense alone we feel justified in including all the dimensions by which the project was informed. What this means is that this chapter outlines some significant dimensions of workplace learning that we consider are worthy of attention if the HPE profession and teacher education/profession are to ensure an efficacious and socially just learning space for pre-service and beginning teachers.

In Part II of this book we use these five dimensions of workplace learning to make sense of the rich field texts gathered across the life of the project. Our discussions across the next five chapters provide a more focused exploration and illustration as to how each dimension played out in practice.

Part II

Understanding the data through the dimensions

5 Social tasks of teaching and learning to teach

Introduction

Very early on in the project, it became apparent to us that the pre-service teacher participants had (at some stage) been told explicitly that satisfactory performance of the various tasks that make up teachers' work would determine their evaluation and indeed ultimate success in the practicum setting, and then allow a seamless integration with the profession postgraduation. However, the specifics of what tasks actually constituted teachers' work were far from clear. This was also reflected in beginning teachers' stories of their first year (later in the study), where they were required to perform various work tasks in order to meet probation requirements and subsequently be officially recognized as a fully qualified teacher. Moreover and seemingly more significant, the relative importance of these various tasks was even less apparent for pre-service and beginning teachers. So we were mindful that decisions made in relation to the tasks/duties that constitute teachers' work, by both pre-service and beginning teachers, were likely to have significant implications for their evaluation, job prospects, community membership, identity and practice. What was not at all clear to anyone involved with the project (participants and researchers alike) was the relative importance of the decisions and what might be appropriate and effective strategies to negotiate the making of such decisions. In our view, teacher education and beginning teacher induction programmes were in a relatively weak position to provide advice on all of this. It was considered that the project might at least provide some future direction in this regard.

Hence we were most interested to know how pre-service and beginning teachers negotiated tacit and contradictory expectations, but more specifically, social tasks (Doyle, 1977) during teaching practicum and the induction year. Concomitantly, we were interested in the ways in which their understandings were likely to be mediated by participation in and negotiation of these social tasks. Given our limited knowledge about the ways pre-service and beginning teachers actively shape their understandings in relation to the community of practice within the particular site of the subject department office, it seemed prudent to give closer attention to how this understanding is shaped through the decisions about, and engagement with, social tasks. We took this position

LIVERPOOL JOHN MOORES UNIVERSITY
LEARNING SERVICES

for a number of reasons. Principally among them, as we claimed in Chapter 4, was the idea that cordial social relations seemed to be critical to success (Tinning and Siedentop, 1985). At this time, little had been written about the tasks systems theory (as elaborated in Chapter 4) and its relationship to learning to become a HPE teacher. We considered that a revisit to this theory offered considerable possibility in making sense of how pre-service and beginning teachers 'engage' with the workplace culture of a HPE department and make decisions about how to become (or not become) a member of that community of practice.

We drew upon workplace learning theory with a particular focus on learning as a social task within communities of practice. For the purposes of this chapter it is important to note that although the focus of the analysis would be guided by Doyle's ideas about task systems and in particular his ideas related to social tasks, we embedded this within a broader framework informed by communities of practice and workplace learning with particular reference to Billett's (2001) work. For this aspect of the study, social task systems enabled us to focus on and analyse the teachers' learning experiences and their engagements with the social task system in the context of communities of practice. Through this understanding we were able to identify emergent themes pertaining to communities of practice that constitute HPE subject department offices, student teachers' understandings of themselves as formed within the space (of the staffroom), and their actions to develop their relationship with the community. In our view, the emergent themes had serious implications for HPE teacher education practice, induction year practices by schools and ways in which these ideas and/or practices might be researchable.

Some notes on methodology for this phase of the study

In keeping with social construction perspectives, we were under no illusion that the stories we gathered were influenced by the interview dynamic (Mishler, 1999; Whelan *et al.*, 2001). There was 'dialectic interplay' (Mishler, 1999, p. 18), whereby the researcher was an active co-constructor of the interviewee's narratives rather than a passive consumer of them. However, in an attempt to express pre-service and beginning teachers' perspectives, all participants were given the transcribed interview and invited to comment on the contents and/or the interview processes. This member-check process enabled another perspective for crystallization (Richardson, 2000).[1] As with all phases of the project, we recognized that there is not one 'truth' to be unveiled but instead multiple truths, which are always partial and constructed.

These particular field texts were analysed using open coding in conjunction with an iterative process of constant comparison (Strauss and Corbin, 1998; LeCompte and Schensul, 1999). Similar ideas were grouped into emergent themes related to pre-service and beginning teachers' learning about becoming an HPE teacher through participation in the department office community of practice (Ryan and Bernard, 2000).

Pre-service and beginning teachers engaging in social tasks

Within pre-service and beginning teachers' narratives of the HPE subject department offices we were able to clearly identify their involvement in organizational
and social tasks. Although both experiences contribute to shaping teachers' learning
(Hodkinson and Hodkinson, 2005), our analysis focused on tasks that were seemingly part of an attempt to move from peripheral to full membership of the HPE
community of practice within particular schools. In what follows we discuss three
interconnected themes of social tasks in relation to Lave and Wenger's (1991) and
Wenger's (1998) community components of shared interests, negotiated meanings,
and repertoires of engagement. Specifically, the tasks are: to demonstrate a shared
interest in sport; an appreciation about belonging to a team; as well as the capacity
to use humour, be easy-going and show interest when engaging in the community.

A shared interest in sport

Sport was a central topic of interest in the subject department offices. As mode
and substance of much of the communication in the department office, HPE
teachers talked, reflected, speculated and analysed both about and through sport.
According to Aaron, a pre-service teacher on practicum:

> In this room there was a lot of talk about sport … or the rugby team … […]
> Or more importantly, what happened on the weekend with different sports,
> not just school sport but also national sport as well. That was basically the
> crux of everything.

Professional and amateur sports were discussed at the international, national, local,
school and personal levels. Sport specialization also determined the particular
interest at certain schools, often reflecting the sporting prowess and reputation of
schools. For example, beginning teachers Mark and Sally (whom we have met
elsewhere) were both placed at a school that specialized in rugby union and
hockey. Within their HPE department there were a number of teachers who were
employed specifically to coordinate these speciality programmes. In addition, international competitive seasons and events sparked sport-related conversations, as did
personal and family interests in exercise and sport such as running, weight training
and golf. Also part of the office culture was the practice of betting and footy-
tipping. Footy-tipping may be an unfamiliar term to some readers so some explanation is warranted. It is reasonable to suggest that there is a recreational gambling
culture in Australia that is relatively benign. As in many developed economies
there is also a much smaller group within the community for whom gambling is a
crippling addiction. Footy-tipping however is low cost – low-gain gambling about
the results of the weekend football rounds – and the most popular sports in which
this occurs are professional rugby league and professional Australian Rules Football (all being the adult male version of the sport). Sometimes these 'gambling'
activities are syndicated through work groups or conducted individually, often

through computer technology. Either way the activity itself provides a point of interaction as part of the culture of many Australian workplaces. Through talk about the football results[2] and related activities, sport became reified, taking on what Wenger (1998) refers to as 'thingness' within the space.

In attempting to make sense of the centrality of sport in the office, Sally indicated that 'everyone was just friendly and asked ... what sports you are interested in, because you know that plays a major role'. Pre-service teacher Mark also suggested that 'everyone can connect to someone via a sport'. In addition to being a shared community interest, sport seemed to function as a repertoire for engagement (Wenger, 1998). Embedded in Sally and Mark's comments are a number of assumptions, the first being that sports which are granted privilege in the office are of interest to all participants and concomitant with this is that female sports were rarely discussed across the entirety of the research sites. Second, just as sport is exulted within Australian culture (McKay, 1991) for contributing towards an 'egalitarian order of society' (Macdonald and Kirk, 1996, p. 62), it is considered a level playing field for social interaction in the department office. We are sure you will be perplexed by the contradictions inherent in these statements.

Participating in sports-related conversations afforded pre-service and beginning teachers opportunities to interact with the other teachers and demonstrate shared interests:

> There was one lady in the staffroom and she was heavily involved with touch football and I immediately had a great relationship with her due to my background in the sport.
>
> (Jonathan, a male pre-service teacher)

Some pre-service teachers who recognized the mediating capability of sport-related conversation for community membership yet themselves lacked past experiences to draw upon took alternative tacks. For example, one pre-service teacher stated:

> I would ask questions of him to clarify, not necessarily clarify but make him feel like he was important by answering them if you know what I mean; like asking questions about different sports.
>
> (Alice, a female pre-service teacher)

Sharing experiences with teachers (particularly the supervising teacher or mentor) in work sites other than the subject office (i.e. sports field, gymnasium) also provided content for office conversations and relationship building. As an example, one pre-service teacher noted:

> I am pretty close to one of the guys because of all the hockey stuff and everything I had helped him with, that we had done and you know he had me around for dinner last week and stuff.
>
> (Josie, a female beginning teacher)

The emphasis on sport in HPE subject departments aligns with enduring historical and dominant notions that the purpose of HPE is to foster participation and competition (Penney and Chandler, 2000; Kirk, 2002). For one pre-service teacher the inability to participate in the language and culture of one sport, rugby, meant that he felt so out of his depth that he left his practicum school and opted to be resituated in a primary school (we have told more of this story in Rossi and lisahunter, 2012). This was despite being an elite soccer player, a football code that had no value in his original practicum school. This privileging or legitimation of shared interests in sport or particular sports in HPE departments went unquestioned, at least publicly. Instead, pre-service and beginning teachers engaged in behaviours to enhance their possibility of participating in the shared interest of the community or denied the community with devastating outcomes.

Negotiated understandings of teamwork

Teamwork, a term almost omnipotent within HPE discourse and yet curiously seriously under-theorized (see Barker and Rossi, 2011), was identified as being not only important, but being part of *the* team was clearly a 'desired state'. Therefore understanding oneself as part of a team emerged as a theme in the project. This is captured in the following sentiment from Roger – a male pre-service teacher – which had widespread support:

> Obviously to work effectively you need to have a good sense of ownership to a team sort of thing, a team approach. You can't go in there and take a different role to everyone else because number one it would be too hard and number two, it's just not right. You've got to go in there and work as a team, helping each other out if they need it.

Within the practicum and first-year setting, pre-service and beginning teachers interpreted and sought team membership using varied methods, and this helped them, over time, to move from the periphery. Collaboration, helping out and getting along were deemed highly important. Cheryl, a pre-service teacher, noted:

> It was sort of like a team culture. Everyone would help each other out. Like they'd swap, someone might do someone else's classes this week because someone else was doing something else. There was quite a sort of family.

Similarly, beginning teacher Larry's perception of the staffroom was that it functioned on a shared ethos, a sense of unity and mutual respect among its members; a place where teachers (or team members) were working as part of a team towards a common goal of providing a positive learning environment for students. He explained that the exchanging and sharing of experiences teachers had with students strengthened and facilitated this shared team goal. He exemplified:

I had this kid, you've got him next, he's in this mood, be careful what you say, what you do, something happened at home.

Despite collaboration being emphasized within the context of teacher education, and in particular within the programme in which our participants either had been or still were enrolled, its significance in the office seemed to surprise participants such as Eric:

I found that you use your colleagues a lot more within the staffroom. The amount of interaction that went on between with regarding to lesson plans and ideas and stuff, I didn't think would be. There wouldn't be so much interaction, a lot more individual, but it's not, it's all about sharing. As much as they tell you that within our classes, it's all about sharing.

Recognizing that fitting in as an HPE teacher included being considered a team player meant that pre-service and beginning teachers alike took up social tasks such as helping out both in and out of the office as a way to demonstrate their commitment to the team. For example, for beginning teachers Millie and Sally (whom we met earlier), both on 12-month contracts, attending and helping out at school events and co-curricular sport was a way to demonstrate their commitment to the school and department in order to enhance the prospect of securing a permanent teaching position permanency. Sally explained:

I thought speech night [awards ceremony] could be boring but I better go, it's my first year and it would be good to be seen to go to that kind of thing. It was fine, I didn't mind going, so I think stuff like that yeah I probably did because I was on contract ... I guess with other stuff, you make sure you are at class on time, you make sure you are at your playground duty, you actively contribute to co-curricular sport, etc. and all of that just so that I guess you kind of get along with people and people see that you are doing the right thing.

Further contributing to supporting teams outside the office facilitated pre-service and beginning teachers' relationships with teachers in the office. Pre-service and beginning teachers were learning that a 'good' HPE teacher values his or her team as a support network for work.

Developing repertoires: humour, easy-going and negotiation skills

Humour was a key repertoire within the staffrooms that pre-service and beginning teachers noticed and attempted to join in. Expressions of it included jokes, pranks and teasing of which pre-service and beginning teachers' played roles as witnesses and targets. As the comments below reveal, being a HPE teacher meant being able to both give and get a joke:

They [teachers] would be playing practical jokes and just trying to laugh and keep the atmosphere light-hearted and not to get too bogged down in stressful situations.

(Danny, male pre-service teacher)

He went on to say:

They made jokes about me now and then but I think that was all part and part of it.

Despite reports of witnessing lewd and sexist jokes targeting women, none were considered offensive:

Often jokes and stuff being sent around emails, often some rude ones, which were pretty funny, some yeah stereotypical blonde jokes and that sort of stuff. But everyone had a good laugh and no one took it to heart.

(Jenny, female pre-service teacher)

They [the male HPE teachers] have a joke, but it's a joke and I know it's a joke and it's not that they're trying to be nasty and it's got nasty undertones, it's just a joke. And I'm just like yeah, I know and then that's it.

(Josie)

According to the pre-service and beginning teachers, teasing and alienation was an appropriate repercussion for individuals engaging in behaviours outside the expectations of the group:

They've got this thing, it's called the whoops tin and anytime you do something wrong or someone picks on something that you did that you stuffed up on, you have to pay a dollar to the whoops tin. And they write it down and bring it up at the PE meetings every week and you can argue your case and, so you have to pay a dollar.

(Rhonda, female beginning teacher)

Passive or dismissive responses by the recipients of the teasing were read as agreement or complicity. Dean, a beginning teacher, described a female teacher who was mocked because of her reluctance to go on a school camping trip as 'a bit of a stereotype you know, the whole blond thing. But she played along with it anyway.' To be part of the community repertoire of using humour, pre-service and beginning teachers took up social tasks that included accepting teasing, and laughing at others' jokes. Yet there were boundaries to the ways they were welcome to participate in community and this was part of the negotiation, which presented a significant struggle. Part of the struggle was learning where they were. Thus, for example, an exchange retold as follows clearly fell outside of the accepted norms, yet seemingly was within the behaviour code generally displayed by the departmental members:

At one stage I thought I pushed it a little bit too far. I was bitching to one of the girls, she was about 5 ft. and we were talking about surfing and I thought I would be a bit of a smart-arse and said, 'So what size board do you ride? A 3 ft. board?' that's pretty small, and I don't think she took it too well. I was a little bit naive, but I sort of made a special effort to get back onside.

(Tess)

In contrast, beginning teacher Millie explained her awareness of being the only female in the staffroom:

Sometimes it's like, can I do this, can I push it this little bit further or should I just leave it?... Just on that annoyance factor. Like because I'm – and it comes with this different sex thing. And because I'm really open and I love to hug or touch or do something else, I have to know when to not touch, hug or jump around and dance and make the boys feel uncomfortable.

In this way Millie was conscious of being the only female in the staffroom and the boundaries to the ways she was welcome to participate in the community, with consideration of this guiding her decisions, actions and interactions.

Maintaining the appearance of being either laid-back, jovial, thick skinned, easy-going, up for a laugh, were social tasks that were identified across a range of department offices. This encouraged altered behaviours either on the practicum or in the induction year. How such behaviours become embodied over a longer term probably needs further consideration and is outside the scope of this project, even though we did witness altered behaviours of the final year practicum finding their way into the first year of teaching for some of our participants.

There were other behaviours that might, in other learning contexts, seem both logical and expected that perplexed our participants. Asking questions, for example, might lead to perceptions of incompetence or being over-conscientious. Thus it was deemed necessary to be cognizant of social and cultural dynamics in the office. To this end, strategic or somewhat tactical approaches were sometimes taken. Beginning teachers Sally and Marty explained that they initially 'stuck together the whole time' because they were both 'new'. Sally explained:

I just ask him questions and he asks me questions so we don't feel like we sound like idiots to everyone else.

In addition, one male pre-service teacher said, 'If you play the game a little bit and get to know them a bit better, that's a good thing.' Similarly, although Denise, one of the pre-service teachers, claimed that 'a bit of sucking up never goes astray', she also cautioned, 'you don't want to be too much of a suck up because teachers will see straight through you'. Efforts were made by pre-service teachers to seem keen, yet not phony, too dependent or underfoot. Cheryl, who found herself 'walking that fine line between looking really keen and getting in the way', aptly expressed this balancing act.

Pre-service teachers' attempts to be unobtrusive influenced their physical and emotional behaviours. They tried not to occupy too much space in the office or consume too much of their supervisor or mentor's time. Pre-service teacher Eric was sensitive to the impact of his presence in the office:

> I was encroaching upon their area within that space, particularly with the person sitting next to me. I don't think they were particularly happy with me being in that little section and doing my work there.

Similar to Eric, Brendan was aware that the HPE office was small and busy. He tried to accommodate to these conditions while still making a good impression:

> It was a matter of you know trying to make sure all of my stuff was out of the road, I mean if I'm doing my work, don't leave it sitting there, make sure that as soon as I'm finished with something it would go back in the bag and thrown into the corner, then I'm kind of, you know, I'm there but I'm not there kind of thing.

Pre-service and beginning teachers noticed that the easy-going, laid-back environment was punctuated with frenetic periods where organizational tasks predominated:

> It [the HPE subject department office] can be a very warm place and at other times, you can almost feel the chill in the air; 'just get down to business' where everyone stays to themselves.
>
> (Jonathan, male pre-service teacher)

In addition to negotiating physical conditions and social dynamics in the office, pre-service and beginning teachers also navigated shifts between social and organizational tasks. This required them to make sense of the office environment in order to react and even anticipate shifts in behaviours. For example, one pre-service teacher, Brian, described how changing tasks occurred in the HPE office at his school:

> One minute he'd be having a joke, telling a story, then he'd go, 'Righto, we've got to work now', sort of thing. You were never sure of your place.

Thoughts on 'fitting in' and 'playing the game'

During the practicum experience and in the induction year our participants engaged in multiple tasks aimed at teaching, organizing and relationship build-ing. Listening to the experiences we were struck by the considerable effort, attention and energy that was expended on various interrelated social tasks aimed at building positive relationships with supervisors or mentors and other HPE teachers at the school. This clearly mattered, as being recognized as a 'good' fit with the HPE teaching community had implications for either a successful practicum or progressing a career.

Hence our participants tried to be recognized as helpful, enthusiastic, easy-going, funny, flexible, collaborative and/or accommodating. However, participating in social tasks to be part of the community required nuanced understandings of the space. Not only were expectations often unspoken or tacitly held, conditions and climate frequently shifted in response to changing demands of HPE teachers' work. As such, there were uncertainties about what behaviours would most positively influence practicum evaluation and rating score, the successful fulfilment of probation requirements and securing a permanent position.

Tinning *et al.* (2001) suggest that pre-service and beginning teachers try to cope with uncertainties of the situation by adopting a strategic game-play approach to either the practicum or a first appointment. Their success in the game is influenced by their capacity to figure out the rules of engagement. However, as Tinning and Siedentop (1985) proposed, in situations where expectations are unclear and the significance of outcome is high (as with the pre-service and beginning teachers in this project), considerable energy may be misdirected and invested into interpersonal relationship building. For both pre-service and beginning teachers, this expenditure could limit their inquiry into curriculum and pedagogical practices, and possibly their own professional learning and development. We make this point because, as we found, there were participants in this study who on the practicum and in the first year of teaching sacrificed asking questions (e.g. about curriculum issues) because they feared it might make them seem incompetent, or otherwise negatively affect their evaluation or future employment.

Accordingly we question the extent to which normalizing processes occur through daily participation in social spaces such as the HPE department office. Perhaps, over time, certain practices, which were once disturbing, come to seem reasonable or 'natural'. In the next chapter, we consider the ramifications for pre-service and beginning teachers' practice through the prism of performance theory.

Notes

1 Following Richardson (2000), we use crystallization to express the possibility of multiple perspectives on the same concept. Unlike triangulation, which uses multiple approaches to understand the 'truth' of a concept, crystallization holds no promise of a knowable truth.
2 This phase of the research took place during the Australian winter.

6 Performance and practice

Introduction

We saw earlier on (in Chapter 5) the importance of maintaining cordial relations as part of the process of being accepted into the community of practice bounded by the entity named the HPE department. This 'performance' was clearly a strategy to move from the periphery towards the centre of the community. We acknowledge that there were limits as to how far outsiders or newcomers could travel from the periphery. Nonetheless, as a strategic device it became evident that crucial to potential for such possible movement was the 'performance' of the outsider or newcomer to particular audiences; in other words, the performance of pre-service and beginning teachers to the full-time members of the department.

This chapter considers how pre-service and beginning teachers 'perform' their 'selves' within subject department offices or staffrooms during the practicum or initial teaching appointment. To this end we were interested in where the performances in HPE teacher education were likely to be most authentic. To do this, we used a conceptual framework informed primarily by the work of Goffman on 'performance' and 'front', supported with Giddens' ideas around protective cocoons and 'going on with things' (as described in Chapter 4). In the discussions of this dimension it is worth noting that many performances of the participating pre-service teachers were considered by the research team to be inconsistent with the coursework ideals and principles within the teacher education programme in which they were enrolled, but in step with the general ethos of most HPE department staffrooms. Beginning teachers' performances were different performances, albeit with links to that of the practicum. For them, new subject positions became available for performance but there was also a shift to something more akin to a negotiation of practice, as we explore in the following chapters of Part II.

Going about this part of the study

This aspect of the study was originally located early on in the project and was prompted by the 'performances' of pre-service teachers. However, once the dataset expanded to include the beginning teachers (pre-service teachers who we tracked into in their first year of teaching) we realized that ideas about 'perform-ance' were not isolated to the practicum phase of teacher education but were applicable to those entering the profession and the way they went about their work. We were conscious that though we were drawing on a theoretical frame constructed around the ideas of Goffman (1959) we did not gather data using the ethnographic processes that characterized his work. The design conventions of his work and the necessary attention to minute social interactions were simply impossible within the context of this research. As a consequence we have relied on the reports of interactions between the pre-service teachers and their super-vising teachers and beginning teachers and their mentors, as well as additional significant others (such as the head of department if he or she were not the super-vising/mentor teacher). We accept that such reports will be filtered through the participants' perceptions of their everyday interactions. This means that we were consciously engaging in second-order interpretations. We acknowledge that such an interpretive design might limit the findings, particularly as we are relying on the interpretive skills of the participants to make sense of what can be complex environments. We considered that the trust established over a prolonged period of association with the project and indeed with us as researchers would encour-age the participants to be as truthful as possible and to attempt to read the depart-ment milieu as accurately as possible.

The dominant performances

During their practicum experience, pre-service teachers spent the great majority of their non-teaching time in HPE subject department offices. We have already advanced the well-supported case that these are significant social spaces for teacher education because of the potential opportunities they afford to interact and forge relationships with other teachers (particularly practicum supervisors). Through this participation, the space offers openings to construct understandings and identities associated with, and valued as, being a HPE teacher. It also com-mences the process of becoming more than a peripheral member of the profes-sional community. It seemed that in order to become a member of the community there were legitimated or valued discourses that had to be performed, and such discourses were sometimes in the visual form of bodily appearance, including what one wears.

Performing valued discourses

It was clear that certain kinds of talk dominated the staffrooms into which the HPE pre-service teachers had been placed. As already established, sport and fitness, as some of you might expect, were significant. Connected to this was an underlying discourse relating to the performance of bodies and this was the per-formance of 'attitude' related to the obesity debate (we prefer not to reify the language of an epidemic or crisis). The coursework that the pre-service teachers had undertaken up to this point had adopted different positions on the obesity question. For example, our participants would have undertaken, as part of their teacher education programme, units or courses of study that related to health promotion. In such courses, obesity was characterized as a serious problem where metaphors such as 'ticking time bombs' and 'economic catastrophe' were not uncommonly associated with an apocalyptic obese future. The course with which the practicum was associated and other courses related to professional practice and teacher education, as opposed to human movement science or exercise science, did not proselytize a particular position on this but rather had encouraged critique and an open mind, and had urged a willingness to draw from a wide range of medical and sociological literature (see Gard, 2011).

However, the coalescence of the particular discourses operating in the HPE staffroom required a certain type of performance that was counterproductive to critique. So, when talking about sport, first it was likely to be what was regarded as male sport that dominated staffroom conversations. This immediately gendered the performance, since the social task required (as identified in Chapter 5) was to get connected to the conversation. This attention to high-performance sport also connected to bodily shape such as might be defined by muscularity, narrow definitions of fitness seemingly mostly to play various codes of football, or hockey or netball – which with the exception of association football or soccer are all Australian winter sports. This seemed to flow seamlessly into judgements about those who did not have such bodily aspirations. The well-rehearsed characterizations of fat people – even those who might be described as modestly overweight according to socially constructed norms (that is, lazy, incompetent, disorganized, unreliable) were in abundance (Gard, 2011; Gard and Wright, 2001, 2005; Tinning, 1985).

> Yeah, everyone was pretty 'fit' looking ... or should I say slim. Even I was told I was 'no shrinking violet' by one of the guys – I just didn't get why they were so obsessed with people's size ... I mean even me! – and I'm an active netball player. I started to wear my representative gear just so that they didn't think I was just some fat slob who couldn't do anything or was useless.
>
> (Tess)

Establishing an alignment to these discourses of sport contributed to our participants' sense of comfort in the environment to which they had been assigned. For example, one pre-service teacher explained:

> I helped him [the Rugby Union coordinator] out with a few Rugby Union things and then after that it was really, really good and, we kind of became mates.
>
> (Philip, male pre-service teacher)

This was particularly the case where the demonstration of knowledge was at a personal level and, in terms of identity performance, was indicative of Giddens'

(1991) notion of ontological security. This sense of being seemed to create a sense of protection from a more hostile gaze. Their embodiment of similar ways of thinking influenced the sense of ease pre-service teachers expressed feeling about department office practices:

> I was quite comfortable. Rugby league and AFL [Australian Rules Football] were the *hot* topics[1] while I was there. They were both in the middle of the season and I like football so it worked out well.
>
> (Peter, male pre-service teacher)

As one might imagine however, within the context of the practicum, possibly more so than in the first year of teaching, female pre-service teachers were at an immediate disadvantage simply because of the time of year when the practicum was undertaken. Given that it was winter, the topics of conversation were dominated by the games ascribed most cultural capital, and in Australia in the winter these, as we previously indicated, are the three main football codes. At one level this may seem like a statement of the obvious. Sport, given that it is often loosely considered to the subject matter of physical education, is frequently a topic of conversation in HPE staffrooms and on occasion in other departments as well. However, it is well recognized that sports experiences are a common feature in the recruitment process in HPE and form part of the subjective warrant for choosing to be a HPE teacher in the first place (Dewar, 1989; Tinning *et al.*, 2001). However, what was reported to us repeatedly was that regardless of their investments in specific sports, the pre-service teachers found they needed a much broader sports vocabulary. The demands of this were noted as the need to be contemporary (what were the key events currently taking place both in Australia and abroad); being highly informed (or at least seeming to be so); and showing prejudice with regard to what sports were worth talking about. So while on the surface this 'performance' seemed relatively straightforward it was fraught with pitfalls, and inevitably those best positioned were those able to improve their sports discourse performance based on the dominant forms of professional sport at the time.

In both the practicum and first-year context, being able to participate in discussions about particular sports of interest in the office afforded certain pre-service and beginning teachers access to contact with key teachers (i.e. supervisors, mentors and sports coordinators) who acted as the 'audience' to this performance participation. In some cases, the necessity of performance spilled into their private lives and, while this was indicative of fuller participation in the community, it required a level of engagement beyond the norm. These interactions offered opportunities to demonstrate impressiveness even when the commitment to some of the sports being talked about was limited. In contrast, those teachers (pre-service or beginning) unable or unwilling to perform the sports discourses found themselves on the periphery of the HPE community in the school. One of the pre-service teachers, Mark, demonstrates how it was desirable to extend his performance to social interactions outside of the school context:

I think a few of [the HPE department] were pretty good friends and would meet up on the weekends for drinks and stuff as well ... I was always invited and I went most Fridays. I'd been invited to the ones on the weekend and went once or twice. They tried to meet up occasionally and I think near the end of the term we went to a volleyball place and stuff. I got invited to that and went along to that as well.... My supervisor was there so I felt a bit obligated to try and be part of it.

Instances like these tended to afford pre-service and beginning teachers opportunities beyond the school boundaries and to potentially deepen relationships with supervisors, mentors, sports coordinators and other HPE staff members. For these participants, learning the value placed on being perceived by the HPE community as a 'good' fit contributed to their perception that the process of 'becoming' was a game (see, e.g. Tinning *et al.*, 2001) with highly specific rules and resources (see Giddens, 1991). The performance of valued discourses, particularly those surrounding sport, meant that the values of these types of social interactions were understood particularly for how they might be later perceived at the time of evaluation, progress or probation reports. One beginning teacher looking to extend her six-month contract explained:

I wanted to get into the rugby league, they're [the HPE department] thinking about doing girls rugby league next year and they're going to need someone to take it ... so I told the HOD, I was like all right, rugby, teach me.... He's like all right. So I go with him on a Wednesday afternoon to training and he teaches me.

(Anne, female beginning teacher)

As we reported previously, others in the project later confirmed how their knowledge of sport had gained them entry into the teachers' social world beyond the confines of the school. Some were even drawn to say how they had become 'good mates' with the teachers in the staffroom, though it is important to acknowledge that no female pre-service participants in this study reported this level of camaraderie.

Importantly, there is another plot to this narrative of discourse performance. Where our participants *lacked* the necessary background, the performance had to be all the more sophisticated, and required alternative strategies such as volunteering for team manager positions (rather than coaching positions) and/or helping other teachers/coaches during their lesson or training sessions. Others developed what we came to call a 'performance of inquiry'. This connected them to the discourses but in more subtle ways. For example, one beginning teacher explained:

I just ask them questions like and I vary my questions between people ... because you make them feel like they are needed and helpful and that you are keen to learn.

(Tess)

Primarily it involved initiating the need for help and to acknowledge the expertise of supervising or mentor teachers as well as other teachers within the staffroom. In other words, this 'front' for social interaction drew the pre-service and beginning teachers who used it into the centre of the staffroom community by showing commitment to learning, rather than exposing their lack of knowledge in certain areas or of contemporary events.

Not all pre-service and beginning teachers were able to perform in this way, not even for the purposes of misrepresentation (see Chapter 4). For those who considered their performance to be completely misaligned with those of the community, their discomfort was palpable. Performing valued discourses was at best awkward and at worst threatening, and, as we explore in Chapter 8, such teachers found it increasingly necessary to seek 'other spaces' within the context of the work of the department. This enabled pre-service teachers to escape the unappealing discourses that ranged from hyper-masculinity to over-emphasis on competitive sport, body shapes, children's motor incompetence, the dismissal of curriculum documents and the rubbishing of university-based knowledge (to list just a few), all topics that had been so heavily critiqued in their university course work.

As we will show in Chapter 8, some teachers chose not to adjust their behaviours to accommodate the social environment of the HPE subject department office. Some, for example, spent their time either in another department office or in other areas of the school altogether. However, it was broadly acknowledged that such action might lead to repercussions related to evaluation in the case of the pre-service teachers, and potential limits to school transfer possibilities in the case of beginning teachers.[2] In short, the capacity to demonstrate an alignment of their interests and those of the HPE subject department was a high-stakes game. A failure to do so could have repercussions such as social isolation, a low rating and/or limited employment opportunities. These were significant concerns for a number of the participants and some fervently believed that this was reflected in how they were evaluated either as pre-service or beginning teacher.

Performances of the body

Expectations regarding body form, bodily maintenance and health within the HPE profession are hardly new (see, e.g. Evans *et al.*, 2004; Hunter, 2004; Kirk, 1997; Tinning, 1985; Vertinsky, 1992). For the most part however it was the degree of scrutiny and regulation that the pre-service teachers noticed most. This meant that the audience for bodily performances within the context of the departmental office was always present. Tess (whom we met a short while ago), for example, decided to sit in certain ways in the staffroom. So, for example, she told us that she tried not to 'sprawl' in the staffroom because it looked as if she was taking up a lot of space – even though other members of the department did this. In a sense she was trying to camouflage her body. She realized that the easiest way to do this was to sit behind the desk she had been allocated rather than 'sit on the comfy chairs', since this would have her out in full view. This sometimes placed her at the periphery of staffroom conversations, but she'd rather this than have her body constantly scrutinized just to see if she (what she called) 'passed muster'. Hence it was clear that it was crucial to manage the impression (see Goffman, 1959) of the body to ensure how the body (that is, its composition) looked, how it was adorned with clothes, was constantly performed to ensure that it was deemed acceptable. At the same time 'other' bodily performances of those outside HPE were more often than not the subject of derision and this was consistent with the performance of dominant discourses discussed above. Not only did the participants of this research have to manage the impression of their own bodies, they also had to perform the 'body talk' directed at others, even when they knew such language was discriminatory and on occasions abusive. As Tess revealed to us later, 'Yeah ... I don't reckon I could really say they hate the fat kids or the unco[3] kids at this school – mostly during lessons they just seem to ignore them.'

Community expectations, values and taken-for-granted norms interconnecting bodies, activity, health and values were explicitly and implicitly conveyed through the words, actions and organizational structures of the HPE department. The normalized process of ascribing characteristics of personality to particular body shapes seemed to be met with little resistance within many HPE staffrooms. Moreover, having a thin, fit-looking body reflected what Macdonald and Kirk (1999) refer to as 'corporeal regimes' (p. 135) where the body becomes a signifier for social and personal behaviour. The individualistic and unproblematic correlation between body shape, health and fitness found in this part of the study confirms previous research findings (Macdonald and Kirk, 1999; Macdonald and Tinning, 1995). The 'playing along' with the general corporeal discourses prevalent within HPE departments, as a form of performance, is inconsistent with one of the key underpinning principles, namely acceptance of difference, which is embedded in the university coursework that these preservice and beginning teachers undertook. This inconsistency could simply reflect the different positions within the broader university programme itself; where there is a valorizing of narrow-minded health promotion discourses, risk reduction and healthy lifestyles juxtaposed with the social justice principle of embracing 'difference'. Of concern for us was that the performance of the preservice and beginning teachers appeared to have some authenticity mainly because the participants identified with the corporeal characteristics within particular social spaces such as the HPE subject department office.

Corporeally 'looking the part' of a HPE teacher was pivotal to being accepted within the department. As part of this, how one looked in what one wore was also significant. Although some pre-service and beginning teachers expressed their dislike for the dominant mode of dress, noting that it was all the same, too jock-like, militaristic, it was nonetheless deemed appropriate 'professional' HPE wear by the university and schools, and consequently they engaged in the performance of appearance. Even though some felt they were perpetuating the 'jock image' that was the basis for their discomfort, they used the front of 'appearance' to consolidate and perform their professionalism. Any challenges to this occurred only at the margins. Through habits of dress style, values and historical constructions of HPE teachers were performed within the department offices in highly explicit ways. Specifically, gender constructions underpinned these norms and, as one pre-service teacher observed, resistance was minimized by the regulatory practices by the boundary keepers. For those who failed to meet the 'standards' or privileged dress style, public commentary (within the staffroom) was sure to follow, and this was invariably derisory and insulting. We talk more about this in Chapters 7 and 8.

Perplexing questions

When drawing on Goffman (1959), we find ourselves in something of a dilemma. When performing, do pre-service and beginning teachers use 'fronts' in the university setting and perhaps revert to a predisposed self when in the practicum or first-year context? We ask this question because, as we have mentioned, the participants in this research were all part of a programme that extolled the virtues of social justice and yet such principles were eschewed in favour of an acceptance (indeed a justification of) behaviour that might be deemed inappropriate. We are compelled to propose that when these pre-service and beginning teachers' performances aligned with those of the department office, their practices (i.e. words and actions) further entrenched these norms within the departmental staffroom. However, we are mindful that the high-stakes environment may have encouraged this performance. It is a performance that of course demonstrates a naturalizing process in which those who are unable to 'fit in' are perceived as 'soft', 'not up to the job' or just plain deviant.

Although our findings, like others' (Brown, 2005; Brown and Evans, 2004), suggest that practicum and first-year performances may lead to a tendency for social reproduction, we argue that there were instances of agency which hold potential for social change. We return to our examples of misalignment between pre-service and beginning teachers' performances and the expectations of the HPE subject department office. Some of our participants engaged in performances that rubbed against the boundaries of what was understood as acceptable, tensions that are played out in social spaces such as the HPE staffroom (see Chapter 8) but also in individuals and the profession (see Chapter 7), tensions captured throughout this book.

Notes

1 We have added emphasis here to illustrate the importance ascribed to this issue by the participant.
2 In the state of Australia where this research took place, the capacity to transfer is earned by employment in difficult locations (remote or country), first-year reports and contractual circumstances (short-term or permanent position).
3 Commensurate with the Australian vernacular habit of shortening words, 'unco' stands for uncoordinated.

7 Identity/subjectivities and the profession/al

The focus of this part of the study

Teacher identity research and literature has sought to understand the emerging teacher as an individual self. This self is shaped by a history within cultural practices prior to teacher education, through teacher education practices introduced through institutions such as our own, and, as part of this, in the school setting as practicum experiences. The associated literature uses the language of identity, identities, subjectivity, subjectivities and a range of other concepts to explore this 'self' and the process of becoming and being a HPE teacher. The credentialing process to be deemed a professional, and to therefore constitute a profession, relies on a clarification as to who or what a teacher must be, through considering certain practices as legitimate and valued and therefore expected or encouraged. Otherwise practices are regarded as inappropriate, unwanted or unacceptable and used to differentiate those who are teachers from those who are not. This scholarship of Initial Teacher Education and HPE teacher identity has a long history (see, e.g. Fernandez-Balboa, 1997; Macdonald and Kirk, 1996; Tinning *et al.*, 2001; Solmon, 1993; Wrench and Garrett, 2012), with Fiona Dowling's (2011) recent work exploring the relationship between physical education teacher education students and their notions of a professional identity. We have established that the subject department office appears to be a key site for influencing curriculum and resource decisions. In addition, and as we have already indicated, the site of the staffroom and the practices of the community within it have a profound influence on teachers' professional identity (Hodkinson and Hodkinson, 2005; McGregor, 2003). However, as we progressed in the study we came to realize that far less was known about how emerging teachers are affected by their participation in staffrooms in terms of their sense of self and their emerging identities or subjectivities as teachers. Work by Rossi (1999) demonstrated that pre-service teachers portray an array of identities (the term he chose to employ at the time) or to have multiple selves, some of which might be identified as strategic, some as compliant and so on. These identities clearly assisted in the day-to-day negotiation of the school workplace environment. However, Rossi's work had no specific focus on the staffroom as a space of workplace learning.

Other recent attempts to understand pre-service teachers' identities and practices describe identity formation as an ongoing process of negotiation (Rossi, 1999) but with a more specific connection to the social and cultural contexts of schools and society (O'Connor and Macdonald, 2002; Rossi, 2000). Furthermore, there was enough in the literature to convince us that pre-service teachers' and teachers' past experiences and discursive histories may be considered as highly influential in relation to identity formation (Devis-Devis and Sparkes, 1999; Macdonald and Kirk, 1999; Rossi and Hopper, 2001), as well as their relationships with school supervising teachers or mentors in the first year of teaching (Brown, 2005; Brown and Evans, 2004). In terms of qualified and experienced HPE teachers' identities – in other words, the identities that dominate the practices within HPE – it is widely accepted that exercise, physical activity and sport occupy a central defining place, as do the connected ideologies of healthism and what we prefer to term body shapism or a preoccupation with body shape as a signifier of health, beauty and sexual desirability. Furthermore, there is ample evidence that many HPE teachers tend to be sexist, elitist, and generally insensitive to social issues (see, e.g. Colquhoun, 1991; Flintoff, 2012), and much of this was confirmed during this study. It is this kind of community into which we place new physical education professionals to learn during the process of 'work'.

This chapter pays close attention to the key relationships within the context of becoming and being a teacher, the relationship between the supervising teacher and the pre-service teacher within the context of the practicum, and between the mentor and beginning teacher. This is within the context of the induction year as being central to the exploration of HPE student teachers' identity formations which, we argue, are mediated through their participation in social and cultural processes of HPE subject staffrooms (see Chapter 5). Before progressing to these relationships we need to remind the reader of our commentary relating to theoretical caution in Chapter 4 surrounding author alignments and identity/subjectivity theory. Recall we suggested that how this theorizing plays out in the academic literature depends to some extent on researcher alignment with particular social theorists. We ask you to bear this in mind as you progress through the chapter.

As we have established, the staffroom acts as a social field albeit at a micro level. It is a contested social space where individuals are offered, or claim, different modes of participation based on positioning or power dynamics. This occurs according to the capital or value they are ascribed (Billett, 2001; Bourdieu, 1989), legitimation practices that constitute what gets to count as valued (capital) in the first place, and perceptions influenced by the field. The interactions and social positioning within the micro social field of the staffroom are influenced by the relative amounts of valued capital individuals are recognized as embodying (such as sports person with an esteemed level of performance). The value granted to one's resources, such as sporting prowess or a thin and able body, are particular to the context and may be cultural, social, physical, symbolic or economic. However, one of the key features that underpinned the entire workplace experience for these pre-service teachers, and therefore influential on the entire project, was their perception of the significance of the suitability rating. This rating was that which they were given at the end of the practicum to indicate their future employability. Together, the experiential perspectives of Bourdieu (1998) and Wenger (1998) enabled us to consider the pre-service teachers as actively shaping identities while at the same time having them shaped by the constraints of power and structure of the community space and beyond.

What emerged from this aspect of the study

Readers will already have a sense through some of the data, themes and narratives we have shared that our findings were less than complimentary to the profession or at least the HPE community of practice within the profession. Recall some of the key themes of the study we have already shared such as 'sports talk' as a feature of day-to-day life in the staffroom; 'how one looked' as a measure of suitability to be in the job; and legitimized portrayals of hyper-masculinity. It is not difficult to get a sense of the hegemonic culture of 'maleness' legitimated as normalized hegemonic heterosexual hyper-masculinity as an explicit feature of some of these workplaces. If we return to Illeris' (2011) point about the importance of workplace climate, it is easy to ask whether anything of significant professional value could have been learned in such environments. What was learned was that it is important to participate in the practices of the community, in the micro field, in order to function with legitimacy and agency rather than be ignored, delegitimated or marginalized within that community. There are two things that spring immediately to mind. First, what seems to be an enduring feature of this study is that teacher educators can hardly take heart in this finding given the critical agenda that has underpinned HPE teacher education for at least the last 20 years (see, e.g. Kirk and Tinning, 1990; Fernandez-Balboa, 1997). Second, and just as important, this analysis must surely challenge the taken-for-granted assumption that learning within a community of practice is inherently effective or good, let alone ideal. The idea that communities of practice may *not* provide for a positive learning experience is not one that has received much attention and would run counter to the positive justifications employed by workplace integrated learning advocates. We believe such a critique is long overdue.

If we take some of the common themes we established across the life of this project, then applying theoretical constructs around ideas of subjectivities can provide further insight to the context of workplace learning within a framework of becoming a teacher. For example, common themes of the role of sport for sharing interests, as a conduit for discussion and a shaper of possible subject positions for new members to the social space, or even as a potential barrier to the inner circle of the HPE community, may be scrutinized. How such a theme in this space may be taken up as part of one's identity or subjectivity is an example of what Goffman (1959) would call 'impression management' – an idea we explored in Chapter 6. So gendered was the sports discourse across the life of the project that it was often an orienting feature in some staffrooms and in others it was a defining feature. We found that the females in the research cohort had to perform their subjectivities with an interest in the sports talk, for example, to 'fit in', in Bourdieuian terms to fit 'the structures constitutive of a particular type of environment' (1977, p. 72). Of course the effect of this was to reproduce 'the objective structures of which they are a product' (p. 72), the objective structures of sport and sport talk. This did not always occur unknowingly, but rather for some as a 'strategy-generating principle' (p. 72) to ensure they were not marooned on the periphery of the practices of the community that constituted the HPE field. Hence, being able to participate in discussions about the particularly gendered sports of interest in the staffroom afforded certain legitimation or value in the form of access to, and positive positioning by, key or strongly positioned teachers. These key teachers held capital in the social space and indeed beyond. For example, the reporting procedures and evaluation by key teachers of both pre-service and beginning teachers heavily influenced the pre-service or beginning teacher's ongoing progress. For the pre-service or beginning teaching having any form of capital or being perceived as having capital legitimated their social positioning within the staffroom, providing a means to move towards fuller community membership (Wenger, 1998). Indeed, the process of moving towards fuller community membership was about capital acquisition and transfer (Bourdieu, 2000) and identifying the rules of what became perceived as a 'game'. This was clearly crucial to the acquisition of capital, in certain practices being legitimated, and in one's social positioning within the teaching group.

Thus, even though this necessitated an adjusted form of conduct for those who did not particularly want to talk about certain forms of sport, the value of being able to talk about sport enabled some of the participants to get closer to the part of the job that interested them the most. Many of the males in the study also had to use such a tactic. Eric, a high-performance rugby union player, used this experience to get closer to the teacher in the staffroom who had interest in and some control over the health education taught within the department. Eric didn't necessarily want to move into health education per se but recognized that it was an area in which he was weak, so he strategically sought to align himself with those who had the expertise in the staffroom. The capital he exchanged was his playing expertise in rugby union, and having benefited from high-level coaching.

For some, though, the exchange of capital through this mechanism was much more difficult. Tom's dispositions, for example, did not allow him easy entry into the community, and the misalignment between his own interests and those of the community left him feeling uncomfortable in the space. As he said: 'Very masculine is the first thing I think of, very masculine. The whole [staff]room was intimidating.' As a consequence, Tom found it necessary to 'absent' himself from the HPE department, all the time using what appeared to be legitimate reasons. Tom chose to spend his time in the science staffroom, science being his second teaching subject. He was not alone in seeking this sanctuary (see, e.g. the story of Sandra in Chapter 1). It was in this social space where he felt his dispositions more closely aligned with the subject positions which characterized that professional community. Sport was not the be-all and end-all. Further based on his descriptions of how the science department functioned, we figured that he was able to trade more capital in the science department because that was where his teaching was ascribed more value in its contribution to the work of *that* community of practice. Hence moving from the periphery of the science department community, or being legitimated there and therefore positioned more strongly, was that much easier and successful. We have noted this phenomenon elsewhere (see Rossi and lisahunter, 2012) where using spatial theory we were able to show that physical absence from the community of which one is allegedly or nominally a part, because of one's dispositions, is tantamount to an act of defiance or more accurately resistance. This space of resistance, Edward Soja's (1996) *Thirdspace*, is discussed in Chapter 8. Being some body – that is, a present body – is made present through a physical, a corporeal presence, but also by being legitimated it was a double move. This double move was Tom's deliberate taking up of a subject position within the field that legitimated him. At the same time Tom was now shaping (and being shaped by) one staffroom by his presence and the other by his absence.

The appearance and competence of the physical body through a corporeal discourse was pervasive throughout the research. We are not at all surprised by this prevalence; nor probably is any reader familiar with HPE teacher education. The HPE literature has ample examples of this ever-present theme beyond the obvious notion of HPE being the site of work on the body. For example, we can look to the early work of Tinning *et al.* (1993), Armour (1999), Macdonald and Kirk (1999), Wright (2000) Gore (2002), and the plethora of contemporary articles that pepper the likes of journals such as *Sport, Education and Society*; *Physical Education and Sport Pedagogy* and the *European Physical Education Review*. However, the role of corporeality as a discourse shaping subjectivities was not quite as we expected. For example, the body form, maintenance (through fitness regimes) and health were on occasions juxtaposed with the bodies of others on the broader staff of a school and the inevitable comparisons were far from complimentary. As described earlier, our research participants reported how other teachers were routinely ridiculed from within the sanctuary of the HPE staffroom. We acknowledge the difficulty pre-service or beginning teachers have in resisting a dominant culture and speaking back to it but the power of the corporeal discourses and the nature and degree to which they were taken up by our participants took us by surprise, mainly because it was the antithesis of the programme our participants were in or had graduated from. For example, one of the pre-service teachers, Patty, expressed views regarding bodies and behaviours that seemed to align seamlessly with those she witnessed in the HPE community where fitness, image, being buff, were simply taken for granted. When the HPE staff was compared to staff in other departments, not only were their overall health, weight and general demeanour criticized, but also assumptions were made about the dubious quality of their work as teachers. Indeed, she emphasized that there was a 'big values gap and attitudes gap between them' (between

HPE and art departmental staff members). In fact Patty's perspective of the situation suggests that she considered her ideas to align with those of the HPE community and was clearly comfortable with this position. There was no indication of dissonance or questioning of values and perspective held by herself or the community, even outside the staffroom, what might be politically an impossible space in which to express such a critique. Assessments regarding body shape, size and maintenance led to judgements (by Patty and other HPE teachers) that the art teachers lack 'self-control, self-discipline, or will-power' (Petersen and Lupton, 1996, p. 25). Corporeality is assumed to reflect values, characteristics, behaviours and lifestyle choices. An ideal of a thin, fit-looking individual emphasizes the idea of corporeal regimes where the body becomes a signifier for social and personal behaviour. Moreover, these corporeal characteristics act as physical capital in the HPE community space (see Shilling, 2003). The unproblematic correlation between body shape, health and fitness found in this study confirms similar findings from previous research studies (Macdonald and Kirk, 1999; Macdonald and Tinning, 1995). Interestingly, there was no indication from Patty of questions about who determines or enforces the norms regarding bodies. For some there was a lack of conscious reflection about the part they were playing in reinforcing oppressive practices.

However, this 'corporeal assessment' of others was not only for those outside the HPE department. Some participants described the often-crushing surveillance of their bodies within the confines of the staffroom, so we were presented with what appeared at least to be a paradox. The members of our research cohort were in environments where capital available through their sporting experiences and achievements could be traded for legitimation or closer proximity to the power of the community, yet their bodies also had to be deemed legitimate. The entrenched durability, then, of the staffroom norms constituted a space where demeaning enforcement practices were tolerated by both teachers and pre-service or beginning teachers. Regulating experiences beyond the HPE community have also been reported by HPE pre-service teachers (Macdonald and Kirk, 1996) and teachers (Sykes, 2001); however, in this study the regulators were colleagues from within the subject department community. The impact of this was also contradictory. At one level there was general disapproval of this conduct. If nothing else it was inconsistent with the values embedded within the socially critical syllabus the teachers and pre-service teachers were supposed to be delivering where discursive oppressions were to be exposed and resisted. This was clearly troublesome as, for many, slipping into the judgemental discourses of the department related to body shape, etc. was relatively easy. It was also troublesome for us as we had little idea how the teachers who were part of this study treated the students with whom they were charged to work.

Corporeal discourses also spilled over into codes of dress and general presentation, as we have also previously discussed. While some found the idea of a 'PE uniform' somewhat demeaning, particularly its historical connections to military-style discipline, in general the idea of 'uniform' – in other words, there being 'one form' of HPE teacher – was widely accepted, and more importantly normalized along gender lines. Indeed, to some extent the university itself played into these common expectations related to appearance or presentation. Those who fell outside of these norms and expectations were ridiculed. Patty described the howls of derision directed at Barb, a pre-service teacher also allocated to the HPE department but who was from another university in the region. One of the reasons for such ridicule was Barb's code of dress, which was not only outside the conventions of a militarized appearance but was heavily feminized. Barb's fondness for the types of skirts and shorts she wore rendered her being a 'really ditzy' or 'such a girl' where yet again the word 'girl' was used in a pejorative sense. This is what is meant by gender performance, as described by Butler (1999, 2004). Barb seemed to accommodate the ridicule, to her face, and accept the perceptions the others had of her because she was female. Patty's unquestioning acceptance of the ideas suggests complicity of the teachers' assessment as at least an unwillingness or inability to challenge their assessment. Interestingly, she later expressed her intention to challenge the norms of attire: 'I think sometimes the dress codes are a little too rigid ... I'd like to think I can try and step outside of these a bit.' For us, trying to make sense of this later, we were torn between interpreting this as demonstrable resistance or simply appeasing the researchers knowing full well how we were most likely to be positioned.

Where there was also some genuine resistance to gendered and corporeal prejudice practised as legitimating norms, these teachers were simply regarded as lacking a sense of humour or not being 'relaxed' enough where their resistance was noticed by others. Often requests by our female participants for teachers to refrain from sex-related banter were routinely ignored and the only line of action then available was to leave the staffroom. In fact it was a male pre-service teacher called David who alerted us to how this was managed by the female teachers. When confronted by such language David said of one of the female teachers: 'She would just put the headphones on [of her iPod] and do her work.' Indeed, when we asked why there was no apparent restraint of such behaviours, David replied: 'It was like they forgot she was there.' The pre-service teachers again were positioned in uncomfortable ways. Regardless of their views on this kind of conduct, the accepted way of being within HPE staffrooms seemed to require one to be 'relaxed'. Should you not be so then you could be courting danger come the point of evaluation.

Generally speaking, the mostly unquestioned acceptance of the practices described here that shaped the social space of the HPE staffroom lead us to suggest that the emerging teachers' own dispositions aligned with the accepted practices in the staffroom. Again, this finding may not be that surprising given the literature indicating that students with values and beliefs similar to those of HPE teachers tend to be recruited into the profession. We propose that when the pre-service or beginning teachers' dispositions matched those of the legitimated participants in the social space (that is, the key or mentor teachers), whether consciously to seek approval or through a non-conscious alignment of the staffroom, their practices (i.e. words and actions) further entrenched the dominant practices. Bourdieu (1990) referred to this dominating set of practices that are taken for granted and reproduced within the social space as the doxa. Doxa contributes to erasing history. It erases what becomes naturalized or normalized, around the very idea of norms, their social construction, and the professional integrity needed to resist such injustice. By making some of the unprofessional practices 'natural' or taken for granted it is much harder to even see what they are. It is even harder to challenge or resist them, and therefore eradicate what are clearly poor practices for the professional development of pre-service and beginning teachers.

Identifying with dominant poor practices, creating generative subject positions as professionals, or something else?

The importance which HPE pre-service and beginning teachers place on building a relationship with the legitimized, credentialed HPE teachers to facilitate participation in the subject department office dynamics, and to reach the desired state of being – namely identification as a HPE teacher – is clearly demonstrated in the lives of those in our study. The strong alignment or felt necessity to align that many of the pre-service and beginning teachers felt with the HPE teachers and the practices in the department office may have contributed to their perception of a 'natural' fit with the community. Our findings in this study confirm other research regarding marginalizing practices by HPE communities (Brown, 1999; Brown and Evans, 2004; Dewar, 1990). Needless to say, the dominant practices concerned our participants and ourselves. Being provided with limiting subject positions to take up or asked to identify with sexist or elitists practices, for example, resulted in two participants rejecting teaching altogether. The alignment between emerging HPE teachers' and credentialed teachers' dispositions, which lent itself to continued marginalizing practices, simply underscored the dissonance between the learning available in some of the workplaces and the ethical underpinning and intellectual orientation of the university programme. Moreover, engaging in communities that support such practices seemed only to further entrench the 'naturalness' of them. There was a definite lack of subject positions available in pre-service and beginning teacher experiences in the workplaces that matched those described by the literature and the university courses as necessary subject positions for educative, equitable and inclusive outcomes through HPE teachers. We would suggest that to create such subject positions is the responsibility of the profession and those who make up the profession. This would require the field, at the micro level of the teachers and their departments, to embody inclusive, generative, educative, etc. practices into which emerging teachers are invited, and invited to constitute their professional self. These could be seen as growth spots that could create/nurture 'critical' subject positions, identified as 'critical staffrooms' to nurture the practices we understand are needed for a more socially just and generative HPE, practices embodied within the professional and the profession.

8 Space and place for/of learning

Introduction

The place of the staffroom is clearly influential in how emerging teachers perceive the subject position of teacher and how they engage with the professional. In this chapter we explore how professional spaces, including the staffroom place, were negotiated dialectically between beginning teacher subjectivities and the physical, representative and representational spaces (Lefebvre, 1991) of the workplace (as described in Chapter 4). Our focus is on demonstrating how knowledge of such dynamics may go some way towards enhancing spaces, places and practices deemed important for the learning or professional development of pre-service and beginning teachers. The responsibility of those constituting the profession to facilitate learning to be a teacher, the justification used for practicum, is a responsibility that suggests agency, or an ability to influence one's own field and change through learning within the practicum or through induction. We established in the previous chapter that agency to negotiate and even change one's field, within the professional learning spaces in the school site and therefore the broader field of HPE teaching, may be affected by the social spaces within which one is placed or places oneself. While there is a large body of literature pertaining to induction and the socialization of teachers, there is only modest research into the notion of professional learning 'spaces' and their significance in the induction and transition processes in the pre-service practicum and the early years of employment. Becoming a teacher 'requires not only the development of a professional identity but the construction of professional knowledge and practice through continued professional learning' (McCormack *et al.*, 2006, p. 95). It is this notion of professional learning space/s, subject positions that pre-service and beginning teachers can take up and participate in the constitution of HPE teacher and profession, that we explore in this chapter.

It is widely acknowledged that locations within and beyond schools have been found to function as spaces for experienced teachers' workplace learning (McGregor, 2003); however, relatively little is known about how the staffroom functions as a professional *learning space* and how, for new graduates, this affects the process of becoming a teacher. As a place, a material and geographically identified space, we were interested in how the staffroom functioned not just as a physical space, but also what might be thought of as social, cultural and emotional spaces for its occupants. We were particularly interested in pre-service and beginning teachers within this place as they are influenced by, but also influence, professional learning.

The staffroom as a space and place for learning at work

The literature emphasizes the transition time/space between pre-service teacher and experienced teacher as important for the development, both positive and negative, of teacher professional identities and its effect on teacher effectiveness and retention (Guarino *et al.*, 2006; Richardson and Watt, 2006). In recognition of this important time/space, substantial efforts and investments in induction and mentoring practices and associated research have been ongoing for more than 20 years (see e.g. the work of Feiman-Nemser, 1996; Guarino *et al.*, 2006; Kelly, 2004; Odell and Ferraro, 1992; Walkington, 2005). The social practices of transitioning from non-teacher to expert are played out through the conscious and non-conscious bodies interacting in the spatiality of restrictions, opportunities and possibilities afforded by multiple social professional spaces (Bourdieu, 1977, 1985). These are in places including the staffroom, the classroom, and the 'between' spaces/places of lunch breaks, staff meetings and so on. However, the place where most non-teaching time is spent is in the departmental staffroom or office. Hence the 'spaces' within this place were of interest to us.

Conceptualizing transition as a learning process and/or a product of professional spaces allows us to consider that it is not constructed as irreversible, temporally or physically fixed, a single moment, unidirectional, or homogeneously experienced. However, it might be reasonable to suggest that the degree to which beginning teachers (and for that matter pre-service teachers) were able to 'resist' spaces or more accurately find spaces of resistance varied significantly. Remember our opening story at the beginning of the book in which Sandra found a space of resistance to the oppressive practices of the PE department through sports coaching (in an area in which she was highly qualified) and in the science department. Also later in the book we heard from Tom who similarly 'absented' himself from the HPE staffroom as a form of resistance. However, the capacity to find what Soja (1996) calls the space of possibility or 'Thirdspace' was not evenly spread across our participants. Pre-service and beginning teachers then may be conceptualized as actively participating in spaces, albeit spaces that have been historically and socially bounded. This suggests that the participation in spaces itself is historically and socially shaped by that space. This is in contrast to the more passive conceptualization of beginning teachers being socialized or inducted into the subject position of fully credentialed teacher. We will argue that this important space/time of learning intersects with the place of the staffroom as an important site for influencing possible professional subjectivities, as we discussed in Chapter 7.

The narratives re-presented below illustrate the main plotlines (Clandinin and Connelly, 1996) of two of our participants' experiences framed by spatiality theory (as described in Chapter 4). After each narrative we offer an analytical discussion to draw out the importance of place and space in relation to their subjectivities, workplace learning and the profession.

Sonny: itinerant teacher in ambivalent space

Energized and enthusiastic on his first day of being a 'real teacher', Sonny arrives at the rural primary school where he had been appointed as HPE teacher for three days a week. His other appointment was as a primary classroom generalist to a different school. In anticipation of this momentous day, he had arrived at the school early, waiting in his car until he saw movement in the administration block. While he would not be teaching students today, as it was a student-free day, he was eager to familiarize himself with the school grounds, available resources and importantly his office space, before meeting the other staff at the staff meeting scheduled for 10 a.m. Having collected the school prospectus and timetable for the day, the pleasant administration woman directed him to his office. Key in hand, he carefully followed her directions to a room under the administration block, next to the main staffroom (common/lunch room). As he turned the key and entered the room, his initial sense of excitement waned. Feeling around for the light switch, he was bemused when he thought it was non-existent. As his eyes adjusted he walked further into the room, scanning his new office space no longer with expectation. His expectations of this space had flown quickly out of the only opening of the room: the door. He eventually found a switch behind some plastic storage crates on the shelves – not where he expected. A weak, single fluorescent light flickered on. In the absence of any natural light Sonny realized that this was the best it would be. Shelves holding a mess of sporting equipment and paperwork lined the left-hand side and back walls of the room. On the right-hand side a small bare desk and chair were crammed in beside the table tennis tables leaning up against the wall. An odd sense of déjà vu overwhelmed him; he had been in a space like this before ... the realization hit him ... the cleaner's cupboard at his old high school.

Sonny was certainly relieved that he had been alone for his initial visit to his office space. While he was somewhat surprised and taken aback by the cupboard-like appearance and limited lighting, he reasoned that he was lucky to have his own office space at all. Having completed his major practicum in a high school and spent irregular and intermittent periods of time in primary schools throughout his undergraduate degree, Sonny didn't really know what to expect of the primary school setting, nor could he recall the primary specialist HPE teachers having or using an office space. While his preference was to work as a primary school specialist HPE teacher, his lack of familiarity within a primary school context was at best disconcerting, and at work absolutely nerve-wracking at worst.

Being the sole HPE teacher at the school, Sonny was responsible for all HPE lessons for all year levels, all the intra-school (tournaments and lunchtime sport) and inter-school sport organization. Sonny was astonished that he had received no advice or direction in relation to his duties as the specialist HPE teacher in his first few days at the school, nor had he been allocated a mentor or received any information about an induction programme. Being proactive, he sought out the deputy principal who vaguely directed him to some paperwork left by the previous HPE teacher. The paperwork was sketchy, containing rough, mostly incomplete unit plans, event programmes and a few contact numbers for district sport. Initially frustrated and overwhelmed with the amount of work and with what appeared to Sonny as a serious lack of support, he started organizing the upcoming swimming carnival [referred to elsewhere as a 'gala' or a 'meet'] and reworked the HPE programme. While Sonny had an understanding that his initial experience and first term would have been far easier with guidance and support, he revelled in the fact that he could navigate this new context with some, if not a large amount of, anonymity and autonomy.

When Sonny wasn't on playground duty or running lunch-time sport, a rare event, he enjoyed visiting the common 'staffroom' for lunch. It was in these infrequent visits to this space that he had befriended the other school specialist teachers from music and LOTE.[1] While Sonny felt quite independent in his development as a HPE teacher, the little time spent with other specialist teachers provided reassurance and aided his understanding of what it meant to be a specialist teacher in this very particular context. Sonny was always pleased when his sporadic visits to the staffroom for lunch corresponded with the other specialist teachers' inconsistent visits because he could let his guard down, ask questions and experience a sense of belonging. Generalist classroom teachers would wander in but usually clustered together in their year-level groupings, otherwise lunching in their classrooms. Sonny's interaction with the generalist teachers was professional and structured, typically occurring when they collected or delivered their classes or during intra- and inter-school sport.

As the first term progressed, Sonny was pleasantly surprised that with such a high teaching load he had limited opportunity and time in his day to spend in his office, which, given that it doubled as the storage cupboard, was not difficult. He organized a lamp to supplement the inadequate light and a fan; however, Sonny did not generally work there. Through a bit of detective work he had found a communal computer and printer in the common staffroom that he accessed during and after school hours, a much-preferred space to his dimly lit and musty office. As the other teachers had computers in their classrooms the common staffroom space was quiet and conducive to work early in the mornings and late after school, the only time Sonny had time for planning and organization.

Professional space: voids and isolation

Issues of school culture and teachers' personal and professional histories have emerged as strong mediating influences in determining the kinds and stability of professional subjectivities that teachers develop in their early professional lives (Flores and Day, 2006). For Sonny, who was rather like an itinerant teacher in his own school, the times where general classroom teachers were timetabled to be 'off class' were either while he was taking their class for HPE or during meal breaks where he was often involved in sports coaching. Although the policy of providing classroom teachers with 'non-contact time' was seen to be a positive move for classroom teachers, there has been no consideration as to the impact this has on the 'specialist' who provides learning experiences for students during this time. In many instances the itinerant space of specialist teachers in primary schools means there is no time or space available for them to communicate, collaborate or participate in professional exchanges with other teachers and certainly not with other HPE teachers, for better or for worse.

The itinerant teacher model[2] is in stark contrast with that of a secondary subject department where many opportunities for 'casual, serendipitous contact as well as more focused social or work-related conversations' were provided (McGregor, 2003, p. 54). Notwithstanding the problems associated with treating subject departments as silos (Talbert, 1995), the *potential* advantages around communities of professional practice stand out. In Sonny's case such a community is missing, as is one based on the broader notion of collegiality discussed as important to teacher professional subjectivities formation (see e.g. McGregor, 2003). This might however be seen as a positive thing when, as we have seen elsewhere in the this study, 'community' is as likely to be imbued with sexism, racism, homophobia, elitism and the like as experienced or observed by many of our participants in their HPE departments.

Neither induction nor mentoring was offered to Sonny and although he expressed satisfaction with teaching and an appreciation of autonomy he also felt professional feedback and interaction to be lacking. Kelly (2004) has shown positive results in the long-term retention and effectiveness of novice teachers who participated in an induction partnership between the teacher education institution and schools. While induction does not necessarily mean that there will be capacity building in the teaching profession, some models showing little if any effect, we were left to wonder what the lack of a good induction programme might mean for teachers such as Sonny who also lack the collegiality and conversations suggested in the literature as necessary for the development of teacher subjectivities.

Physical space – ambivalence of the subject

Numerous studies (e.g. Kim and Taggart, 2004; Paechter and Head, 1996; Thompson, 2003) illustrate the ambivalent or low status in which HPE is held in the school system. For Sonny, the ambivalence of the school system towards

HPE is also reflected in the ambivalent professional spaces made available to him. The poorly lit storage room did not match the desk and classroom space of the generalist teachers, and required him to relocate to do some of the procedural or planning tasks of a teacher, such as those needing access to computers. The temporal space where teachers congregated in the central staffroom was not available to Sonny, as his coaching and sports team management work occurred at these times. Even the temporal space allocated for generalist teachers to plan did not include Sonny, as this was precisely the time allocated for him to teach. Isolation clearly has a freedom in terms of the subject positions a pre-service or beginning teacher might take up but it also has a loss when compared to experiences such as Angel's below.

Angel: at 'home' with the 'staffroom' family

Angel experienced nothing but guidance and professional support from the moment she received her first teaching position at a rural Catholic college. While at times overwhelming, the busy and chaotic transition into the school, and ultimately her teaching career, was smooth, facilitated by an induction morning devoted exclusively to beginning teachers and teachers new to the school. It was on this morning that she was introduced to the school's administration team, the HODs, and importantly her mentor, a female HPE teacher with three years' experience. The induction provided an opportunity for Angel to receive information about the school's policies, procedures and expectations. Angel felt very valued and welcomed, thankful for the opportunity to ease into starting and to gain a clear understanding of expectations of her by the school in professional standards (e.g. dress, extra-curricular commitments, resource sharing and development) and professional development.

Angel and her housemate Mandy, also a beginning teacher at the school, had met some of the teachers at a barbeque they had been invited to prior to their induction. This, coupled with Mandy being by her side today, offered Angel confidence as she entered the staffroom for the first time, meeting and greeting the other teachers on staff. Housing all the staff from all subject areas, the staffroom space was long and narrow, a corridor-like room with benches running the length of the walls. Each teacher (the majority of whom were female), is allocated one and a half metres of bench space and corresponding storage space directly overhead where shelves contour the walls. This space allocation is more than enough for Angel, but for some teachers it is an obvious challenge to keep their stacked folders of units and resources within their allocated space, spilling into others' space. Some teachers own their laptops and keep them on their desks; however, Angel makes use of one of the six communal computers at one end of the staffroom. Apart from peak times before and after school, gaining access to a computer is unproblematic. Similarly, resources such as unit plans, lesson plans and worksheets are very accessible in this communal space. The reworking of, addition to and sharing of resources is explicitly encouraged, a value clearly immersed within the staffroom context across all subject areas. To Angel, the physical layout of the space embodies and encapsulates this strong sense of openness, cooperation and collaboration among teachers, regardless of teaching areas, giving access to an invaluable resource, namely other teachers.

Like the other teachers, when Angel is not teaching or on playground duty she is hanging out or working in the staffroom. She affectionately likens the staffroom to a safe place,[3] a home or haven at school away from the students. At times, a fun, relaxed atmosphere permeates the staffroom, everyone being silly and filling the room with laughter. This inclusive social atmosphere transfers beyond school hours to social gatherings and staff functions on weekends. In times of work, Angel experiences a sense of togetherness and belonging through the continual questioning and inquiries about her progress and teaching, not only from her heads of department and mentor but also from other staff. Their selfless time giving, answering questions and general concern for her development as a beginning teacher are clearly evident. These feelings of being immersed in the staffroom and the school are in stark comparison to her practicum experience where she felt insignificant and transient. As a beginning teacher she is now privy to the behind-the-scenes happenings of the school, more able to effectively engage with relevant information about students, teaching and the school. Similarly her access to support and development of comfortable, stable professional relationships signify the disparity between Angel's experience of now being a teacher and that of a pre-service teacher the year before. As the semester progresses, the induction and mentoring process is complemented with beginning teacher meetings scheduled every fortnight and the sharing of a homeroom class with an experienced teacher.

Smooth transitional professional space in place: induction, scaffolding and mentoring

Unlike the initial confusion and anxiety experienced by many novice teachers (Tickle, 1994, 2000), including Sonny in our first narrative in this chapter as well as others included in this volume, Angel experienced a strong sense of openness, support and cooperation within her staffroom and with her staff. Young (2000) argues that new teachers not only need to become experts in the technical aspects of teaching, but also to develop the professional capacity to deal with conflicts between their personal and professional lives. Angel was given many opportunities for this, within and beyond the staffroom. Although assigned a mentor and given a specific induction to the school, she quickly identified individuals who could help answer her specific questions, those who were easily accessible in the mixed subject and common staffroom and with whom she had met through the induction day, in-service days, staffroom functions, and social functions outside the school. The physical staffroom was cohesive, open and included all teachers other than the administration. The physical space reflected how Angel felt in relation to the staff and moved beyond the materiality of the place as she maintained her teacher subjectivities into other places in the town evidenced when participating in the staff netball weekend team and weekend staff trips.

The literature supports mentoring and induction programmes to facilitate the transition from pre-service to credentialed teacher and to transmit the culture of the system to the beginning teacher (Huling-Austin, 1990; McCulla, 2005; Smith and Ingersoll, 2004). For Angel, this mentoring took place in the staffroom but was not confined to the staffroom, supporting Nespor's (2002) notion that the functions of specialized spaces are often not as bounded as perhaps they are represented. Nevertheless, in this case the staffroom was a significant space for the beginning teacher to collaborate and interact in professional exchanges as well as bond or connect with other staff. This reinforces the finding of McCormack *et al.* (2006) that while formal induction programmes and mentoring are useful, 'collaborative, informal, unplanned learning from colleagues and former peers was also reported as a most significant and valuable source of support' (p. 95). Angel felt very comfortable with the challenges of being a beginning teacher as her needs for professional contact were met with positive relationships. She was scaffolded in terms of the necessary information to understand expectations of her by others and that she could expect of colleagues and students. For Angel, the staffroom was a central place where all teachers were physically located regardless of their specialist subject areas. It was also a place that represented a professional space where she felt she could influence and contribute to as time went by. This place also linked with other spaces where the social relations were reinforced despite relocation. This included staff social events within and beyond the school and indicated strength of relations that were not only constructed with and within the place of the staffroom but endured relocation.

The Soja and Lefebvre trialectic: spaces of embodied possibility

We have already learned from Lefebvre (1991) that space is culturally and historically shaped. We indicated in Chapter 4 that this shaping or 'production' of space is made possible by the interactions of those within it, according to their perceptions, to evoke that which may be represented in the form of subjectivities formed through relationships and practices. Moreover, we claimed a little licence earlier by playing with language to suggest that the shaping of workspaces, as they have been identified across this study, is brought about through the practices of the community within those spaces. Through participation then, the space is experienced as embodied. If we follow Soja (1996), both of the participants in this chapter experienced and participated in the 'planned' nature of the 'Firstspace'; space with a material reality designed for a purpose. However, the differences in the experience of this reality could not have been starker. The planned space of Sonny was not conducive to what he wanted to achieve, the space was isolated, physically unappealing and offered few possibilities. The consequence was that Sonny needed to remove himself from the space in order to engage in overlapping spaces and this tactic enabled him to participate in the community of other primary school curriculum 'specialists'. This was not so much resistance, but certainly it created a space of possibility, and for Sonny this was crucial given his sense of isolation.

Angel experienced the staffroom space as not a Firstspace but as a Third-space. The level of support for Angel to experiment, be influential, be supported, allowed her to perform her subjectivities in ways that could be maintained. The practices of the community then in Angel's case were confirming and support-ive, and drew her towards the centre.

When we reflect on this we are drawn to Phil Hubbard's (2002) idea that it is not so much what spaces are, but what spaces 'do'. In the narratives provided here the embodied spaces as experienced by the participants did quite different things. As Massey (2005) says, space has to be understood through its multiplic-ity and not through any assumed singularity. She contends that space should be seen as the sphere of possibility. While we support and are attracted to this idea, it is easy to see here that our two participants perceived the realm of possibility quite differently. For both, the physical space governed action; for Angel however, possibility was evident across the space trialectic.

Where the stories leave us

While supportive and affirming induction and mentoring practices clearly exist in experiences such as Angel's, and are shown to be important in teacher profes-sional development and retention, their implementation seems to be 'patchy' at best (McCulla, 2005, p. 37). As a profession wishing to attract quality teachers and hold a more respected status within society, we (the field of the teaching profession) must ask ourselves: to what extent do we expect and practise the cre-ation of supportive and affirming professional workplaces for new teachers? How might the staffroom (general or subject specific), a distinctive space where professional culture and power relations are practised, facilitate or resist different forms of social space that make possible the teacher subjectivities needed to transform student learning? Stoll *et al.* (2006) suggest that advancing profes-sional spaces through professional learning communities seems to hold promise for capacity building for sustainable development although not without cautions.

Kelly's (2004) work demonstrates that induction does indeed matter, that a meaningful induction experience has lasting effects on teacher quality and reten-tion. However, Feiman-Nemser (1996) makes the point that for beginning teach-ers to learn the ways of thinking and acting associated with new kinds of teaching, they need to be placed with mentors who are already reformers in their classrooms or schools and to develop collaborative environments. Conceptualiz-ing the staffroom not just as a physical space but also as an opportunistic profes-sional learning space that is perhaps underutilized or under-represented, or even (if inadvertently) totally absent may provide a more usable platform for analysis. Given 'schools that provided mentoring and induction programs, particularly

LIVERPOOL JOHN MOORES UNIVERSITY
LEARNING SERVICES

those related to collegial support, had lower rates of turnover among beginning teachers' (Guarino *et al.*, 2006, p. 201), we could imagine a more productive staffroom and staff for those in Sonny's (and others in the study) situation if the space were to be conceptualized as a learning space and a professional place as opposed to being just an organizational place, somewhere to 'dump your gear'. In this way the space moves beyond its simple materiality and becomes a space of possibility. It is probably apparent to most that Angel's situation seemed more akin to a positive experience. Ideally, ongoing research to track each of these teachers would have provided a better understanding of the complexities of the outcomes of induction, mentoring and professional spaces for new teachers. Even though we have stated that boundaries in field-based research are largely artificial, research projects themselves invariably have to be bounded by the mundane exigencies of budget, time and workload.

Notes

1 LOTE (Language Other Than English) is a key learning area in the state-based syllabus suite of documents developed for primary schools. Teachers of LOTE are most often specialist teachers of a particular language.
2 We acknowledge that this model may be unfamiliar to some international readers. An itinerant teacher is a teacher who serves many schools. A potential parallel in the UK might be the peripatetic music teacher. In Australia there is now limited recognition of the specialist primary HPE teacher; however, Queensland still supports and employs specialist HPE teachers. Inevitably, given the small size of some schools especially in rural and remote regions in which they are located, a permanent HPE teacher is untenable. It is not uncommon for itinerant teachers in Australia to cover over 1000 kilometres (approximately 600 miles) per week.
3 This is consistent with Illeris' (2011) work and his ideas on safe workplaces being learning workplaces.

9 The micropolitics of being a new worker

Introduction

In Chapter 6 you read that pre-service teachers used a number of 'fronts' as part of their performance and that what beginning teachers experienced was a somewhat different performance to that advocated in the teacher education programme in which they were enrolled, albeit with links to that of the practicum. In this chapter then, and following on from Chapter 8, we highlight the importance of the *politics* of transition rather than simply its *structural elements* in the construction and negotiation of beginning teachers' learning, and illustrate how the HPE subject department office has the capacity to (re)shape beginning teacher learning. We now draw on the analytical tool of micropolitical literacy (as described in Chapter 4) to show how beginning HPE teachers' micropolitical experiences in the workplace context of the staffroom have the potsential to (re)shape beginning teachers' learning.

Narrative inquiry and beginning teacher contexts

This chapter is informed by a narrative inquiry approach, an it represents what has been termed elsewhere (Christensen, 2013) *micropolitical staffroom stories;* that is, the stories which beginning teachers told of their micropolitical staffroom context. Here we report on the experiences of some of the participants who were transitioning to teaching positions and their first year. We present two of the narratives to draw attention to how beginning teachers negotiate the micropolitical context of the HPE staffroom and how this impacts upon their lives, learning and development as beginning teachers.

The narratives we have developed for this chapter have 'been both carefully composed and selected' (Clandinin, 2006, p. 48), informed by the micropolitical perspectives of the beginning teacher. The narratives of Millie and Sally, whom we met in earlier chapters, emerge from what is a developing and ongoing micropolitical plotline of their first year of teaching. The plotlines are drawn from the stories they described emanating from their staffroom contexts. The narratives are partial representations of their accounts more broadly, adapted and written in the interest of constituting a particular kind of story

(Sarup, 1996). Millie and Sally were chosen for their similarity in situation; that is, they went into an exclusively HPE teacher staffroom. Both of these young women commenced their programme of study in 2005, Sally entering at the age of 18, directly from school, and Millie at 19, after working in retail for one year. Millie had also completed the Honours programme path. For their first teaching appointment, both participants were appointed on six-month contracts (rather than a permanent position) in secondary schools,[1] which were subsequently extended for a further six months.[2] Their narratives also capture the differences, diversity and complexity of beginning teachers' experiences of learning to 'read', navigate and influence the micropolitical reality (Curry *et al.*, 2008; Kelchtermans and Ballet, 2002a, 2002b). While both participants transitioned into HPE staffrooms – Millie at an urban school and Sally at a large regional school – the staffroom contexts were different. Millie was the only female in a staffroom with five males. One of these male teachers and the HPE HOD were, like her, new to the school. In contrast, Sally found herself in a large HPE staffroom housing eight other HPE teachers, with an equal number of males and females. The acting HOD was not situated in the staffroom with the HPE teachers, but down the hall in his own office. At Christensen School, Sally was offered and participated in a formal induction and beginning teacher programme, and allocated a mentor from within the HPE staffroom. At McRiver School, Millie was not offered a formal beginning teacher programme or mentor, and described her induction as self-directed, online and brief. We use these two, particular yet very different, exemplar narratives to draw attention to, evoke and illustrate the complexity of beginning teachers' micropolitical experiences and learning in the staffroom. Each narrative is followed by an analytical discussion about the beginning teachers' micropolitical learning.

Millie: the frustrating curriculum story

Millie transitioned from a pre-service teacher and into the subject position of qualified teacher via the HPE staffroom at the large McRiver School. While settling quickly and comfortably into building relationships, and engaging and participating in staffroom activities, Millie was often beleaguered with frustration. This was due to the lack of clear direction, cohesiveness and collaboration in relation to the HPE department's planning, pedagogy, curriculum and assessment. Millie remembered the first curriculum-planning meeting she attended at the beginning of Term 1. The HPE teachers were required to map their departments' curriculum in accordance with the new State Curriculum Assessment and Reporting Framework. Having just completed her university studies, which focused heavily on this Framework, Millie was aghast at the lack of understanding and subsequent conversations regarding the considerations and implementation of the Framework and its subsidiaries throughout this meeting. However, Millie did not feel comfortable speaking up and voicing her opinions regarding this issue. She explained:

I just said … I can't help you because I don't know, like when we were doing the activity I was like, 'cos I haven't been here I don't know how your programme works. And they were fine with that.

Furthermore, Millie was intimidated by the reaction of the staff to Louis, an experienced teacher new to the staffroom, who had voiced his concerns and ideas. Millie referred to Louis as 'the ideas man', and perceived that the other HPE teachers had little respect for him as a consequence. Millie explained that he had not been tactful or sensitive to being a newcomer to the staffroom and department; a staffroom with occupants who had been part of the staffroom story for a considerable length of time. Millie referred to these occupants as 'the legendary teachers'. While Millie felt she had a significant in-depth understanding regarding the Framework, she perceived that she did not know how the school programme worked. She chose to position herself within the staffroom by 'going with the flow' and not 'rocking the boat', as she considered that '[t]hey know what they are doing; people don't like change you know'. In this way Millie chose an approach that best fit in with the story of the staffroom, enabling her to maintain what Tinning and Siedentop (1985) described as 'cordial relations' (see Chapter 5). Similarly, Millie considered that this sensitivity and awareness of being a beginning teacher and new to the staffroom also made life easier for the other HPE teachers:

> They had no preconceptions about me, they know I am a newbie…. Like while I know what I think and what should happen I don't have experience and I think that makes it easier for them. Because I am not in their faces this is how you should be doing it.

Although Millie expressed this sensitivity and awareness of being positioned, and positioning herself as 'the newbie' (her choice of word), her frustration regarding curriculum and assessment within the department deepened as the teaching term progressed. In her planning of units, resources and assessment Millie had found it increasingly difficult to negotiate and decipher the department's inconsistent expectations, programme structures and requirements:

> Everywhere you look the sports that we are covering are different…. You look at one document and it says this sport and then another document it says these sports and I'm like well what are we doing?

While a deeply frustrating issue for Millie, she didn't perceive that the inconsistent and non-collaborative approach to planning was an issue for the other HPE teachers, describing it as 'that is how it has always been'. Millie suspected that the HPE/HOD's approach to 'easing people into it', and being respectful of 'the legendary teachers', facilitated and continued this disorganization and way of operating. This ongoing staffroom story bumped up against Millie's understanding of best practice in terms of curriculum planning and pedagogy that she developed and practised in her university degree.

Similarly, Millie was dumfounded to learn that criteria and standards did not exist within the department for the practical assessable components of HPE courses.[3] While her HOD had explained that he understood the theory behind practical criteria and standards, Millie was dismayed by his suggestion to simply grade students based on her 'gut feeling' and 'judgement'. For Millie this was unacceptable and conflicted directly with everything she had been taught regarding assessment best practice at university and considered this approach entirely unfair for students. It was not unsurprising though when Millie explained that she did not speak up about this issue. She sarcastically justified that 'I can't say anything because I'm a first year and I know nothing'. Instead, Millie had resolved to make her own criteria and standards. So as to not 'rock the boat', she used the criteria and standards as an assessment tool but did not make it obvious that they were missing from the unit. Agentically she used the tools to aid in decision-making because she did not have the experience of years of teaching to fall back on. This approach both protected her interests as a beginning teacher while maintaining 'cordial relations' within the staffroom.

Later in the year, with a term cycle of teaching and assessment completed and another underway, Millie said that her frustration had only deepened in relation to the staffroom's disorganized and non-collaborative approach to planning, curriculum, assessment and reporting. This process of change, according to Millie, was progressing far too slowly:

> We're still in a debate [about the curriculum] – we've only just, like we go around in circles.... He's [the HPE HOD] very diplomatic and like plants the seeds with the old ones who have been there ages and don't really like change. Plants the seed, and then he will bring it up a few weeks later and then he doesn't force anything. Like he doesn't go well this is what we have to do and this is how we're going to go about it. He gets everyone slowly onside whereas I see that as pussyfooting around.

Millie's annoyance was clearly evident as she portrayed her perception of why her HOD took this current approach to managing the department's curriculum. Millie was annoyed at the HOD's approach but understood it as a sensitivity towards 'the legendary' teachers. In particular, Millie commented on Terry's (one of the legends) influence in the staffroom: 'I think everyone just kind of looks up to him. He's a very smart man ... like he doesn't – he's not one of these people who goes out of his way to make you see how smart he is. But he's very smart and like because he's been there so long.' Millie noted Terry's influence as 'subtle', 'silent' and 'not in your face', an influence she deemed manifested in the interactions and actions of the other staffroom occupants. Acknowledging and respecting this influence, Millie drew distinction between the teaching philosophies and pedagogical approaches that 'the legendary' teachers and 'newbies' attempted to embody: 'Okay they [the legendary teachers] use 20-year-old textbooks or worksheets that are crap. So they're just oldies like chalk and talk. I don't know what the – we all get to the one exam, but how we get there, I don't know.' However, Millie, as a beginning teacher, adamantly and with respect expressed that she would not disclose her frustrations to the 'old timers' 'Because they've been there forever and they like it and that's what they know, that's what they've always done.... I just would never put them in that position.' On the contrary, Millie indicated that the HOD was the problem. He was not fulfilling his position. Millie was resolute that, in relation to the changing curriculum and all that it entailed, there 'had to be a point where he puts his foot down' with respect to the department's curriculum organization and assessment practices.

Millie's frustration with the staffroom curriculum story also manifested in her discussions about the reporting process, a process she had experienced for the first time at the end of Term 1. She reflected that her current approach to this frustration was quite different to the approach she had employed at the beginning of the year where she 'would have just planted the seed, um do we have a criteria sheet for this, put it as a question not a demand'. Millie had found the marking and reporting process quite difficult because she considered it to be very subjective and with no moderation process in place. She resorted to asking many questions that bordered on excessive in order to access the information and support she felt she required. Millie perceived this was met with frustration from colleagues: 'they [the other HPE teachers] were getting like a little bit frustrated with me because I was like, well what would you give for this because I am on this?' Millie justified that she was trying to moderate her judgements in line with the other HPE teachers: 'Like you've got an idea, but I'm just like, how do I know that my idea is right?' Millie confessed that she didn't bother addressing this issue of moderation with the HOD, as she didn't expect that she would receive a straight answer or solution. Millie was aware that she was responsible and answerable for the grades she reported for her students, and in order to protect her professional self 'made sure that I could justify it before I did it. Because if someone came to me, why did you give this kid his mark, then I could say well, dah, dah, dah.'

During her first semester in the staffroom, and as she managed to move beyond her first experience of the reporting process, Millie developed a better understanding of how to read the staffroom and its occupants. 'I know when to open my mouth and when to keep it quiet' and 'I'm certainly getting better at putting things – expressing things'. Further, she supposed that this change in approach was because she had become 'more comfortable with people' and had 'a better understanding of the space'.

Millie's tension of being a 'newbie'

Captured in Millie's narrative is her shift in micropolitical knowledge and practices as she came to understand and make connections with the frustrating curriculum story of the HPE staffroom at McRiver School. While conservative in her approach to the curriculum early in the year, her micropolitical strategies and practices evolved throughout the year. Still sensitive to 'the legendary teachers' and maintaining cordial relations (Tinning and Siedentop, 1985), a particular positioning intended to establish and safeguard the 'professional' working conditions she desired (Kelchtermans and Ballet, 2002a), Millie had developed other, more reactive strategies in order 'to get things done'. In this way the frustrating curriculum story and the lack of accountability afforded by the staffroom (and school) context shaped how Millie came to understand and practice, both in the staffroom and classroom. Similarly, as a beginning teacher, Millie had developed ways to position herself and her practices, steering clear of living and telling stories that may have conflicted with the dominant and dominating staffroom story. Over time, how Millie positioned herself progressed to a less defensive, yet more strategic and hidden approach as she became 'more comfortable with people' and had 'a better understanding of the space'. As Kelchtermans and Ballet (2002a, 2002b) designate, Millie became more satisfied and confident with her micropolitical literacy, her ability to understand and participate in the micropolitical context of the staffroom in such a way as to protect her desired working conditions.

Millie's narrative also portrays the tension between her image of good teaching, curriculum planning and assessment cultivated at university, and the notion of acceptable practice within the staffroom. While this tension existed for Millie, as a 'newbie' she perceived that she did not have authority or influence within the staffroom. Instead, the 'legendary teachers', those not in positions of formal authority but nevertheless positioned powerfully, (re)produced and maintained their desired working conditions through informal non-authoritative means, by using their influence in maintaining the prevailing staffroom story through reproducing long-standing and often outdated practices, and ridiculing and dismissing the ideas and practices of the 'newcomers'. Of concern, this prevailing staffroom story, as shared by Millie, did not necessarily represent sound practice advocated for in the State Assessment and Reporting Framework.

Although Millie complied by employing passive strategies such as 'holding her tongue' and 'going with the flow', in essence to allow congruence with the frustrating curriculum story, she retained private reservations about doing so (Smyth, 1995). Millie's narrative also highlights her proactive strategies such as 'excessive questioning' and playing on being positioned as 'the newbie' to gain information she required in order to protect her professional interests and commitment to curriculum and assessment best practice. This all in a contradictory micropolitical context where she perceived she had no influence. As a beginning teacher, Millie felt powerless to change the practices constituting the ongoing reality of this prevailing social space.

Sally: alignment with curriculum rather than sport specialization people

Sally was appointed to the large regional Christensen School where she shared the HPE staffroom with eight other HPE teachers. Of the people in the staffroom she described:

[W]e kind of have different sorts of people in the staffroom. Like, they actually said to me in a PE meeting, oh you're a curriculum person, what do you think about this? Like everyone's meant to be curriculum people, but they look at some of us, mainly all of us from the same uni and go, you're a curriculum person.

When Sally referred to 'us', she was referring to members of the HPE staff who had graduated from the same university degree as she. Sally, Jane, Clare and the acting HOD were positioned by the staffroom occupants as 'the curriculum people', 'because we actually care about what we're teaching'. Conversely, Sally termed the other staffroom occupants who were responsible for sport specialization and excellence programmes 'sports specialization people'. While Sally noted this distinction, she described a healthy respect between these two loosely coupled groups 'the curriculum people' and 'sport specialization people', each group appreciating the core work focus and contribution of the other.

Sally believed that she was well supported by the other 'curriculum people' in the staffroom. For Sally this support was professional and also personal; she had connected and become friends with a number of 'curriculum people' who had the same values and beliefs as her own. She explained that this was the case 'probably because they're from the same uni degree, but partly because they're the kind of people that I am'. Sally actively socialized with Clare, Jane and the HOD outside of school, including playing 'basketball together on Wednesday nights'. She considered that this helped her connect within the staffroom:

Because when we socialize outside we talk about things as well, kind of helps you like Clare and I will go for walks most afternoons and you know we'll talk about if we've got any problems and discuss what we should do about them.

For Sally, the curriculum people were 'the ones I talk to about serious stuff. They're the same. We talk about the serious stuff all the time.' In addition, Sally said that when she needed support or had questions regarding planning, curriculum, assessment and teaching 'they're the people that I go to because I guess I know them better as well, because I'm socializing with them'. Typically, Sally would approach Clare and Jane 'because Tim's [the HOD] downstairs. He's not actually in our staffroom.' Sally considered that Clare probably provided her with the most support 'because I talk to her a lot' and '[w]e're just stuck together all the time'. While Clare was Sally's official mentor, Sally surmised that their relationship would be unchanged if this was not the case, because Clare 'tends to think exactly the same as me anyway and … if I've got the problem she probably has too'. Sally reflected on her relationship with Jane – 'Jane is young, around my age – and she just wants to learn everything as well'. Sally discussed concerns, issues and queries with the other curriculum people inside and outside the staffroom.

Reflecting on her initial entry into the staffroom, Sally described her challenge to figure it all out, who does what, what goes where, pondering that '[n]ow it's good because now I know who to go to for whatever'. Halfway through Term Two Sally contemplated that her understanding of the staffroom and its occupants had developed and deepened during her time at the school. Sally considered that the functioning and dynamics of the staffroom 'was pretty obvious from the start' and was 'easy to pick up ... because everyone's got their role'. She noted:

> There are certain people that do certain jobs. Like, you learn what people are like. Like Clare and I get there early and then Marty gets there and then Jane gets there. Everyone else kind of like rolls in whenever. There are people that always get the notices from the office because they're there so they pretty much always bring them, so that's their job. Everyone really just gets along – like, the basketball/hockey guys do their thing.... The hockey dudes do their thing ... the curriculum people, we do our thing.

Although Sally identified these diverse roles within the staffroom, she explained that 'everyone is still really friendly and helpful and all of that'. Sally portrayed a respectful, inclusive staffroom atmosphere where 'everyone is completely different. I think, because there are so many separate things there's no one that really, rules the roost. Everyone stands up for themselves, which is good.' Sally considered that this inclusive, respectful atmosphere of the diverse staffroom had manifested over time. She supposed that 'there are things that go on because that's the way it is. That's the way it works ... I guess it's worked like that for however long. So, now we've gotten used to it like that.' She explained that while the 'hockey dudes (teachers with a preference for hockey) ... will get shitty if basketball (the school sport group) gets stuff because two of the deputies are basketball guys and so basketball gets whatever they want and people can do anything in basketball', they did not take it out on the 'basketball guru' because 'I think they're used to it ... they know that it's just the way the cookie crumbles'.

While Sally acknowledged the shared value of co-curricular activities within the staffroom, for her, 'curriculum stuff comes first and I make sure that all of my stuff is done and I know where I'm at, and I know what's going on and improving – so I've been improving'. Sally perceived that she was supported in her endeavour for ongoing teaching improvement by the other 'curriculum people'. It was the 'curriculum people' to whom Sally turned and trusted in relation to teaching and curriculum issues and support:

> If it's something about theory I definitely ask them [curriculum people] because no one else [in the staffroom] knows anything about theory and they don't care. [I know this] because they grab their stuff two minutes before their lesson and go, oh, what am I meant to be doing today? Oh yeah, that. I'm not handing the assignment out yet. I'm not ready – and everyone else is handing it out in the same week.... They don't write supers [lessons/work for replacement teachers], they're going to be away because they don't care. Well, I don't know if it's that they don't care, maybe just not bothered.

Sally drew important distinctions between how her and Marty (another beginning teacher from a different university in the HPE staffroom) behaved in and negotiated the staffroom. She considered that she and Marty had different priorities and interests. She considered Marty to be coordinating the rugby union sports specialist programme at the school and aligning himself with the 'sport specialization people' rather than the 'curriculum people'. Similarly, Sally perceived that she and Marty had different values in relation to socializing within and outside the staffroom with colleagues. Socializing, for Sally, was an important aspect of the staffroom. Sally deliberately and actively attempted to be social at Christensen School:

> I think I've been trying to be quite social because I want to make friends and I want to have a good time. So, first term, I pretty much did anything that anyone said, like, do you want to come and do this, I said yeah – that would be good … I just wanted to make friends. I think that that helps. If you say no too many times people aren't going to want to invite you anymore.

On the contrary, Sally explained that 'we [the curriculum people] tried to include Marty, we invite him places but he always says nah I'm busy'. Sally considered that Marty's declining of offers and subsequent lack of socializing had affected his interactions and relationships within the staffroom:

> Because I know that the other people always go oh Marty never does anything. I don't think he cares because it's not really with the boys because the boys like, I mean, (a) he is getting married and is busy with family stuff, and (b) because the boys are very busy with hockey stuff.

While Sally and the 'curriculum people' socialized regularly outside the staffroom, her perception was that the other staffroom occupants did not. Although Marty was friendly with the 'sport specialization people' within the staffroom and school, she explained: 'I don't know that he wants to be social with the "curriculum people" [but he] might think something completely different.'

Sally's alignment

Sally's narrative illustrates how she came to understand and accordingly practise her micropolitical knowledge in relation to the *curriculum and sport specialization stories* of the HPE staffroom at Christensen School. These stories framed the possibility of what she came to know, how she positioned herself and was positioned as either a 'curriculum person' or a 'sport specialization person', and consequently how she negotiated her interactions within the staffroom. Sally occupied the same HPE staffroom as another beginning teacher, Marty. However, her story captured dramatic differences in how she and Marty perceived and navigated the staffroom. While Sally acknowledged the sport specialization and curriculum stories of the staffroom, a dichotomy emerged in her account of *how* they connected with, and positioned themselves in relation to, the particular staffroom stories. Sally considered herself a 'curriculum person', and she associated, socialized and strategically aligned herself with other 'curriculum people' within the staffroom who she perceived had similar values, interests and beliefs and had attended the same university as her.

Sally's positioning and alignment with the curriculum story according to her interests, values and beliefs shaped how Sally practised her micropolitical knowledge in the staffroom, reflected in whose opinions she valued, whose advice she sought and in whom she confided. Flores (2001) noted how prior experience, as a student, has powerful influences on teachers. Sally's narrative also captures the interwoven nature of her personal and professional life. Sally's alignment with the curriculum people served not only her professional interest and commitment to curriculum and pedagogy, but also her personal interests of making new friends. Having moved to a large regional town, for Sally, her officially allocated mentor not only provided strong professional support but also personal support outside of the school context. While Sally described their working relationship as 'professional', she considered her mentor a friend, a relationship that had developed over time. For Sally, the staffroom provided not only a professional place and space, but also a social space where she could develop relationships that were reinforced and endured despite relocation outside the school (lisa-hunter *et al.*, 2011). As such, Sally's micropolitical strategies and practices were focused towards initially developing, and subsequently maintaining, these types of supportive personal and professional relationships; relationships based on shared values and beliefs.

The (re)shaping micropolitical staffroom stories

The two narratives by Millie and Sally presented and discussed above draw attention to how the social space of the staffroom significantly shaped and reshaped the beginning teachers' micropolitical learning, positioning and practices throughout their first year of teaching. Both beginning teachers' experiences were bounded and structured by the uniqueness of people, practices and relationships of the staffroom space. While some researchers (see, e.g. Hodkinson and Hodkinson, 2005; Wilson and Demetriou, 2007) have highlighted the complexity of interrelations among individuals, departments and school contexts in professional learning and development, and others (see Curry *et al.*, 2008; Kelchtermans and Ballet, 2002a, 2002b; Schempp *et al.*, 1993) have depicted the micropolitical context of the school as an important influencing factor for beginning teachers' professional development, the narratives in this study point to the significance of the micropolitical context of the staffroom in beginning teacher learning and development.

Given that both Millie and Sally spent the majority of their non-teaching time in the HPE staffroom, the staffroom occupants, both individually and collectively, with their own micropolitical knowledge, interests and agendas (Ball,

1987), acted as informants of those fundamental cultural codes that govern discourse, modes of interaction, values and standards of the profession (Keay, 2005; Schempp *et al.*, 1993). They also shaped the micropolitical situations and relationships that the beginning teachers encountered and negotiated. The staffroom space and historical narratives shaped the content of micropolitical learning (Kelchterans and Ballet, 2002a); that is, *what* beginning teachers came to know (Craig, 1998). The narratives depict the staffroom as a place where beginning teachers encounter a contact zone of contested stories, of possibilities where different staffroom occupants' interests and agendas meet, collide and compete for fulfilment and recognition. Beginning teachers enter this social space and attempt not only to understand the space, but also to decipher and negotiate the space in such a way as to fulfil their own interests and agendas.

While the staffroom stories bounded *what* beginning teachers came to know, *how* they interacted and came to learn micropolitically in the staffroom was reflected in their pursuit to protect their desired working conditions, interests and agendas. Thinking narratively, Connelly and Clandinin (1995) perceive that beginning teachers are active agents (shaped by past and present experiences), pulling themselves into the future with their own inevitable social agendas. Guided by past and present experiences and future agendas, beginning teachers attempt (to varying degrees of success) throughout their first year to develop and practise the necessary knowledge and capacity to negotiate the context of contested stories, the processes of power and struggles of interests (Kelchtermans and Ballet, 2002a) within the staffroom. The beginning teachers drew on previous understandings, values, beliefs and experiences, such as those fostered in their university studies, pre-service teacher experiences, and their new experiences of a staffroom to make sense of, and participate in, the staffroom. Given the contextually specific nature of micropolitical learning, over time and through continuing engagement with the staffroom occupants, beginning teachers became more micropolitically 'literate'. They developed a more in-depth understanding of the nuanced space and place through consciously interacting with prevailing staffroom stories. Beginning teachers' micropolitical learning was reshaped by their increasing capacity to engage with, navigate (cope) and accordingly position themselves in relation to the staffroom context, in such a way as to protect their desired working conditions and interests. Overwhelmingly, across our participants' narratives, beginning teachers' interests and agendas (shaped by their past and present experiences) were guided by who they wanted to be professionally. This was illustrated through Millie's and Sally's exemplar narratives in their commitment to quality curriculum and assessment (cultivated at university) and subsequently how they practised micropolitical literacy, both proactively and reactively.

Notes

1 At the time of this research, secondary schooling in the State of Australia in which this study was conducted is typically Years 8 to 12 with students commencing Year 8 in the year they turn 13 years of age.

2 It is important to note that in Australia, other than in the private and denominational schools sectors, the state (in this case Queensland) is the employing body and 'assigns' graduates to teaching positions – we make other references to this process throughout the text. There is an increasing trend for principals (headteachers) to manage their own recruitment. However, this is limited by the necessity to staff schools in rural and remote regions, which as one might appreciate are not as sought after as schools closer to the coastal regions.

3 This has been a long-held expectation in the HPE subject area in Queensland and other parts of Australia.

Part III

Implications for policy, practice and research

10 The power of policy in shaping teaching and teacher education

Introduction

> The greatest resource in Australian schools is our teachers. They account for the vast majority of expenditure in school education and have the greatest impact on student learning, far outweighing the impact of any other education program or policy.
>
> (Jensen, 2010, p. 5)

Despite the centrality of quality teaching to student learning, '"policy" has assumed an increasingly pivotal role in the educational system' (Sykes *et al.*, 2009, p. 1). The purpose of this chapter is to return to our starting point and more closely consider education policies (and their underpinning ideologies) that are framing HPE teacher education and teachers' work as well as those that could or should assist in optimizing the workspace of teachers. In addition, we consider it important to attend to the silences in the pre-eminent policies. The repository for Australian education policies suggests:

> All educational organisations maintain a body of policies be they administrative, teaching, human resource, legal or some other type. Combined, they help create the effective operation of educational institutions and the effectiveness of the learning which occurs in them.... Such policies do not simply appear. They are created following reviews of existing processes and procedures and usually following some level of research locally, within the wider Australia setting or internationally.
> (Aussie Educator: www.aussieeducator.org.au/education/other/policy.html)

Importantly, it is worth adding to the above description of policies that they also reflect a socio-political position on values, priorities and resources. Our specific interest is in what polices could assist HPE teachers to become and be professionally engaged, supported and recognized.

The opening quote in this chapter reminds us that policy is always *framed* whereby framing a social or policy problem provides an interpretive schema that assists people to understand the question at hand. 'Framing techniques are used to *diagnose* particular conditions as problematic, to offer a *prognosis* for improving or addressing those considerations, and to consolidate the *identities* of groups on various sides of an issue' (Rosen, 2009, p. 277). From this perspective, polices are a social framework that 'provide background understanding for events that incorporate the will, aim, and controlling effort of an intelligence' (Goffman, 1986, p. 22). These 'doings', such as policy enactments, 'subject the doer to "standards", to social appraisal of his [*sic*] action based on its honesty, efficiency, economy, safety, elegance, tactfulness, good taste, and so forth. A serial management of consequentiality is sustained, that is, continuous corrective control' (Goffman, 1986, p. 23). In other words, policy, in the form of practice, is something that, as Goffman (1959) might say, is performed. Ball (2003) takes a rather more pejorative stance on the idea of performance. He suggests that given the audit culture within which we now exist (see our opening chapters for more on this), teachers are compelled to 'perform' in ways consistent with certain compliance measures. This contrasts somewhat with Goffman (1959) who argued, as we saw in Chapter 6, that one 'presents' oneself in everyday life on a number of fronts that are drawn upon to suit the social parameters of context. This social interactionism (which tends to define Goffman's work) as we identified earlier is a performance. Ball (2003) would argue however that there are greater limits to the agency of teachers when it comes to performativity given that performance is shaped by compliance to externally imposed standards, and the measures of the attainment of those standards that are reflective of contemporary policy.

The frame then, for many of the policies that shape or inform teachers' work and its corollary problems, solutions and controls, is clearly reflective of neo-liberalism. As we discussed earlier in the opening chapters, neo-liberalism frames most of what gets done in the name of work. As a frame for teachers' work policies, neo-liberalism drives particular aspects of teachers' work, how teachers are valued, and significantly, processes for teacher regulation and recognition. Davies (2005, p. 8) has noted, 'The language and practices of neoliberal managerialism are seductive. They lay the grounds for new kinds of success and recognition', primarily marked by student academic achievement, individual teacher monitoring and rewards, flexibility in workplace conditions and new, entrepreneurial partnerships.

> 'Education' is no longer just about what happens in classrooms and schools, but increasingly about rules and regulations promulgated in state capitals and the federal government designed to improve student academic performance and social development as well as the management and operation of schools they attend.
>
> (Sykes *et al.*, 2009, p. 1)

With the introduction of a range of teacher education, teacher and teaching policies, in some senses what might be referred to as a policy network (Ball, 2012), it is crucial to be mindful of how the policies have been framed by accountability, performativity and individualism (Ball, 2012). While much of the discussion here is set within the contemporary Australian policy context, it is very much a case of neo-liberal agendas fashioned in line with those in the UK, USA and other neo-liberal economies (Evans and Davies, 2014; Macdonald, 2014).

Pathways into teaching

More mature readers familiar with teacher education research in the 1970s to 1990s may recall questions addressed; for example, who is attracted to the (PE) teaching profession, what should be the priorities of a university-based teacher education programme, what configurations and tasks make for effective practicum experiences, and how should beginning teachers be supported to effect positive change in schooling (e.g. Dewar, 1989; Lortie, 1975; Macdonald, 1995; Zeichner, 1986)? We alluded to some of these questions in Chapter 1. However, since the rise and spread of new instantiations of managerialism in the 1990s, much of the scholarship on teacher education has focused on seeking to understand the impact of policy, and thereby programme, changes that have recast university-based teacher education and teachers' performances as 'problems' that require school-based, market-oriented solutions.

The HPE pre-service and beginning teachers in our project were graduates of a four-year, university-based programme integrating disciplinary, pedagogical, professional and school-based practicum learning experiences. Many of their teaching colleagues would have undertaken a three-year undergraduate degree plus a one- or two-year diploma/Masters as their teacher preparation. As we indicated in Chapter 1, despite being challenged, these models have endured to date in some countries such as Australia, New Zealand, Finland, Scotland and the USA, while elsewhere the role of universities in teacher education has diminished. The language of challenge to university-based preparation is common (see Chapter 1 for an example) and follows neo-liberal discourses that argue something like this: economies rely on a well-educated workforce; schooling is not meeting national expectations for student performance in international testing regimes; teachers and teaching are failing our students; conventional teacher education is failing to produce effective teachers; effective practices can be prescribed in standards frameworks; and focusing on practical skills provided by competitive teacher education and schooling markets will produce more effective teachers. A new private provider of teacher education in the USA, Relay Graduate School of Education, notes on its website: 'Announcing a new plan to strengthen teacher preparation, the White House featured Relay GSE among U.S. education leaders "exploring new and innovative efforts to make teacher preparation more hands-on, relevant, and effective"' (see www.relay.edu, accessed 4 May 2014; see also Hibernia College in the UK).

The School Direct policy in England explicitly privileges 'hands-on' training whereby schools can request teacher training places, select candidates, manage the training programme and invite university input if/as required. 'School Direct

– [is] the new way into teaching.… If you're looking for school-led training, School Direct is the option for you. With School Direct you'll be training in a school from day one' (www.education.gov.uk/get-into-teaching/teacher-training-options/school-based-training/school-direct, accessed 4 May 2014). The School Direct policy sits alongside government support for academy (aka charter) schools that represent a growth in deregulated school governance, curriculum and employment systems (Ellis and Maguire, 2014). McNamara and Murray (2013, p. 14) describe School Direct as 'an ideologically driven understanding of teaching as essentially only a "craft" rather than a complex and fundamentally intellectual activity; an apprenticeship model of teacher training that can be located entirely in the workplace.' The Australian government is watching these policy 'initiatives' with great interest and the Teacher Education Ministerial Advisory Group is inviting public input into directions for teacher education's pedagogical approaches, subject content and professional experience while at the same time considering support for the expansion of the charter schools network and increasing student financial contributions to their tertiary education. In contrast, it is worth noting that Finland, whose schooling outcomes have been the envy of countries worldwide, has strengthened its research-based teacher education to require a Master's degree for comprehensive and upper-secondary school teaching (Sahlberg, 2011).

Against this national and international policy backdrop, we return to what it may mean to teacher education, teacher identity and workplace learning using the experiences of our project participants as the referent. HPE teacher education in Australia still tends to attract school-leavers who are seeking a university experience in a programme with which they have a personal affinity. Using the language of 'subjective warrant' (Lawson, 1983, 1986, 1988), the project participants and their peers nationally still tend to value (and perform) particular stereotypical versions of sport, body shape, health and fitness. As discussed in earlier chapters, this profile has, on the one hand, been criticized for its propensity to lead to inequitable practices in schooling (see Wrench and Garrett, 2012), yet on the other has generated a cadre of HPE teachers who are usually young, vibrant contributors to the school community and who value their content knowledge and curriculum expertise (Kirk and Macdonald, 2001). Our sense is that a School Direct model of HPE teacher education would attract a different cohort – possibly older 'trainees', those with a sport-specific talent suited to the school's differentiated market position, or those seeking a change of career with a background in exercise and/or health sciences. Even with such a shift in profile, we argue that the same subjective warrant would most likely endure, thereby perpetuating some of the dominant cultures and conversations in staffrooms outlined in earlier chapters.

Participants such as Millie and Sally defined their expertise as curriculum and assessment knowledge reflecting emphases in their university-based teacher education programme. Their knowledge and skills were developed in a spiral curriculum in several courses across three of the four years of their ITE programme. This university background became integral to their subjectivities (and perceived strengths) in their workplaces, ones they are unlikely to have developed in an abbreviated, school-based apprenticeship model. Further, several participants recruited the reflexive dimension of their ITE programme to make sense of the HPE departmental practices and to find solutions that purposefully challenged, acquiesced with or removed them from what they considered were inappropriate practices. In contrast, the School Direct model of ITE, in which the 'trainee' is looking for employment within their host school, would seem to limit any resistance to what the pre-service teacher may consider inappropriate or unprofessional practices and they position themselves and perform in concert with the dominant school and staffroom cultures. This tension was clear in Tom's' experiences in Chapter 6, and in Holly's, whose story we have told elsewhere (see Rossi, 2012) as they managed their performance in such a way as was deemed appropriate by her or his supervising teacher in order not to jeopardize their practicum result.

We are also interested in how the different models of ITE can support learning during the practicum and induction. It may be that where schools have a 'stake' in quality learning outcomes for their 'apprentices', significant, coordinated and accountable resources are more likely to be available to support the teachers as experienced by Sally and Angel. As pathways into teaching in many countries seem to increasingly value the technical (over theoretical), training (over education), apprenticeship (over professional), school-based (over university-based), intensive (over developmental), and trainees (over students) it will be important to track the impact of these policy shifts on the production and/ or reproduction of particular forms of HPE workplaces and practices.

Standards as representations of teachers' work

Integral to neo-liberal shifts from government to governance in education has been the introduction of various agencies that provide both guidelines and accountability processes for quality assurance of programmes and practices. Frequently, agencies over the past 20 to 30 years have been charged with creating and implementing a range of standards for teacher education, the practices and priorities for teachers in different subject areas, in different roles and in different career stages, and teacher misconduct. For example, in England, *Teachers' Standards* (2013, p. 3) 'define the minimum level of practice expected of trainees and teachers from the point of being awarded qualified teacher status (QTS)'. In the USA, the National Board for Professional Teaching Standards (NBPTS) oversees the creation and certification of teachers of different subject and year levels, including PE teachers. As with all NBPTS standards, the 13 PE teaching standards are based on five core propositions:

Proposition 1: Teachers are committed to students and their learning.

Proposition 2: Teachers know the subjects they teach and how to teach those subjects to students.

Proposition 3: Teachers are responsible for managing and monitoring student learning.

Proposition 4: Teachers think systematically about their practice and learn from experience.

Proposition 5: Teachers are members of learning communities.
(See www.nbpts.org/sites/default/files/documents/certificates/Aaag/
EMC_PE_AssessAtaGlance_05.22.13_Final.pdf.)

PE teachers in the USA can choose to move into the competitive certification processes (through portfolio and content knowledge examinations) provided by Pearson.

In Australia, the National Professional Standards for Teachers (NPST) also outline what teachers 'should know and be able to do' but in a different configuration to that in England and the USA. Across seven standards and four career stages (Graduate, Proficient, Highly Accomplished and Lead), the Australian standards:

define the work of teachers and make explicit the elements of high-quality, effective teaching in 21st century schools that will improve educational outcomes for students.... They present a common understanding and language for discourse between teachers, teacher educators, teacher organizations, professional associations and the public.

(Australian Institute for Teaching and School
Leadership [AITSL], 2011, p. 2)

Table 10.1 summarizes the NPST, offered as an example of how teaching standards are typically represented.

The NPST are framed by discourses that highly value what is seen to be a core of teachers' work. In relation to the narratives in our study, these standards resonated (to varying degrees) with the experiences of teachers such as Angel, Sally and Larry but did not with many of the experiences of teachers such as Millie. As we read in Chapters 5 and 8, Angel and Sally were encouraged and supported in their staffrooms to develop their professional knowledge and teaching and learning practices through engagement with their colleagues and their local communities.

What is particularly interesting about these standards (whether they be from England, the USA or Australia) is the emphasis placed on the individual teacher's responsibilities to his or her students, peers and community. We concur that these are and should be significant. However, nowhere does the document indicate what the rights of teachers might be in terms of their work environment that should support the demonstration of the standards. For example, Millie's school-based experiences of teaching, curriculum planning and assessment (as depicted in Chapter 9) were in direct contrast to those advocated for in her teacher

Table 10.1 Australian National Professional Standards for Teachers

Domains of teaching	Standards	Focus areas and descriptors
Professional knowledge	1 Know students and how they learn. 2 Know the content and how to teach it.	Refer to standard at each career stage, i.e.:: • Graduate teachers • Proficient teachers • Highly accomplished teachers • Lead teachers
Professional practice	3 Plan for and implement effective teaching and learning. 4 Create and maintain supportive and safe learning environments. 5 Assess, provide feedback and report on student learning.	
Professional engagement	6 Engage in professional learning. 7 Engage professionally with colleagues, parents/carers and the community.	

Source: adapted from: www.aitsl.edu.au/verve/_resources/AITSL_National_Professional_Standards_for_Teachers.pdf, available from www.aitsl.edu.au.

education programme and correspondingly by the NPST. Her staffroom context did not support or encourage the creation of innovative and effective teaching and learning practices or the development and implementation of clear, fair and valid assessment tasks. This scenario raises the potential of policy to do positive work. If teachers are policy-literate, they can draw on policies such as teaching standards to possibly open professional conversations that can benefit them and their students.

A corollary document to the NPST in Australia is the Australian Teacher Performance and Development Framework (AITSL, 2012a). This document calls for the 'creation of a performance and development culture in all Australian schools' (AITSL, 2012a, p. 2). It continues: 'Research is unambiguous in showing that a successful approach to effective performance and development relies on creating a strong and supportive culture in a school' (AITSL, 2012a, p. 3). While arguing for flexibility in the approach to implementing a performance and development cycle, the document does recognize 'the entitlement of teachers to receive feedback and support' (AITSL, 2012a, p. 5). This entitlement is further articulated in the Australian Charter for the Professional Learning of Teachers and School Leaders (2011) which encourages professional learning that is relevant, collaborative and future focused embedded within a learning culture, underscored by 'a shared responsibility and commitment' (2011, p. 1). It is worth musing upon the outcomes for Millie had she encountered a school staffroom context that embraced and was committed to ongoing, collaborative, professional learning as articulated in these policies. Perhaps more of her energy and time would have been spent on developing her teaching and learning practices rather than negotiating the disorganized, 'messy' and underdeveloped curriculum, assessment and reporting practices with which she was confronted in her first year of teaching. Indeed, had the following AITSL statement applied to Millie, her first year in teaching may not have been so frustrating or so exhausting to the point of debilitation.

Although it is useful to note that the latter document is also predominantly framed by teachers' individual responsibility and silences on the schools' responsibilities, there is some acknowledgement by the responsible policy organization, AITSL, for a broader remit:

> The next step is for all involved in Australian education to take a deliberate, structured and long-term approach to building a culture that provides a satisfying and challenging environment in which all Australian teachers can improve their practice and the outcomes their students achieve.
>
> (AITSL, 2012b, p. 8)

Australia is yet to adopt a systematic appraisal process, as will be discussed below. Yet we are encouraged to read of policies that have a stronger focus on school culture and the support of teachers' work than is evident in many of the international sets of teaching standards. If the standards were reviewed, our data suggest that domains such as 'professional engagement' or 'professional responsibilities' are broadened to read as, for example, 'engage in professional learning in and through a supportive environment'. Lessons from Finland could also be instructive for Australia where central to Finnish ways of thinking about professional development is the concept of professional learning communities (Sahlberg, 2011; see also Chapter 2) that structures time for teachers to collaborate, research and reflect.

Teacher appraisal and feedback

Central to the teacher standards and quality discourses is discussion about teacher inspection, appraisal and feedback. The case has been made that Australian teachers are dissatisfied with how their work is currently evaluated and that policy work that has focused on developing teacher standards is not germane to effective teacher development (Jensen, 2010). National and international data are presented by an independent policy 'think tank', The Grattan Institute,[1] to argue for empowering school principals to instigate rigorous teacher appraisal and feedback protocols that support targeted teacher development, recognition and promotion. The Grattan Institute (Jensen, 2011, p. 3) consequently proposed to governments the importance of more effective policies and processes given:

> Systems of teacher appraisal and feedback that are directly linked to improved student performance can increase teacher effectiveness by as much as 20 to 30%. This would not only arrest our decline but lift the performance of Australia's students to the best in the world.

Jensen's 2011 report frames the issue as one of correlation between teacher effectiveness and student performance outcomes. It goes on to argue that teacher appraisal systems need to be matched to the values and goals of individual schools, and appraisal methods should be varied to capture the different aspects of the teachers' role: 'Schools must decide the objectives and benchmarks against which performance is assessed' (Jensen, 2011, p. 9). It is important to remind ourselves that this advice (and possibly policy precursor) is located within the neo-liberal frame in several ways: focusing on *individual* teacher performance; linking teacher performance to student (academic) outcomes irrespective of context; positing appraisal power within individual schools; and laying the foundations for competition for differential salaries. As we have argued elsewhere, understanding the policy frame can assist the PE profession in understanding, predicting, supporting or resisting particular education trajectories (Macdonald, 2014).

This Australian discourse sits in contrast to Ontario's appraisal system, explained as follows:

> The Teacher Performance Appraisal System provides teachers with meaningful appraisals that encourage professional learning and growth. The process is designed to foster teacher development and identify opportunities for additional support where required. By helping teachers achieve their full

potential, the performance appraisal process represents one element of Ontario's vision of achieving high levels of student performance.

(www.edu.gov.on.ca/eng/teacher/appraise.html)

The policy frame here of supporting learning communities emphasizing 'learning', 'growth', 'development' and 'full potential' as the backbone of the appraisal system would have been welcomed by many of the early-career HPE teachers who were looking for support for their professional growth within and beyond their subject department.

The notion of teacher 'inspection' adds poignancy to debates around school/ teacher quality and appraisal. In England, for example, the Office for Standards in Education, Children's Services and Skills – Ofsted) has recently revised its inspectorial system as a response to 'an increasing emphasis on international league tables … [in which] England is viewed as underperforming against comparable countries' (Baxter and Clarke, 2013, p. 702). Ofsted's inspection of schools (and individual teachers within the schools) aims to:

> provide information to the Secretary of State for Education and to Parliament about the work of schools and the extent to which an acceptable standard of education is being provided. This provides assurance that minimum standards are being met, provides confidence in the use of public money and assists accountability, as well as indicating where improvements are needed.

From the appraisal performed by inspectors, detailed school ratings are produced as well as interventions and monitoring. While there is a body of research that considers the stress of the inspectorial system on schools and teachers, interventions suggest that inspections may also serve to interrupt unprofessional workplace micropolitics and challenge the doxa where it is deemed to undermine contemporary and creative practices.

It is reasonable to suggest that many international appraisal priorities and options seem to be more about power over individual performances rather than empowering teachers to reflect holistically upon their work (with notable exceptions such as Finland). Would Millie and Larry, both of whom had been frustrated and disappointed by the lack of feedback and support they had received in relation to their teaching planning and practices, have found their workplace and work more rewarding if they were subject to a rigorous appraisal and feedback system? While an appraisal system might from one framing perspective seem to have draconian overtones and gatekeeping roles, from another perspective what is under consideration in Australia could be a policy of support and development that provides a safe space for systematic, professional conversations.

School culture and teachers' well-being

While the Australian education policy landscape is relatively silent about teachers' rights, working conditions and welfare, overarching international documents do raise aspects of the conditions of teachers' work (Cooper and Alvarado, 2006; OECD, 2006; UNESCO, 2012). A UNESCO/ILO (2009, p. 22) report, building on those organizations' policy heritage in teachers' *rights* and responsibilities, reports:

> At the same time there is a generalized decline in the teaching and learning environment. Teachers no longer feel respected or safe in their working environment.... Many teachers in developing countries report feelings of professional isolation and lack of support.

International consensus draws attention to school organizational factors and the consequences if these are ignored:

> Although salaries can make a difference in terms of teacher recruitment, teachers generally report the importance of good working conditions in making a decision to stay in teaching. A number of school organizational factors play a crucial role in teacher turnover, including inadequate support from school administration, student motivation and discipline problems, and limited teacher input into and influence over school policies. These factors also affect the motivation and commitment of those teachers who stay at the school.
>
> (UNESCO, 2008, p. 5)

International concern for the broader school culture is also captured in the concept of the health-promoting school articulated by the World Health Organization (WHO) in 1998 as 'A healthy setting for living, learning and working' (WHO, 1998, p. 1). The health-promoting school concept can explicitly address the work environment for teachers as manifested in the following policy advice that, when a school community pursues the goals of a health-promoting school, 'A safer and less stressful working environment for staff can be an outcome' (DECS, South Australia, 2001). One of the key features of health-promoting schools – as one might imagine – is the environment in which pupils and teachers come together. This is important, as it is not difficult to see how health promotion might be taken as a concern of curriculum subject matter. Also of significance here is the essential role that school organization and ethos has to play in the promotion of participants' well-being. Research on teachers' well-being is building with some schooling systems in Australia and elsewhere, instigating programmes that seek to promote teacher well-being, although this work sits outside the powerful standards policy network (e.g. Parker and Martin, 2009; Pillay *et al.*, 2005).

Parker and Martin (2009) concluded that interventions focusing solely on the organizational/school level and not at the individual teacher level (such as through appraisal and mentoring) may not enhance workplace well-being as it was individual 'buoyancy' that they found to be significant. The importance of support at both the individual and collective level was also advice provided by

McCallum and Price (2010) to generate 'the promotion of positive personal and physical identities as well as a sense of belonging ... and empowerment in their new role' (p. 32). The overarching health-promoting schools concept then would, on paper at least, seem to provide the type of policy guidance to create a safe, supportive and healthy workplace (see Chapter 1) in which pre-service and beginning teachers could develop their skills and professionalism that Illeris (2011) argues is critical for learning and quality workplace performance.

Inevitably, as a collective in this book, we have been particularly concerned (if not on occasion disturbed – see the opening scenario to the book) with the stories from our participants who related incidences of what could be conceived of as harassment and bullying in their workplaces. Riley *et al.*'s (2012) research into staff bullying in Australian schools indicates widespread bullying with the most reported forms of bullying perceived to be: information is withheld which affects performance; questioning of decisions, procedures and judgement; tasks are set with unreasonable or impossible targets or deadlines; attempts to belittle and undermine work; and recognition, acknowledgement and praise are withheld. Interestingly their work is important in the light of our study, given that it too addresses the space of the 'department', ranging from how workloads are allocated, to how work is recognized and respectful communication expected. In response to their data, Riley *et al.* (2012) adapted the National Safe School Framework to create a profile for how the bullying of teachers can be reduced through changes to the workplace culture (including the subject department). The Framework identifies 'nine elements to assist Australian schools to continue to create teaching and learning communities where all members of the school community both feel and are safe from harassment, aggression, violence and bullying' (MCEECDYA, 2011, p. 2). Such a position is entirely consistent with Illeris' (2011) recent work where he suggests that the best conditions for workplace learning are those that are 'safe'. Remember: by safe, Illeris was referring to workplaces that were supportive of innovation and intellectual and practical risk-taking, and imbued with a sense of constructive feedback aimed at improving practice within the individual worker but also at improving the workplace itself. As Illeris (2011) says, 'the interaction between basic security and inspiring challenges is the first and most fundamental balance of a good workplace learning environment' (p. 132).

A safe schools framework that had a focus on teachers and their work could have significantly helped Holly, whose story we referred to earlier. Holly, at times, felt as though she had been cut adrift to sink or swim in the most crucial professional experience prior to graduating as a teacher. Her strong sense of mission (for example, trying to motivate reluctant participants) garnered almost no support from other staff in the department who seemed to consider such children a 'lost cause'. This had a profound affect not only on Holly's professional development but also on her whole sense of self and ultimately her decision to pursue further study rather than enter the profession. Other pre-service teacher tales paint a similar picture. Gareth, for example (whose story we tell in full elsewhere: see Rossi and lisahunter, 2013), was placed in a school that had a sporting Centre of Excellence. Ordinarily this would be a 'dream' placement for a HPE pre-service teacher. However, Gareth's lack of expertise in the sport that was the focus of excellence meant that he mostly looked incompetent, lacking in knowledge and skills of the game, and he therefore came across as a 'poor' teacher. There was little support provided to develop the necessary skills to be effective. Rather, Gareth was often ridiculed (by pupils as well as by teachers) for what were perceived as his inadequacies. A safe schools framework, embedded in the environment in which Gareth found himself, might have led to far more favourable learning outcomes – the very purpose of the practicum in the first place. The beginning teachers in the study may also have benefited from working within the context of a safe schools framework. Millie's experience, for example, in assessing children's work in HPE is salutary. Given that conventional practice within her department was to use 'gut feeling' rather than evidence-based practice, she was forced to develop criteria and standards through subterfuge in order to avoid undermining the more experienced teachers in the department. Having to portray 'best practice' as a device to overcome her inexperience (Millie identifies this as a strategy in Chapter 9) is hardly the basis for a 'safe' workplace.

Conclusion: policy possibilities

Relatively little in the high-profile policy network of teacher education, teaching standards, and professional appraisal and learning connects with the challenges faced by several of the beginning teachers in our research. Framed by neo-liberal concerns for performativity (Ball, 2003) in student outcomes, the human, embodied, emotional and aspirational aspects of teachers' work have been largely backgrounded in policy development. That said, we are encouraged by policy possibilities offered through, as examples, the Australian Charter for the Professional Learning of Teachers and School Leaders, safe schools, health-promoting schools, teacher well-being programmes and school culture surveys. The rising use of school culture surveys completed by parents and teachers can be a valuable instrument for detecting professional collaboration, affiliative and collegial relationships, and staff efficacy or self-determination (Wagner, 2006). Such a policy network takes a more holistic and inclusive approach to schools as professional learning organizations. As Comber and Nixon (2009, p. 344) argue, 'Teachers' working conditions need to be altered in order for them to participate in education as scholars and as researchers, not merely as the technicians and implementers of someone else's curriculum and pedagogy', and without safe, consistent and respectful support and guidance this might prove extraordinarily difficult.

Lingard (2011) suggests that it is a difficult time in which to change the nature of teachers' work in many countries given the top-down inter/national policy priorities. However, like Lingard, as a group of researchers we can see some extensions to the current policy network that could create a collaborative and democratic professionalism with teachers and principals, and quality partners, working together not only on pedagogy and assessment but on the broader school environment. If we ask different questions, recruit different frames and their associated policies and practices, we avoid 'searching for resolutions to our dilemmas in the wrong places, namely, in precisely those official discourses which are intended to play a game which is not of our choice' (Mahony and Hextall, 2000, p. 94), that seek to frame teachers' responsibilities but less so teachers' professionalism and well-being.

Note

1 The Grattan Institute (based in Melbourne) is, as we indicate, a politically independent think tank and was helped into existence by two prominent members of the main opposing political parties in Australia. A Labor Prime Minister eventually launched the Institute in 2008. Funding is sourced from an independent endowment, State (Victoria) and Federal governments but also from BHP Billiton (a global resources company) and the National Australia Bank. It is meant to mimic the Brookings Institute in Washington, DC. Inevitably, like any think tank that claims to be independent, the 'Grattan' is subject to political criticism and charges of bias.

11 Learning to teach physical education in the workplace

Some concluding thoughts

The contribution of this book to the literature and the field

We acknowledge that many books on workplace learning have a central organizing feature that tends to encompass ideas around situated learning, communities of practice, affordances, limiters, and other constraints and enablers. The work of the likes of Billett (2001) and Boud and Garrick (1999) has generated significant findings and theorizing around some of these concepts and concerns. This work has itself been informed in some of these (e.g. Wenger, 2000). Other work has drawn more from the idea of the culture of the workplace (see Illeris, 2011), and workplace learning in school teaching is developing (Hodkinson and Hodkinson, 2005).

This book however departs from previous work in three main ways. First, the book had its genesis in a series of events that we recount in the opening chapter. These events gave focus to the pilot study, the subsequent funded study, an Australian Research Council Discovery Project, and ultimately, this book. The central and original concern of that series of events was the nature of the learning experience of pre-service teachers within the final, and high-stakes school-based practicum. However, as you will recall, the central concern of the project was only part of the story. One of the distinguishing features of this book, and what separates it from others of its type, is the exclusive attention to the professional subject area of Health and Physical Education, to use its most common Australian name and the name we have used throughout this book, and the role of the HPE departmental office or staffroom in the development of aspiring teachers. There were other 'turns' that help to distinguish this book. The theoretical and methodological turns to some extent revolved around personnel in the research but also the reflexive nature of our work over time where field texts interacted with our continual reading of the literature and posed new questions to what we were witnessing in the field texts. Therefore, connected to this, the book is framed by five what we have called dimensions, rather than a single organizing theme or framework. This made life messy for us at times, yet in the end was far more informative in terms of the sense we were able to make of the data.

The second departure for this book is that we have included transitional stories. That is, the transition from pre-service to qualified teacher while at the same time maintaining our central focus on the departmental office. This aspect of the overall study drew heavily (though not exclusively) on the doctoral work that emerged from the project.

The final departure of the book is that the field texts are represented mostly through themed and narrative accounts. We say mostly here because again, the move towards narratives was an evolutionary feature of the whole project but it will be apparent to readers that we move in and out of both methods of representation across the entirety of this book. This is consistent with the various stages of the project itself. The narrative turn (see Barone, 2001; Clandinnin and Connelly, 2000; Mishler, 1999) by which we predominantly represent our participants is an attempt to place them increasingly at the heart of the book. These narratives are based on their stories. We perhaps need to clarify our position. The narratives in this book were created from a range of data sources across the life of the project. We did not restrict our data collections to lengthy talk-fests or 'focus' groups. We also used photo evidence, photo elicitation, observation protocols, document analysis, syllabus and work programme analysis and context analysis. All of these field texts were subject to a very critical and rigorous process of analysis using a specific theoretical lens identified in Chapter 4 and represented in Part II of the book. As Atkinson and Delamont (2006) inform us, narratives are embedded in organizational culture, so the narratives we created from the field texts, while potentially generative, were not developed to necessarily identify constant patterns in teacher development, even though patterns were evident to some extent. Rather, the purpose was to capture a wide variety of stories that would demonstrate the differences in experiences rather than the similarities. This we considered would be of more use to the field and would make a stronger contribution to the academic literature.

We were not, as by now you may have gathered, especially convinced by the position of letting the participants speak for themselves, as espoused by literature associated with participant voice. We considered this to be a somewhat laboured idea to the point of being a cliché as well as a potential cop-out. We would not expect a scientist to distribute a series of graphs and then suggest that the graphs somehow speak for themselves. This may seem like a trite comparison but it is all too easy to abdicate the responsibility to do the analytical work expected of a researcher by claiming fidelity to voice. It is a cautionary note that Atkinson and Delamont (2006) also make. As they say, 'It is a common failing, for instance, to imply that informants' voices "speak for themselves", or that personal, biographical materials provide privileged means of access to informants' personal experiences' (p. 166). Nonetheless, we considered our use of narratives to be not only justified and appropriate but also effective in their capacity to portray a message.

Therefore we would state that the contribution of this book is that it is constituted by a set of narratives developed of emerging HPE teachers across the transition period from the final pre-service practicum to induction year through a range of theoretical lenses that kept a steady (but in the end not exclusive) focus on the department office or staffroom as a research site. In this we believe we are unique.

What did we learn?

We think an important caveat is necessary here. It is sometimes easy for research to get ideologically ahead of itself and become more than a little rant about the need for reform and policy changes. The attraction of such action is probably obvious. Within the context of an audit culture (Ball, 2003, 2012) the desirability to have 'impact' is significant. A relatively easy way to do that is to shout about everything one considers wrong or poor about teacher education, the role of the practicum, and the HPE departmental office. Just about every ideological evangelist may have something to say about this and we have flirted with some of this throughout the text. So, to ensure that the reader genuinely knows our position, we think there is a need to spell it out clearly in case it has been missed up to this point.

Not all the experiences of all the participants in this study were poor experiences. It is reasonable to suggest that some of the participants had experiences as pre-service teachers that were uplifting and motivating, and as a consequence they were committed to enter the teaching profession and excited about becoming a HPE teacher. The induction experiences of the same participants were not always as fulfilling. Some of the participants had modest experiences in their final practicum and opted to enter the profession in spite of these experiences rather than because of them. Others opted out. At the point of induction, many of those opting in found teaching to be much more rewarding than the practicum experience. What may be said however, and with some confidence, is that a sizeable proportion of the participants in the pre-service section of this study had experiences that convinced them *not* to enter teaching and a sizeable proportion moved into beginning teacher subject positions that were not reflective of educative and socially just practices and profession. We regard this loss of human resource and contradiction to the idea of education to be unacceptable given the cost alone of developing teachers. Remember: these participants did not 'fail' the practicum component of their programme, nor were they regarded as unacceptable to the profession. Essentially they just did not like what they saw and experienced. Not only is this a loss to the profession; it is also a sad indictment of the impact of some of the in-school teacher education requirements specifically within HPE teacher education but also of some of the processes of induction into the profession. In short, then, were all the experiences negative ones? No, of course not. However, to take that message surely misses the point.

Let's think about it this way. We now exist in a culture where the exigencies of a market mentality override almost everything we do, including what we do in education and more specifically teacher education. Apple has commented widely on this but in an article in 2007 he suggested that when certain conditions are in place that 'mimic' market mentality something strange occurs (see our commentary on this in Chapter 2). As he says, 'standardized and competitive labor processes begin to dominate the lives of the newly marketized workers' (p. 5). Drawing on Habermasian ideas, Apple suggests that the implication of a shift to a marketized labour force, rather than, say, an investment in the teaching profession, is about having 'systems' colonize our lifeworlds (hence the attention to Habermas). In other words, we must work/function within systems in order to actually 'be' part of the lifeworld. This seems to represent an absurd contradiction that Apple goes on to pick up. Classical liberalism, the genetic master of neo-liberalism, holds that the freedom of the individual is sacrosanct and the state has no role to play in interfering with the individual. This is other than the enforcement of contracts upholding property law and criminal law under the common laws of a country and ensuring no harm befalls others as a consequence of one's actions.

Classical liberalism then upholds the principle of liberty, and perhaps the most widely read treatise on this is Stuart Mills' *On Liberty*. Neo-liberalism (which should be first understood as a theory of political economy – see Harvey (2005) for more on this) is perhaps a more extreme version of this with an odd but added contradiction. That is, though the mantra of neo-liberalism is personal liberty, the construction of the citizen under this guise is one that behaves as the state both desires and then designs. It is a case of centralized liberty – an oxymoron if ever there was one. So where are we going with this? Well, one of the key words Apple identifies is *'standardized'* (see above). If we stay with this logic for a moment, it suggests that in public life we must 'measure up' to an accepted 'standard' behaviour or practice. Once we can set standards of practice, then measuring performance (on the surface at least) becomes all too easy. What this means then is that, for example, in order to be measured as a pre-service teacher, it surely means that everyone has to have the same (as far as is possible) experience to be measured against. This, as we have shown throughout this book, was clearly not the case. Neither was this the case in the induction year for our participants in that part of the study. To be perfectly clear: we do *not* support the standardization of teaching or of teacher development.

Moreover, all our participants had different experiences – however, this is clearly not our central concern. The key concern for us, and an important finding – or perhaps reaffirmation is better – is that it was not so much that the experiences were different for our participants but that it was the *quality* of the experience that varied so much. We would not expect all experiences to be identical. This is neither logical nor desirable and probably not even feasible. However, we do consider it important that attention is given to the quality of the experience as both a moral and professional obligation on the part of the school but more specifically in this case on the part of the central site of concern for this research, namely the departmental office or staffroom.

So it would be trite to say that we found that the participants had different experiences both within the pre-service component and the induction part of the study. Rather, we need to emphasize that the difference in the quality of the experience in both of these aspects of the study had an impact on whether participants entered or remained in the profession and this for us was a significant concern. Hence, on the one hand, we have a profession that (like most others) provides opportunities for work-based or work-integrated learning that will vary across the many sites where such learning takes place. At the same time, we have a set of centralized 'measures' (or ways of making judgements) to assess, first, the suitability of teachers to enter the profession, and second, the *quality* of that teacher once she or he is part of the system (see Chapter 10). Once in the profession, the variability of experiences available to teachers is almost incalculable and yet as a profession we seem unable to agree upon an 'at least' set of principles by which we induct new teachers into the profession in their first year. As if this were not bizarre enough, the teacher standards agenda will ensure that teachers are measured against proscribed standards regardless of the circumstances of their appointment. The incongruity of laissez-faire marketized educational systems and centrally controlled standards makes little sense.

Getting a sense of what happened through the lens of the five dimensions

Coming to terms with social tasks

Our analysis using the lens of social tasks suggested that assumptions are made regarding willingness of pre-service and beginning teachers to 'join in' and 'naturally' navigate the social task system that is not only relevant to becoming a HPE teacher but is seemingly pertinent to the localized nature of the departmental office. As we said in Chapter 5, this perspective is both naïve and simplistic, and presents an image of the of department office as a sort of benevolent society. In fact, according to our participants, the social dynamics are highly nuanced and require a game-like approach. In our view, the complexity that pre-service and beginning teachers must negotiate in striving for an excellent evaluation, fulfilling probation requirements and securing a permanent job warrants specific attention in teacher education and beginning teacher programmes.

We propose that teacher education and beginning teacher programmes increase opportunities for pre-service and beginning teachers to examine social dynamics of HPE and potential implications for their understanding and participation in social tasks. Specifically, we recommend that pre-service and beginning teachers engage in conversations with peers and teacher educators, read stories about the practicum 'game' (see Tinning *et al.*, 2001), and engage in reflection both prior to and during their practicum and first year in order to explore perceptions, expectations and experiences related to teachers' work.

In addition to supporting pre-service and beginning teachers to better play the practicum and induction year game, as partisan teacher educators (see Liston and Zeichner, 1991; Tinning, 2002; Cochran-Smith, 2004) we actively support the explicit State or government education ministry expectations that HPE teachers' practices will be underpinned by principles of equity, diversity and supportive environments, not just in Queensland where this study took place, but internationally as a broader imperative. Taking such a stance leads us to question the social spaces into which pre-service and beginning HPE teachers are striving to negotiate and participate fully and not just fit in. In other words, we are bothered by some of the condoned community practices that exist in certain HPE subject departments and which we witnessed first hand. For example, it seems to us that the pre-service and beginning teachers' experiences of teasing, sexist jokes and comments in the office contradict state expectations that teachers work in/for supportive spaces and equity (Queensland HPE, 1999). We suggest that this is a long way from what Illeris (2011) might describe as a 'safe' or healthy environment (lisahunter, 2010; see also Chapter 10).

This dimension of workplace learning raised questions for us regarding our responsibilities in sending pre-service teachers into contexts that we came to describe as toxic for some. Politically, selecting some HPE departments as 'appropriate' and not others would be a public relations minefield. Practically, even if such selectivity was politically justifiable, it is not an option for most teacher education programme providers, since invariably there are simply not enough practicum sites to be choosey. With this in mind, we continue to question how we might better support pre-service teachers so that they can demonstrate skills needed for successful evaluation, while at the same time challenge behaviours of inequity, inequality or exclusion in their schools. For beginning teachers, questions surrounding support and teacher education preparation are clearly raised and we alluded to these in the chapters in Part II, and we explore them further below. It is our contention that there is ample evidence that points to the need for more in-depth examination of the dynamics in various school spaces in relation to HPE pre-service and beginning teachers' learning to be a teacher.

Performing in the 'game'

The analysis, guided by the social task dimension, inevitably informed our understanding of the realms of performance in which the pre-service and beginning teachers engaged. Indeed, the performance within the context of the 'game' provided further insights as to how the negotiation of the HPE departmental space was undertaken. Of greater importance however was the sense of challenge to those of us charged with the responsibility of preparing teachers for the field. This was particularly the case when we were compelled to return to a question we posed earlier. Where are the performances in HPE teacher education likely to be most authentic? This part of the study demonstrated that there are various ways in which social processes of HPE communities are played out. By returning to our earlier question we are forced to ask a further question at this juncture: Were the performances of the pre-service teachers within the practicum and the performance of the beginning teachers in the first year performances of misrepresentation (Goffman, 1959)? The strong alignment many of the pre-service and beginning teachers felt with the HPE teaching community (even if the alignment took longer for some) and the practices in the department office contributed to the seeming naturalness of the perspectives. We are aware of such alignments from the work on recruitment that appeared in the 1980s (see Lawson (1983, 1986) and Dewar (1989) as examples of this work). So we could expect that through daily practices these pre-service and beginning teachers will reify and reproduce these same behaviours, norms and ways of being an HPE teacher. However as we noted earlier, the university programme of which these participants were a part is founded upon non-discriminatory practices, gender equity, social justice and a critique of some of the conduct within the social and cultural practice of sport. It is not clear whether the principles of the university course work are washed out as Zeichner (1983) suggests; whether the high-stakes context encourages performances of compliance; whether our practices as teacher educators are really not as socially critical as we may like to think; or – and not the least worrying – whether the front used when the pre-service teachers are 'in session' at the university is the performance of misrepresentation. Whether it is one, none, or a combination of all of these possibilities, it does suggest that somewhere in the process of HPE teacher education and the transition into the first year, the pre-service and beginning teachers attempt to idealize the performances required within the process. In doing so, they conform to Giddens' (1991) idea of maintaining a division between their self-identity and their performance. As we said, this is somewhat perplexing for those in the business of preparing HPE teachers, and perhaps in teacher education more generally. In our view the practicum (and to an extent the first year of teaching) does come across as theatre. There is clearly a front and back stage (Goffman, 1959), and the pre-service and beginning teachers have to 'pick' their performances when they are on front stage accordingly and plan them to have effect when they are on back stage. To do this, irrespective of any notions of authentic self (if there is such a thing), the participants used a number of fronts to negotiate the tricky waters of the subject department office, and this is particularly so in this case as so much rides on the overall performance.

We are further perplexed in terms of understanding these performances. We have to try to understand whether the fronts used during the practicum and the first year were performances of identity (as Goffman suggests), whether they were attempts at accumulating capital and a positive positioning within the social space (Bourdieu, 1977), or whether they were strategies for coping with the social task demands of the environment. Giddens (1991) can be of assistance here, since his idea of the self being routinely created and sustained reflexively suggests that the pre-service teachers in this study used fronts as part of their identity performance but reflexively adjusted self-narratives to deal with the phenomena encountered during the practicum. The great majority of our research cohort in this study show remarkable dexterity in managing the variety of possibilities within the context, and the idea of multiple selves cannot be overlooked.

However, there is reason for concern because as this research, like Brown (2005) and Dewar (1989) have demonstrated, the fronts used in the practicum setting have the propensity to contribute to the naturalization of practices and social (re)production. Furthermore, our findings indicate the power of the practicum in that through practice in workplaces, such as the subject department office, norms supported by and even 'played out' in pre-service teacher performance become further entrenched and assumed. Through their daily practices as pre-service teachers and then beginning teachers, these socially constructed norms become sustained. For example, although it is as long ago as 1985 when

Tinning first argued that the HPE profession was implicated in reproducing the cult of slenderness, we still witness such processes in HPE department communities. Although as a profession we may talk more about matters of difference and change, certain norms have a stubborn tendency to endure.

Subject positions and identity: doing and being a HPE teacher

This practicum and the induction year experiences we drew on clearly revealed the importance HPE pre-service and beginning teachers placed on building a relationship with the legitimized, credentialed HPE teachers. This was to facilitate participation in the subject department office dynamics and reach the desired state of being: recognition and identification as a HPE teacher. The strong alignment which many of the student teachers felt with the HPE teachers and the practices in the department office may have contributed to their perception of a 'natural' fit with the community. Needless to say, the findings concerned us in many ways. Some of the alignments among our research participants and credentialed teachers' dispositions lent themselves to the social reproduction of marginalizing practices. At the same time these alignments simply underscored the dissonance between the learning available in some of the workplaces and the ethical underpinning and intellectual orientation of the university programme. We have now expressed this concern a number of times. Moreover, our participants' engagement in communities that supported such practices further entrenched the doxa or seeming 'naturalness' of them. Through engaging in such practices, some of our participants were embodying the very oppressive practices they knew to be antithetical to socially just practices, arguably re-enabling these practices. Perhaps they were making these practices part of their identity, as alternative subject positions were unavailable with which to identify.

We can report that there were a modest number of instances where ideas and expectations that tended to define the HPE staffroom could be challenged by our participants. Given this, we propose that actions of the emerging HPE teachers that pushed at the doxa of the HPE community may be able to contribute to clearing the way for broader notions of legitimate identities or subject positions. Over time, such practices may work towards reshaping the social field to accept alternative dispositions, although the evidence in the field currently is not heartening. Each of the authors, despite embodying or at least trying to create subject positions for attention to social justice, are at once evidence of success and failure of such a project. Bourdieu did warn that change could take generations!

We would have liked to be able to report more instances of our emerging teachers offering resistance to practices that contravened what we considered to be the ethics of the university programme. However, our findings remind us of the power of the social space of the HPE subject department for emerging teachers and their need to conform (e.g. to facilitate a good grade or performance rating) within that community of practice. It also reminds us of the enduring nature of the field of HPE that is perhaps not unfairly stereotyped as being full of bullies and buffoons (McCullick *et al.*, 2003). Drawing on Wenger (1998) and Dowling (2011), we suggest that the pre-service teachers' and beginning teachers' participation in the departmental office as a structure of the profession may be likened to a form of apprenticeship where being accepted by the other HPE teachers (particularly their supervisor) can legitimize fuller community membership. In this way, community participation acts as a conduit into the HPE department membership while also contributing to (re)producing its normalized practices and as such re-embodied as a practice within emerging teachers' practices.

For teacher educators, the findings in this study suggest that we need additional information regarding the HPE teaching community, the normalizing practices and habits shaping various workspaces within schools, and the impact these have on emerging teachers' identities and/or subjectivities. A deeper understanding of these complicated social dynamics may assist us in disrupting the dominance and unproblematic acceptance of certain doxa that marginalize emerging teachers and what is deemed 'good' practice within the teaching profession. This deeper understanding may also support teachers (new and experienced) to recognize their own capacity to generate equitable, supportive and inclusive learning and teaching communities. Such understanding also provides a launching point for other discussions about what practices should and could constitute teachers' work and to what extent these practices and people constitute and are constituted by a profession and its professionals. It also allows us to ask who wants to identify as what, in terms of those employing HPE teaching as an identity, as a way of being, and whether the 'what' or way of being is acceptable. At the same time it allows us to ask what subject positions can be created to invite particular practices, or ways of doing into what constitutes HPE teachers' work.

Department staffrooms and spatiality

Given the considerable variability across schools in how workplaces sustain the social task dynamics and the complexities of the workplace climate (Hayes *et al.*, 2006: Talbert and McLaughlin, 2002), the spatial arrangement of the staffroom where teachers work and/or meet is clearly an important site for the constitution of professional subjectivities (Grosz, 1994) of the pre-service and experienced teacher (Hodkinson and Hodkinson, 2005: McGregor, 2003) as well as the more obvious expectations of it being a site where curriculum and resource decisions are influenced. It is a social space (Bourdieu, 1985; Lefebvre, 1991) in which certain behaviours, attitudes and dispositions are sanctioned and reinforced while others are perhaps marginalized, dismissed or ridiculed. As we have now seen, pre-service teachers and beginning teachers alike must read, understand, negotiate, reconstruct, reproduce, resist or reconstitute what is acceptable and what is not within this space. White and Moss (2003, p. 8) noted that the experience for many beginning teachers was one:

> where a silent rage exists. While grappling with issues of professional identity, these teachers have been astounded at both the complexity of teaching and the lack of professionalism within the profession.

In a climate where recruitment and retention of quality teachers is difficult (see, e.g. Liu *et al.*, 2000; Organization for Economic Co-operation and Development (OECD), 2004; Preston, 2000; Ramsay, 2000; Richardson and Watt, 2006), where teacher resignation in challenging schools, often staffed by beginning teachers, is high (Ferfolja, 2008, p. 69), a better understanding of this place would seem to be vital. This is particularly so because while many authors have attempted to provide stronger theorization around the idea of 'spaces' in schools (Clandinin and Connelly, 1996; Clandinin *et al.*, 2009; McGregor, 2003, 2004b; Nespor, 1997, 2002; Paechter, 2004) we would argue that there is still only modest theorization and research about the spatiality of teachers' work. This includes attention not just to the symbolic and social space but also the physical space. Again within the context of the neo-liberal imaginary (Ball, 2012), we consider this to be crucial.

Within the context of this study, new teachers and beginning teachers who were able to read the social spaces presented to them when entering a new situation were afforded greater capacity to be favourably positioned within that space. In Angel's case (presented in Chapter 8), for example, the subject position of teacher was consistent and seamless across spaces so her negotiation of these spaces was relatively smooth compared to that of Sonny. While the physical/material places were important in symbolic value and the opportunities they afforded, the interrelationships within those spaces were still a critical factor in the experiences of beginning teachers. Kostogriz and Peeler (2007) refer to this as orientation in social space or a deciphering of produced space. This is 'an ability to navigate-perceive, decode and make sense of or "read" different locations and places that have been historically produced and have acquired cultural-semiotic meanings' (p. 109). It is clear to us that there is an important question to ask of the teacher education process. Just how well are pre-service teachers prepared to be able to orient themselves successfully in new spaces and more clearly participate in those practices that shape the subjectivities needed for a more effective educational system? How different spaces might be negotiated by different beginning teachers also needs further investigation to build on the work of Ferfolja (2008) and Kostogriz and Peeler (2007), among others.

Given that the spatial arrangements of the staffroom where teachers work and/or meet is clearly an important site for the constitution of professional subjectivities, our work also suggests that the physical space in which pre-service teachers and beginning teachers are located needs serious consideration. Some schools and their education ministries, councils, boards and funding bodies could note this more generally for all their teachers, with the poor physical spaces, the lack of resources and even the location within the school not just being an issue for emerging teachers. It nevertheless needs to be taken into account when discussing what sorts of spaces and places we want for our profession and the subject positions into which we invite new professionals.

Confronting the micropolitics of the departmental office: barking shins on reality

The need for formal induction and beginning teacher programmes has already been established (Carver and Feiman-Nemser, 2009; Darling-Hammond, 2000, 2003; Kelly, 2004; Wang *et al.*, 2008). Quality mentoring and induction programmes facilitate the transition from pre-service to practice (Ingersoll and Smith, 2004) and help early career teachers to form a professional identity (Feiman-Nemser, 2001). Similarly high-quality and meaningful induction programmes are considered critically important in the development of beginning teachers' capacity for continued professional learning and growth (Feiman-Nemser, 2001), retention and support of beginning teachers and quality teaching in schools (Darling-Hammond, 2000, 2003; Guarino *et al.*, 2006; Kelly, 2004). Conversely, research confirms that the majority of learning in the first year of teaching is informal, reactive and implicit (see, e.g. Williams, 2010; Wilson and Demetriou, 2007, and more recently Christensen, 2013), and that this type of learning is often undervalued in a system that focuses on formal learning (Williams, 2010). Williams (2010, p. 217) suggests that 'encouraging early career teachers to become aware of their non-formal and unplanned learning is likely to be as important as ensuring that formal learning needs are met'.

The narratives in Chapter 9 highlight the highly personal, contextualized and informal micropolitical learning of beginning teachers within the staffroom context. They remind us that pre-service and beginning teachers develop their professional identities in the politically impregnated organizational context of a school (Ball, 1994), and a staffroom more particularly. Kelchtermans and Ballet (2002a, p. 766) contend 'that any micropolitical learning involves elements of a "politics of identity": establishing, safeguarding, restoring one's identity as a teacher is a central dynamic in professional development'. Professional identity development is one of the most challenging aspects of professional learning for beginning teachers (McCormack *et al.*, 2006), and learning in the staffroom is predominantly informal, unplanned and serendipitous (Hodkinson and Hodkinson, 2005; Knight, 2002b). Given this, the narratives in this study depict that what beginning teachers are learning micropolitically within the staffroom, and how they are understanding and practising micropolitical literacy, is not necessarily always positive for professional development, practice and learning. This is a problem that we have repeatedly referred to in this book. Furthermore, the processes and strategies that beginning teachers employ in pursuit of their interests, desired working conditions and professional identities may not contribute to the development of positive micropolitical identities for beginning teachers. We posit that these micropolitical identities are those that will enable and empower them to participate in and move from space to space with the confidence, belief and strategies to proactively, assertively and effectively engage in and influence their professional contexts.

We did not intend to position all micropolitical experiences and learning in the staffroom as negative or destructive. We said the same about the practicum experiences of the pre-service teacher. Moreover, we have already identified the work of Billett (2001), who describes unplanned and unpredictable learning as being potentially rich, assisting learning in ways that are quite different from what happens in formal educational settings. However, it is when we hear stories such as Millie's and Sally's (see Chapter 9) or Holly's (about whom we have written elsewhere: see Rossi, 2013) that we are obligated to think further. How can negative or destructive micropolitical learning be avoided or minimized? What is the role of universities and schools to prepare beginning teachers for this complex staffroom space given the highly contextualized nature of micropolitical learning? We would argue that this is seldom considered in the 'preparation for the workplace' discourse. How can beginning teachers who are, and can be, active agents 'in controlling the direction of biography and social structures in the socialization process' (Solmon *et al.*, 1993, p. 313) be catered for in the transition from university to the school and staffroom context? And similarly, how can schools and staffrooms be organized and structured to improve, enhance and support the quality of beginning teachers' micropolitical learning in the staffroom? These questions are worthy of further discussion here, and in doing so we consider the implications and significance of this part of the study.

Williams (2010) suggests that some informal activity during the induction year is highly valued and genuinely developmental, but not without caution. Similarly, Patrick *et al.* (2010, p. 277) portray that those informal elements of induction 'such as collegiality, good communication and a welcoming workplace environment should not be underestimated'. Individuals within the HPE department 'play a role in the development of new teachers both in the induction process and also less formally as "standard setters"' (Keay, 2005, p. 139). As highlighted by Sally's and Millie's micropolitical staffroom stories, unless carefully managed, the informal relationships, interactions and prevailing stories within the staffroom are likely to perpetuate the status quo and traditional norms rather than promote positive professional development and innovation (Carter and Francis, 2001; Keay, 2005).

The narratives in this study call for increased awareness of the positioning and practices of other teachers, particularly in the staffroom, in the provision of informal induction and support for beginning teachers. Following Knight, who suggests that '[i]f much learning is informal and subliminal, then a lot of professional developmental learning comes from what departments *do*. Good practices make for good learning. Improve practices and learning follows' (Knight, 2002a, p. 294), more attention needs to be paid to the staffroom (and its occupants) as a micropolitical context in which emerging teachers transition, learn and develop professional and micropolitical identities. Efforts to establish positive and supportive staffrooms that support, as opposed to hinder, the development and learning of pre-service and beginning teachers is desirable. This study further reinforces previous research which suggests that '[t]he staffroom is a potential location for professional learning communities and teacher induction (however informal) to build capacity for sustainability' (lisahunter *et al.*, 2011, p. 35). Although the importance of having access to a community, or 'family', of support during induction and creating positive organizational climates and school environments such as professional learning communities which facilitate the development of supportive professional relationships is evident (Carter and Francis, 2001; Tellez, 1992), the informal relationships and practices in the staffroom should not be seen as a substitute for other, more formal induction activities. Similarly, given that how beginning teachers negotiate the micropolitical context of the staffroom is shaped by their past experiences, current situations, and future plans and actions (Clandinin, 1992), the development of the staffroom as a potential professional learning community and site for beginning teacher induction and support must be guided by a vision of good teaching and an understanding of teacher professional learning (Feiman-Nemser, 1996).

Concluding commentary

As we reach a conclusion to this book we find ourselves in a strange position. We are all, to a person, advocates for both the teaching profession and Health and Physical Education as a subject area in schools albeit with qualification. Yet we emerged from this project with a sense of disappointment. We have stated clearly and often that not all of the experiences of either the pre-service or beginning teachers (some of these were the same person) were poor all of the time. So one might reasonably ask whether what we report here is widely applicable to all school HPE departments in all jurisdictions. If not, some might argue that our findings are much ado about nothing. We are not at all confident in suggesting this. We contend that the regularity of the findings and stories across the life of this project and anecdotal stories in a range of other countries give us cause for concern. Elsewhere, much has been written about teacher attrition and we are not in a position to discuss that here. However, on the grounds of attrition alone, the experiences described in this book not only cannot be condoned, they will do little to sustain a vibrant HPE community. Of the 18 participants in this study, fewer than 50 per cent remained in teaching by the time the study was completed and fewer still by the time this book went to press. Even though some of our participants decided to teach science (for a range of career reasons) it means that still fewer ventured into HPE teaching. It is not unreasonable to suggest that the experiences within the context of either the final practicum or the induction year were significant in participants deciding to exit teaching. Thus, though we do not seek to generalize the findings beyond the confines of this study, we are compelled to offer them as a cautionary tale.

Alongside Dowling's (2011) call to reassess teacher education recruitment policies and develop broader PE teacher professional identities, we also echo her appeal for the 'taken-for-granted' notions of teacher professionalism to be systematically re-analysed. Hence, such an analysis cannot just be of teacher educators but of the wider professional field, including the teachers and emerging teachers who enact the practices that constitute the field. As part of the field, the analysis needs also to include government and bureaucratic directors, employing bodies, and of course policy-makers. Although an analysis is important it is insufficient, since it is in the practices embodied by participants in the field that constitute both the participants and the field at the same time. Therefore we would suggest that those within the field must be able to justify what they consider represents good practices. Subject departments must be able to provide educative, supportive, professional and socially just environments for emerging teachers to practise being the type of citizen expected within teaching and, as such, departments and their participants must be held accountable for this. We hope this book provides some impetus to discuss how we can encourage more socially positive practices and learning spaces in such places.

There is much scope for further discussion and research around the conceptualization of the practices, the processes and the products of what has previously been 'metaphored' as transition, induction, transformation, socialization, enculturation and probation. Other metaphors such as migration, mobilization, circulation and co-construction to describe what happens in the space between the pre-service teacher and the fully credentialed teacher may offer us greater insights into 'becoming a teacher' or taking up practices of teaching and being an agent of change through teaching to enhance the profession, and at the same time the educational experiences of young people in our schools. Hence we need to further explore how best to support school administrators and teachers in creating learning spaces that are supportive, safe and in the broader sense 'healthy' (Illeris, 2011; see also Chapter 10), and where formal and informal induction and support are both valued at school and in the staffroom. This is crucial in order to maximize learning, identity development of beginning teachers, and/or agentic subject spaces into which pre-service and beginning teachers can step.

Furthermore, given the importance of all of the participants within the HPE staffroom who play a significant role in shaping the micropolitical space and subsequently pre-service and beginning teachers' micropolitical learning, identity development and potential subject position creation, the awareness and importance of establishing the staffroom as a professional learning community can perhaps be advocated for and structured through ongoing professional development opportunities for all staffroom occupants. Following Curry *et al.* (2008), possibilities may include the ongoing opportunities for beginning teachers and staffroom occupants to participate in professional discussions that reflect on and inquire into their experiences of the micropolitical context of the school and staffroom, their micropolitical identities and subject positions, and subsequently their development of micropolitical literacy. This approach to understanding and developing the staffroom as a professional learning community needs to be systematically supported (Horn and Little, 2010), reinforced and promoted by departmental HODs, schools, state-employing authorities and universities.

The discussions here and in Chapter 9 point to induction and support that addresses both formal and informal situations for beginning teacher learning. While acknowledging the significant impact of quality formal induction, Williams (2010, p. 217) problematizes such valuing 'of the very kinds of non-formal learning that are, from their very nature, not amenable to legislation or central or local directive'. Both Williams (2010) and McCormack *et al.* (2006) suggest that the way forward in this dilemma is through the creation of a school ethos which places importance on both structured induction programmes and professional discussions where beginning teachers and teachers alike are encouraged and welcomed to contribute. In support of this conclusion, the narratives also highlight the necessity to support those practices, interactions of people (HODs and staffroom members) and places that comprise the micropolitical staffroom in the development of the aforementioned ethos. Attention needs to be paid to the development, delivery and maintenance of both informal and formal beginning teacher induction and support in the staffroom.

The role of teacher education

Teacher education programmes need to provide opportunities and learning experiences that not only expose pre-service teachers to staffrooms, but also open up for discussion the staffroom as a potential (if not probable) location for professional learning and development. We believe there is a need for explicit attention in teacher education programmes to address the broader dimensions in the realities of schools and school departments as we have discussed throughout this book. Future research needs to explore the capacity for teacher education programmes and practicum experiences to facilitate and structure learning experiences that create awareness and offer opportunities for pre-service and beginning teachers to practise and develop their capacity to negotiate the complex learning spaces into which they enter as a pre-service teacher and then into which they transition fully credentialed. There is unpredictability and messiness in the reality of schools and staffrooms (Ball, 1987). Given this and the current climate of concern for teacher retention and effectiveness, beginning teachers require support in negotiating the multi-dimensional reality of the staffroom context. So, too, the ongoing development of staffrooms as potential sites for professional learning and development need to be pursued and prioritized, more attention being focused on the development of effective teachers who remain in the profession.

And finally...

In Australia, as with most of the developed world, education is in a constant state of 'reform'. We have discussed these reforms at length throughout the book. Given the ideological landscape that education and more importantly educational policy represents, this is hardly any surprise. However, most reform, even when teacher education (pre- or in service) is implicated, seldom considers the nature of professional learning that might be available within or through the workplace. Most policy only ever tinkers at the edges of what to us seems of paramount importance. Much reform is largely focused on getting teacher education and teacher development out of the hands of universities and academics positioned as distanced from reality and into the hands of 'real people' at the 'chalk-face', or into the hands of other providers who might claim expertise and capacity to educate teachers in economically, or more likely ideologically, preferable ways. Based on our field texts and the stories we collected, this does not exactly present as informed or wise policy. We do not advocate all pre-service and beginning teachers to have the same experience, and to even assume that this can happen is nonsense. However, we consider it to be non-negotiable that the learning made available through the workplace and, in the specific case of this study the departmental office or staffroom, must be of higher quality. It needs to conform to all decent ethical standards and should be comparable as a professional learning space across all sites and participants. At such a point, then, workplace learning might at least align with international policy standards of teacher development within the context of a safe and healthy learning environment. We look forward to such a development.

Bibliography

Altrichter, H. (2001) 'Micropolitics of schools', in N.J. Smelser and P.B. Baltes (eds) *International Encyclopedia of the Social and Behavioral Sciences* (pp. 13594–13598).

Andersen, Hans Christian (1837, 2008) *The Annotated Hans Christian Andersen*, (ed.) M. Tatar and J.K. Allen (trans. J.K. Allen), New York: W.W. Norton, 'The Emperor's new clothes' originally published in 1837.

Apple, M. (2004) 'Creating difference: Neo-liberalism, neo-conservatism and the politics of educational reform', *Educational Policy*, 18(1): 12–44.

—— (2007) 'Education, markets and an audit culture', *International Journal of Educational Policies*, 1(1): 4–19.

Archer, M.S. (2007) *Making Our Way in the World*, Cambridge: Cambridge University Press.

Armour, K. (1999) 'The case for a body-focus in education and physical education', *Sport, Education and Society*, 4(1): 5–16.

Atkinson, P. and Delamont, S. (2006) 'Rescuing narrative from qualitative research', *Narrative Inquiry*, 6(1): 164–172.

Aussie Educator: www.aussieeducator.org.au/education/other/policy.html (accessed 13 October 2012).

Australian Council of Deans of Education (1998) *A Class Act: Inquiry into the Status of the Teaching Profession/Senate Employment, Education and Training References Committee*, Canberra: ACDE.

—— (2005) *Teaching Tomorrow's Teachers: ACDE Submission to the House of Representatives Inquiry into Teacher Education*, Canberra: ACDE.

Australian Institute for Teaching and School Leadership (2011) *National Professional Standards for Teachers*, Melbourne: AITSL.

—— (2012a) *Professional Learning of Teachers and School Leaders*, Melbourne: AITSL.

—— (2012b) *Australian Teacher Performance and Development Framework*, Melbourne: AITSL.

Bacharach, S. and Lawler, E. (1980) *Power and Politics in Organisations*, San Francisco, CA: Jossey Bass.

Ball, S. (1987) *The Micro-politics of the School: Towards a Theory of School Organization*, London: Methuen.

—— (1998) 'Big policies/small world: An introduction to international perspectives in education policy', *Comparative Education*, 34(2): 119–130.

—— (2003) 'The teacher's soul and the terrors of performativity', *Journal of Education Policy*, 18(2): 215–228.

—— (2006) *Education Policy and Social Class*, London: Routledge.

—— (2012) *Global Education Inc.: New Policy Networks and the Neo-liberal Imaginary*, London: Routledge.

Barker, D.M. and Rossi, A. (2011) 'Understanding teachers: The potential and possibility of discourse analysis', *Sport, Education and Society*, 16(2): 139–158.

Barone, T. (2001) 'Pragmatizing the imaginary. A response to a fictionalized case study of teaching', *Harvard Educational Review*, 71(4): 734–741.

Baxter, J. and Clarke, J. (2013) 'Farewell to the tick box inspector? Ofsted and the changing regime of school inspection in England', *Oxford Review of Education*, 39(5): 702–718.

Beck, J. (1999) 'Makeover or takeover? The strange death of educational autonomy in neo-liberal England', *British Journal of Sociology of Education*, 20(2): 223–238.

Beck, U. (1992) *Risk Society: Towards a New Modernity*, (trans. Mark Ritter), London: Sage.

—— (2000) *The Brave New World of Work*, Oxford: Polity Press.

Bernstein, B. (1996) *Pedagogy, Symbolic Control and Identity*, London: Taylor & Francis.

Billett, S. (2001) *Learning in the Workplace*, Sydney: Allen & Unwin.

Blase, J. (1991a) 'The micropolitical orientation of teachers toward closed school principals', *Education and Urban Society*, 23(4): 356–378.

—— (1991b) 'The micropolitical perspective', in J. Blase (ed.) *The Politics of Life in Schools: Power, Conflict, and Cooperation*, Newbury Park, CA: Sage (pp. 1–18).

—— (1991c) *The Politics of Life in Schools: Power, Conflict, and Cooperation*, Newbury Park, CA: Sage.

Boud, D. and Garrick, J. (1999) *Understandings of Workplace Learning*, London: Routledge.

Bourdieu, P. (1977) *Outline of a Theory of Practice*, Cambridge: Cambridge University Press.

—— (1984) *Distinction: A Social Critique of the Judgement of Taste*, London: Routledge.

—— (1985) 'The social space and the genesis of groups', *Theory and Society*, 14(6): 723–744.

—— (1986) 'The forms of capital', in J.G. Richardson (ed.) *Handbook of Theory and Research for the Sociology of Education*, New York: Greenwood Press (pp. 241–258).

—— (1989) 'Social space and symbolic power', *Sociological Theory*, 7(1): 14–25.

—— (1990a) *The Logic of Practice*, Cambridge: Polity Press.

—— (1990b) 'The scholastic point of view', *Cultural Anthropology*, 5(4): 380–391.

—— (1994) *In Other Words: Essays Towards a Reflexive Sociology*, Cambridge: Polity Press.

—— (1998) *Practical Reason: On the Theory of Action*, Stanford, CA: Stanford University Press.

—— (2000) *Pascalian Meditations*, Stanford, CA: Stanford University Press.

—— (2004) *A Sketch of Self Analysis*, Cambridge: Polity Press.

Bourdieu, P. and Johnson, R. (1993) *The Field of Cultural Production: Essays on Art and Literature*, Cambridge: Polity Press.

Bourdieu, P. and Wacquant, L.J.D. (1992) *An Invitation to Reflexive Sociology*, Cambridge: Polity Press.

Brown, D. (1999) 'Complicity and reproduction in teaching physical education', *Sport Education and Society*, 4(2): 143–159.

—— (2005) 'An economy of gendered practices? Learning to teach physical education from the perspective of Pierre Bourdieu's embodied sociology', *Sport Education and Society*, 10(1): 3–23.

Brown, D. and Evans, J. (2004) 'Reproducing gender? Intergenerational links and the male PE teacher as a cultural conduit in teaching physical education', *Journal of Teaching in Physical Education*, 23(1): 48–70.

Brown, J. (1992) *The Definition of a Profession: The Authority of Metaphor in the History of Intelligence Testing, 1890–1930*, Princeton, NJ: Princeton University Press.

Bullock, A. and Trombley, S. (1999) *The New Fontana Dictionary of Modern Thought*, New York: HarperCollins.

Butler, J. (1993) *Bodies That Matter: On the Discursive Limits of Sex*, New York: Routledge.

Butler, J. (1999) *Gender trouble: feminism and the subversion of identity*, Updated 2nd edn, New York: Routledge.

—— (2004) *Undoing Gender*, Boca Raton, FL: Routledge.

Butt, T., Burr, V. and Epting, F. (1997) 'Core construing: Self discovery or self invention?', in G.J. Neimeyer and R.A. Neimeyer (eds) *Advances in Personal Construct Psychology*, London: Elsevier (vol. 4, pp. 39–62).

Carter, M. and Francis, R. (2001) 'Mentoring and beginning teachers' workplace learning', *Asia-Pacific Journal of Teacher Education*, 29(3): 249–262.

Carver, C. and Feiman-Nemser, S. (2009) 'Using policy to improve teacher induction: Critical elements and missing pieces', *Educational Policy*, 23(2): 295–328.

Charlton, A. (2011) 'Man-made world: Choosing between progress and the planet'. *Quarterly Essay*, 44: 1–72.

Christensen, E. (2013) 'Micropolitical staffroom stories: Beginning health and physical education teachers' experiences of the staffroom', *Teaching and Teacher Education*, 30: 74–83.

Clandinin, D.J. (1986) *Classroom Practice: Teacher Images in Action*, London, and Philadelphia, PA: Falmer Press.

—— (ed.) (1992) *Narrative and Story in Teacher Education*, Philadelphia, PA: Falmer Press.

—— (2006) 'Narrative inquiry: A methodology for studying lived experience', *Research Studies in Music Education*, 27: 44–54.

Clandinin, D.J. and Connelly, F.M. (1996) 'Teachers' professional knowledge landscapes: Teacher stories, stories of teachers, school stories, stories of schools', *Educational Researcher*, 25(3): 24–30.

Clandinin, D.J. and Connelly, F.M. (2000) *Narrative Inquiry: Experience and Story in Qualitative Research*, San Francisco, CA: Jossey-Bass.

Clandinin, D.J. and Murphy, M.S. (2009) 'Relational ontological commitments in narrative research', *Education Researcher*, 38(8): 598–602.

Clandinin, D.J., Downey, C.A. and Huber, J. (2009) 'Attending to changing landscapes: Shaping the interwoven identities of teachers and teacher educators', *Asia-Pacific Journal of Teacher Education*, 37(2): 141–154.

Clifford, J. (1983) 'On ethnographic inquiry', *Representations*, 1(2): 118–146.

Cochran-Smith, M. (2004). *Walking the Road: Race, diversity, and social justice in teacher education*, New York: Teachers College Press.

Cochran-Smith, M. and Fries, M.K. (2001) 'Sticks, stones, and ideology: The discourse of reform in teacher education', *Educational Researcher*, 30(8): 3–15.

—— (2005) 'Researching teacher education in changing times: Politics and paradigms', in M. Cochran-Smith and K. Zeichner (eds) *Studying Teacher Education: The Report of the AERA Panel on Research and Teacher Education*, Mahwah, NJ: Lawrence Erlbaum Associates (pp. 37–68).

Cohen, L., Manion, L. and Morrison, K. (2007) *Research Methods in Education*, London: Routledge.

Colquhoun, D. (1991) 'Health based physical, the ideology of healthism and victim blaming', *Physical Education Review*, 14(1): 5–13.

Colquhoun, L. (2005) 'Teacher training in a class of its own. Letters to the editor', *The Australian Higher Education Supplement*, 21 December.

Comber, B. and Nixon, H. (2009) 'Teachers' work and pedagogy in an era of accountability', *Discourse: Studies in the Cultural Politics of Education*, 30(3): 333–345.

Commonwealth Department of Education, Science and Training (2003) *Commonwealth Review of Teaching and Teacher Education*, Committee for the Review of Teaching and Teacher Education, Canberra, Commonwealth of Australia, Retrieved from www.dest.gov.au/schools/teachingreview/documents/Agenda_for_Action.pdf.

Connelly, F.M. and Clandinin, D.J. (1995) 'Personal and professional knowledge landscapes: A matrix of relations', in D.J. Clandinin and F.M. Connelly (eds) *Teachers' Professional Knowledge Landscapes*, New York: Teacher College Press (pp. 25–35).

Cooke, M., Irby, D. and O'Brien, B.C. (2010) *Educating Physicians*, San Francisco, CA: Jossey-Bass.

Cooper, J.M. and Alvarado, A. (2006) *Preparation, Recruitment, and Retention of Teachers: Education Policy Series*, Paris, UNESCO.

Coulter, C.A. and Smith, M.L. (2009) 'The construction zone: Literarary elements in narrative research', *Educational Researcher*, 38(8): 577–590.

Craig, C. (1998) 'The influence of context on one teacher's interpretive knowledge of team teaching', *Teaching and Teacher Education*, 14(4): 371–383.

Cuban, L. (2008) *Frogs into Princes – Writings on School Reform*, New York: Teachers College Press.

Curry, M., Jaxon, K., Russell, J.L., Callahan, M.A. and Bicais, J. (2008) 'Examining the practice of beginning teachers' micropolitical literacy within professional inquiry communities', *Teaching and Teacher Education*, 24: 660–673.

Darling-Hammond, L.A. (1995) *A License to Teach: Building a Profession for 21st Century Schools*, Boulder, CO: Westview Press.

—— (2000) 'How teacher education matters', *Journal of Teacher Education*, 51(3): 166–173.

—— (2003) 'Keeping good teachers: Why it matters, what leaders can do', *Educational Leadership*, 60(8): 6–13.

Darling-Hammond, L. and Snyder, J. (2000) 'Authentic assessment of teaching in context', *Teaching and Teacher Education*, 16: 523–545.

Davies, D. (2005) 'The (im)possibility of intellectual work in neoliberal regimes', *Discourse*, 2(6): 1–14.

Davis, B. and Sumara, D. (2000) 'Curriculum forms: On the assumed shapes of knowing and knowledge', *Journal of Curriculum Studies*, 32(6): 821–835.

Denzin, N. and Lincoln, Y. (2005) *The Sage handbook of qualitative research*, Thousand Oaks: Sage Publications.

Department of Education (2011) *Teachers' Standards*, London: Department of Education.

Department of Education and Curriculum Services (2001) *An Introduction to Health Promoting Schools in South Australia*, Adelaide, South Australia.

DEST (2003) *Australia's Teachers: Australia's Future, Advancing Innovation, Science, Technology and Mathematics – Main Report,* Review of Teaching and Teacher Education Final Report, Canberra: Commonwealth Department of Eduaction, Science and Training.

Devis-Devis, J. and Sparkes, A.C. (1999) 'Burning the book: A biographical study of a pedagogically inspired identity crisis in physical education', *European Physical Education Review,* 5(2): 135–152.

Dewar, A. (1989) 'Recruitment in physical education teaching: Toward a critical approach', in T. Templin and P. Schempp (eds) *Socialization into Physical Education: Learning to Teach,* Indianapolis: Benchmark Press (pp. 39–58).

—— (1990) 'Oppression and privilege in physical education: Struggles in the negotiation of gender in a university programme', in D. Kirk and R. Tinning (eds) *Physical Education, Curriculum and Culture: Critical Issues in the Contemporary Crisis,* London: The Falmer Press (pp. 67–100).

Dewar, A. and Lawson, H.A. (1984) 'The subjective warrant and recruitment into physical education', *Quest,* 36(1): 15–25.

Dodds, P. (1986) 'Stamp out the ugly "isms" in your gym', in M. Pieron and G. Graham (eds) *Sport Pedagogy,* Champaign, IL: Human Kinetics (pp. 140–150).

Donnelly, K. (2004) *Why our Schools are Failing,* Sydney: Duffy & Snellgrove.

Dowda, M., Sallis, J.F, McKenzie, T.L., Rosengard, P. and Kohl, H.W. (2005) 'Evaluating the sustainability of SPARK physical education: A case study of translating research into practice', *Research Quarterly for Exercise and Sport,* 76(1): 11–19.

Dowling, F. (2011) 'Are PE teacher identities fit for postmodern schools or are they clinging to modernist notions of professionalism? A case study of Norwegian PE teacher students' emerging professional identities', *Sport, Education and Society,* 16(2): 201–222.

Doyle, W. (1977) 'Learning in the classroom environment: An ecological analysis', *Journal of Teacher Education,* 28(6): 51–55.

—— (1981) 'Accomplishing writing tasks in the classroom', paper presented at the American Research Association Annual Conference, Philadelphia, PA, 3–7 April.

Ellis, V. and Maguire, M. (2014) ' "The market will (not) decide": School Direct, the state and the provision of teacher education in England', paper presented at the American Education Research Association Annual Conference, Philadelphia, PA, 3–7 April.

Ellström, P. (2001) 'Integrating learning and work: Problems and prospects', *Human Resource Development Quarterly,* 12(4): 421–435.

Evans, J. and Davies, B. (2014) 'Physical Education PLC: Neoliberalism, curriculum and governance. New directions for PESP research', *Sport, Education and Society,* DOI:10.1080/13573322.2013.850072.

Evans, J., Davies, B. and Wright, J. (eds) (2004) *Body Knowledge and Control: Studies in the Sociology of Physical Education and Health,* London: Routledge.

Feiman-Nemser, S. (1996) *Teacher Mentoring: A Critical Review,* ERIC Digest. ED#449147.

—— (2001) 'From preparation to practice: Designing a continuum to strengthen and sustain teaching', *Teachers College Record,* 103(6): 1013–1055.

Ferfolja, T. (2008) 'Building capital in pre-service teachers: Reflections on a new teacher-education initiative', *Australian Journal of Teacher Education,* 33(2): 68–84.

Fernandez-Balboa, J.M. (1997) 'Physical education teacher preparation in the postmodern era: Toward a critical pedagogy', in J.M. Fernandez-Balboa (ed.) *Critical Postmodernism in Human Movement, Physical Education, and Sport,* Albany, NY: State University of New York Press (pp. 121–138).

—— (1999) 'Poisonous pedagogy in physical education', AIESEP, World Congress Proceedings, Long Island, NY, Adelphi University, AIESEP.

Fitzclarence, L. (1993) 'Social violence and physical activity', in D. Kirk (ed.) *The Body, Schooling and Culture*, Geelong: Deakin University.

Flanagan, E. (2012) *Navigating Staffroom Stories: Beginning Health and Physical Education Teachers' Micropolitical Experiences of the Staffroom*, unpublished Ph.D. thesis, The University of Queensland, Brisbane.

Flintoff, A. (2012) 'Playing the "Race" card? Black and minority ethnic students' experiences of physical education teacher education', *Sport, Education and Society*, iFirst article, 1–22. DOI:10.1080/13573322.13572012.13745397.

Flores, M.A. (2001) 'Person and context in becoming a new teacher', *Journal of Education for Teaching*, 27(2): 135–148.

Flores, M. and Day, C. (2006) 'Contexts which shape and reshape new teachers' identities: A multi-perspective study', *Teaching and Teacher Education*, 22(2): 219–232.

Flyvbjerg, B. (2004) 'Five misunderstandings about case-study research', in C. Seale, G. Gobo, J.F. Gubrium and D. Silverman (eds) *Qualitative Research Practice*, Thousand Oaks, CA: Sage (pp. 420–434).

Friedman, M. (2002) *Capitalism and freedom. 40th Aniversary edition* (originally published in 1962), Chicago: University of Chicago Press.

Furlong, J. (1996) 'Re-defining partnership: Revolution or reform in initial teacher education', *Journal of Education for Teaching*, 22(1): 39–56.

—— (2013) *Education – An Anatomy of the Discipline. Rescuing the University Project?*, London: Routledge.

Gard, M. (2011) *The End of the Obesity Epidemic*, London: Routledge.

Gard, M. and Wright, J. (2001) 'Managing uncertainty: Obesity discourses and physical education in a risk society', *Studies in Philosophy and Education*, 20(6): 535–549.

—— (2005) *The Obesity Epidemic: Science, Morality and Ideology*, London: Routledge.

Giddens, A. (1984) *The Constitution of Society: Outline of the Theory of Structuration*, Cambridge: Polity Press.

—— (1991) *Self Identity and Modernity*, Stanford, CA: Stanford University Press.

Glatter, R. (1982) 'The micropolitics of education: Issues for training', *Education Management Administration Leadership*, 10: 160–165.

Goffman, E. (1959) *The Presentation of Self in Everyday Life*, London: Penguin.

—— (1974) *Frame Analysis: An Essay on the Organization of Experience*, New York: Harper & Row.

—— (1986) *Frame Analysis: An Essay in the Organization of Experience* (2nd edn), Boston, MA: Northeastern University Press.

Gore, J. (2002) 'Pedagogy, power, and bodies: On the un(der)-acknowledged effects of schooling', in S. Shapiro and S. Shapiro (eds) *Body Movements: Pedagogy, Politics and Social Change*, Cresskill, NJ: Hampton (pp. 75–95).

Gorely, T., Holroyd, R. and Kirk, D. (2003) 'Muscularity, the habitus and the social construction of gender: Towards a gender-relevant physical education', *British Journal of Sociology of Education*, 24(4): 429–448.

Grant, C. and Sleeter, C. (1985) 'Who determines teacher work: The teacher, the organization, or both?', *Teaching and Teacher Education*, 1(3): 209–220.

Gray, S. and Whitty, G. (2010) 'Social trajectories or disrupted identities? Changing and competing models of teacher professionalism under New Labour', *Cambridge Journal of Education*, 40(1): 5–23.

Greenberg, J., McKee, A. and Walsh, K. (2013) *Teacher Prep Review*, Washington, DC: National Council on Teacher Quality.

Griffey, D.C. (1991) 'The value and future agenda of research on teaching physical education', *Research Quarterly for Exercise and Sport*, 62(4): 380–383.

Grosz, E.A. (1994) *Volatile Bodies: Toward a Corporeal Feminism*, St Leonards, NSW: Allen & Unwin.

—— (1995) *Space, Time and Perversion: Essays on the Politics of the Body*, New York: Routledge.

—— (1999) 'Bodies-cities', in M. Shildrick and J. Price (eds) *Feminist Theory and the Body*, Edinburgh: Edinburgh University Press (pp. 381–387).

—— (2001) *Architecture from the Outside: Essays on Virtual and Real Space*, Cambridge, MA: MIT Press.

Groundwater-Smith, S., Deer, C.E., Sharp, H and March, P. (1996) 'The practicum as workplace learning: A multi-mode approach in teacher education', *Australian Journal of Teacher Education*, 21(2): 29–41.

Guarino, C., Santibanez, L. and Daley, G. (2006) 'Teacher recruitment and retention: A review of the recent empirical literature', *Review of Educational Research*, 76(2): 173–208.

Hargreaves, A. (1994) *Changing Teachers, Changing Times*, London: Falmer Press.

Harvey, D. (2005) *A Brief History of Neoliberalism*, New York: Oxford University Press.

Hastie, P. and Siedentop, D. (1999) 'An ecological perspective on physical education', *European Physical Education Review*, 5(1): 9–27.

Hayek, F.A. (2007) *The Road to Serfdom – Text and Documents*, the definitive edition, edited by Bruce Caldwell, Chicago, IL: University of Chicago Press.

Hayes, D., Mills, M., Christie, P. and Lingard, B. (2006) *Teachers and Schooling: Making a Difference*, Sydney: Allen & Unwin.

Hill, A. (2008) 'Learning in the workplace: New forms of learning for preservice teachers', retrieved 4 April 2011 from http://ro.uow.edu.au/edupapers/46.

Hodkinson, H. and Hodkinson, P. (2005) 'Improving schoolteachers' workplace learning', *Research Papers in Education*, 20(2): 219–232.

Hodkinson, P. and Hodkinson, H. (2004) 'The significance of individuals' dispositions in workplace learning: A case study of two teachers', *Journal of Education and Work*, 17(2): 167–182.

Horn, I.S. and Little, J.W. (2010) 'Attending to problems of practice: Routines and resources for professional learning in teachers' workplace interactions', *American Educational Research Journal*, 47(1): 181–217.

Hoyle, E. (1982) 'Micropolitics of educational organisations', *Educational Management Administration Leadership*, 10: 87–98.

—— (1986) *The Politics of School Management*, London: Hodder & Stoughton.

Hubbard, P. (2002) *Thinking Geographically: Space, theory, and contemporary human geography*, London: Continuum.

Huling-Austin, L. (1990) 'Teacher induction programs and internships', in W.R. Houston (ed.) *Handbook of Research in Teacher Education*, New York: Macmillan (pp. 535–548).

Hunter, L. (2004) 'Bourdieu and the social space of the PE class: Reproduction of doxa through practice', *Sport Education and Society*, 9(2): 109–131.

Illeris, K. (2011) *The Fundamentals of Workplace Learning*, London: Routledge.

Ingersoll, R. and Smith, T. (2004) 'Do teacher induction and mentoring matter?', *National Association of Secondary School Principals Bulletin*, 88(638): 28–40.

Jackson, J.A. (2010) 'Professions and professionalization', *Sociological Studies*, 3: 23–24.

Jensen, B. (2010) *What Teachers Want: Better Teacher Management*, Melbourne: Grattan Institute.

—— (2011) *Better Teacher Appraisal and Feedback: Improving Performance*, Melbourne: Grattan Institute.

Jesson, J. (2000) 'Caught in the contradictions: New Zealand teacher education', in A. Scott and D.J. Freeman-Moir (eds) *Tomorrow's Teachers: International and Critical Perspectives*, Christchurch, NZ: Canterbury University Press.

Jones, O. (2012) *Chavs – The Demonization of the Working Class*, London: Verso.

Keay, J. (2005) 'Developing the physical education profession: New teachers learning within a subject-based community', *Physical Education and Sport Pedagogy*, 10(2): 139–157.

Kelchtermans, G. and Ballet, K. (2002a) 'Micropolitical literacy: Reconstructing a neglected dimension in teacher development', *International Journal of Educational Research*, 37: 755–767.

—— (2002b) 'The micropolitics of teacher induction. A narrative-biographical study on teacher socialisation', *Teaching and Teacher Education*, 18(1): 105–120.

—— (2002c) 'Learning how to play the game: The development of micropolitical literacy', in R. Huttunen, H.L.T. Heikkinen and L. Syrjälä (eds) *Narrative Research: Voices of Teachers and Philosophers*, Jyväskylä: SoPhi (pp. 219–240).

Kelly, L. (2004) 'Why induction matters', *Journal of Teacher Education*, 55(5): 438–448.

Kelly, G. (1955) *The Psychology of Personal Constructs*, New York: Norton.

Kenway, J. and McLeod, J. (2004) 'Bourdieu's reflexive sociology and "spaces of points of view": Whose reflexivity, which perpsective', *British Journal of Sociology*, 25(4): 525–544.

Kim, J. and Taggart, A. (2004) 'Teachers' perception of the culture of physical education: Investigating the silences at Hana Primary School', *Issues In Educational Research*, 14(1): 69–84.

Kirk, D. (1997) 'Schooling bodies in new times', in J.M. Fernandez-Balboa (ed.) *Critical Postmodernism in Human Movement, Physical Education, and Sport*, Albany, NY: State University of New York Press (pp. 39–63).

—— (2002) 'Physical education: A gendered history', in D. Penney (ed.) *Gender and Physical Education: Contemporary Issues and Future Directions*, London: Routledge (pp. 24–38).

Kirk, D. and Macdonald, D. (2001) 'The social construction of the physical activity field in higher education: Towards a research agenda', *Quest*, 53(4), 440–456.

Kirk, D. and Tinning, R. (1990) *Physical Education, Curriculum, and Culture: Critical Issues in the Contemporary Crisis*, Philadelphia, PA: Falmer Press.

Kirk, D., Macdonald, D. and Tinning, R. (1997). 'The social construction of pedagogic discourse in physical education teacher education in Australia', *The Curriculum Journal*, 8(2): 271–298.

Knight, P. (2002a) 'A systemic approach to professional development: Learning as practice', *Teaching and Teacher Education*, 18: 229–241.

—— (2002b) 'Learning from schools', *Higher Education*, 44: 283–298.

Koerner, J.D. (1963) *The Miseducation of American Teachers*, Boston, MA: Houghton Mifflin.

Kostogriz, A. and Peeler, E. (2007) 'Professional identity and pedagogical space: Negotiating difference in teacher workplaces', *Teaching Education*, 18(2): 107–122.

Kozol, J. (2005) *The Shame of American Education: The Restoration of Apartheid Schooling in America*, New York: Crown.

Krugman, P. (2007) *The Conscience of a Liberal*, New York: Penguin.

Lagemann, E. (2000). *An Elusive Science: The Troubling History of Education Research*, Chicago, IL: University of Chicago Press.

Larson, M.S. (1978) *The Rise of Professionalism: A Sociological Analysis*, Berkeley, CA: University of California Press.

Latour, B. and Woolgar, S. (1979) *Laboratory Life: The Construction of Scientific Facts*, New York: Sage.

Lave, J. and Wenger, E. (1991) *Situated Learning: Legitimate Peripheral Participation*, Cambridge: Cambridge University Press.

Lawson, H.A. (1983) 'Toward a Model of Teacher Socialization in Physical Education: The Subjective Warrant, Recruitment, and Teacher Education', *Journal of Teaching in Physical Education* 2(3), 3–16.

—— (1985) *Reflexivity: The Post-modern Dilemma*, London: Hutchinson.

—— (1986) 'Occupational socialization and the design of teacher education programs', *Journal of Teaching in Physical Education*, 5(2): 107–116.

—— (1988) 'Occupational socialization, cultural studies, and the physical education curriculum', *Journal of Teaching in Physical Education*, 7(4): 265–288.

LeCompte, M. and Schensul, J. (1999) *Analyzing and Interpreting Ethnographic Data*, Walnut Creek: AltaMira Press.

Lefebvre, H. (1991) *The Production of Space*, Oxford: Blackwell.

Levine, A. (2006) *Educating School Teachers*, Washington, DC: The Education Schools Project.

Lingard, B. (2011) 'Changing teachers' work in Australia', in N. Mockler and J. Sachs (eds) *Rethinking Educational Practice Through Reflexive Inquiry*, New York: Springer (pp. 229–245).

lisahunter (2010) ' "Healthy staffspace" as a professional workplace learning goal: Iterability, legitimation and practice', paper presented at the Australian Association of Research in Education Annual Conference, Brisbane, 29 November to 2 December.

lisahunter, Flanagan, E., Rossi, T., Tinning, R. and Macdonald, D. (2010) 'Healthy staffspaces in teaching: Ideas for sustaining a profession', paper presented at the Australian Teacher Education Association Annual Conference, Townsville, 4–7 July.

lisahunter, Rossi, T., Tinning, R., Flanagan, E. and Macdonald, D. (2011) 'Professional learning places and spaces: The staffroom as a site of beginning teacher induction and transition', *Asia-Pacific Journal of Teacher Education*, 39(1): 33–46.

Liston, D. and Zeichner, K. (1991) *Teacher Education and the Social Conditions of Schooling*, New York: Routledge.

Little, J. (1990) 'The persistence of privacy: autonomy and initiative in teachers' professional relations', *Teachers College Record*, 91(4): 509–536.

Liu, E., Kardos, S., Kauffman, D., Preske, H. and Johnson, S. (2000) *Barely Breaking Even: Incentives, Rewards, and the High Costs of Choosing to Teach*, Cambridge: Harvard Graduate School of Education.

Lortie, D. (1975) *Schoolteacher*, Chicago, IL: University of Chicago Press.

Louis, K.S., Marks, H.M. and Kruse, S.D. (1996) 'Teachers' professional community in restructuring schools', *American Journal of Education*, 33(4): 757–798.

Lovell, T. (2003) 'Resisting with authority: Historical specificity, agency and the performative self', *Theory, Culture and Society*, 20(1): 1–17.

Macdonald, D. (1995) 'The role of proletarianization in physical education teachers', *Research Quarterly for Exercise and Sport*, 66(2): 129–141.

—— (2013) 'The new Australian Health and Physical Education curriculum: A case of/ for gradualism in curriculum reform?', *Asia-Pacific Journal of Health, Sport and Physical Education*, 4(2): 95–108.

—— (2014) 'Is global neo-liberalism shaping the future of physical education?', *Physical Education and Sport Pedagogy*.

—— (in press) 'Teacher-as-knowledge-broker in a futures-oriented HPE', *Sport, Education and Society*.

Macdonald, D. and Kirk, D. (1996) 'Private lives, public lives: Surveillance, identity, and self in the work of beginning physical education teachers', *Sport Education and Society*, 1(1): 59–76.

—— (1999) 'Pedagogy, the body and Christian identity', *Sport Education and Society*, 4(2): 131–142.

Macdonald, D. and Tinning, R. (1995) 'Physical education teacher education and the trend to proletarianization: A case study', *Journal of Teaching in Physical Education*, 15(1): 107–119.

Macdonald, D., Hutchins, C. and Madden, J. (1994) 'To leave or not to leave: Health and physical education teachers' career choices', *The ACHPER Healthy Lifestyles Journal*, 41(3): 19–22.

Macdonald, D., Kirk, D. and Braiuka, S. (1999) 'The social construction of the physical activity field at the school/university interface', *European Journal of Physical Education*, 5(1): 31–51.

Mahony, P. and Hextall, I. (2000) *Reconstructing Teaching: Standards, Performance and Accountability*, London: Routledge.

Malen, B. (1994) 'The micropolitics of education: Mapping the multiple dimensions of power relations in school politics', in J. Scribner and D. Layton (eds) *Politics of Education Association Yearbook*, New York: Falmer Press (pp. 147–167).

Marsh, C. (1987) 'Curriculum theorizing in Australia', *Journal of Curriculum Theorizing*, 7: 7–29.

Marshall, C. and Scribner, J.D. (1991) '"It's all political": Inquiry into the micropolitics of education', *Education and Urban Society*, 23(4): 347–355.

Massey, D. (2005) *For Space*, London: Sage.

Maton, K. (2003) 'Pierre Bourdieu and the epistemic conditions of social scientific knowledge', *Space and Culture*, 6(6): 52–65.

Mayer, D., Luke, C. and Luke, A. (2008) 'Teachers, national regulation and cosmopolitanism', in A.M. Phelan and J. Sumison (eds) *Critical Readings n Teacher Education – Provoking Absences*, Rotterdam: Sense Publishers (pp. 79–98).

McCallum, F. and Price, D. (2010) 'Well teachers, well students', *Journal of Student Wellbeing*, 4(1): 19–34.

McCormack, A., Gore, J. and Thomas, K. (2006) 'Early career teacher professional learning', *Asia-Pacific Journal of Teacher Education*, 34(1): 95–113.

McCulla, N. (2005) 'Creating graduate, university and employer links through research in supporting the professional work and learning of newly-qualified teachers', *Change: Transformations in Education*, 8(1): 32–43.

McCullick, B., Belcher, D., Hardin, B. and Hardin, M. (2003) 'Butches, Bullies and Buffoons – Images of physical education teachers in the movies', *Sport, Education and Society*, 8 (1), 3–16.

McCullick, B.A., Lux, K., Belcher, D.G. and Davies, N. (2012) 'A portrait of the PETE major re-touched for the early 21st century', *Physical Education and Sport Pedagogy*, 17(2): 177–193.

McGregor, J. (2003) 'Making spaces: Teacher workplace typologies', *Pedagogy, Culture and Society*, 11(3): 353–377.

—— (2004a) 'Editorial: Space and schools', *FORUM: For Promoting 3–19 Comprehensive Education*, 46(1): 1–4.

—— (2004b) 'Speciality and the place of the material in schools', *Pedagogy, Culture and Society*, 12(3): 347–372.

McKay, J. (1991) *No Pain, No Gain? Sport and Australian Culture*, Sydney: Prentice-Hall.

McKenzie, T.L. and Lounsbery, M.A.F. (2009) 'School physical education: The pill not taken', *American Journal Of Lifestyle Medicine*, 3(3): 219–225.

McLeod, J. (1987) *Ain't No Making It: Levelled Aspirations in a Low Income Neighbourhood*, Boulder, CO: Westview Press.

McNamara, O. and Murray, J. (2013) 'The School Direct programme and its implications for research-informed teacher education and teacher educators', in L. Florian and N. Pantic (eds) *Learning to Teach*, York: Higher Education Academy.

McNay, L. (2003) 'Agency, anticipation and indeterminancy in feminist theory', *Feminist Theory*, 4(2): 139–148.

Merriam, S.B. (1998) *Qualitative Research and Case Study Applications in Education*, San Francisco, CA: Jossey-Bass.

Metzler, M. (2009) 'The great debate over teacher education reform escalates: More rhetoric or a new reality?', *Journal of Teaching in Physical Education*, 28: 293–309.

Miles, M.B. and Huberman, A.M. (1994) *Qualitative Data Analysis: An Expanded Sourcebook*, Thousand Oaks, CA: Sage.

Mill, J.S. (2009) *On Liberty and Other Essays*, Foreword by Jonathan Riley, New York: Kaplan Publishing, originally published in 1859.

Miller, A. (1987) *For Your Own Good: Hidden Cruelty in Child-rearing and the Roots of Violence*, London: Virago.

Ministerial Council for Education, Early Childhood Development and Youth Affairs (MCEECDYA) (2011) *National Safe School Framework*, Melbourne: MCEECDYA.

Mishler, E. (1999) *Storylines: Craftartists' Narratives of Identity*, Cambridge, MA: Harvard University Press.

Moon, J. (2004) *A Handbook of Reflective and Experiential Learning: Theory and Practice*, London: Routledge Falmer.

Morgan, J. (2000) 'Critical pedagogy: The spaces that make the difference', *Pedagogy, Culture and Society*, 8(3): 273–289.

National Board of Employment, Education, and Training (NBEET) (1994) *Workplace Learning in the Professional Development of Teachers*, Canberra: NBEET.

Nespor, J. (1997) *Tangled Up in School: Politics, Space, Bodies, and Signs in the Educational Process*, Mahwah, NJ: Erlbaum Associates.

—— (2002) 'Studying the spatialities of schooling', *Pedagogy, Culture and Society*, 10(3): 483–491.

Nias, J. (1991) 'Changing times, changing identities: Grieving for a lost self', in R.G. Burgess (ed.), *Educational Research and Evaluation*, London: Falmer Press.

Nilges, L. (2001) 'The twice-told tale of Alice's physical life in wonderland: Writing qualitative research in the 21st century', *Quest*, 53(2): 231–259.

O'Connor, A. and Macdonald, D. (2002) 'Up close and personal on physical education teachers' identity: Is conflict an issue?', *Sport Education and Society*, 7(1): 27–55.

Odell, S. and Ferraro, D. (1992) 'Teacher mentoring and teacher retention', *Journal of Teacher Education*, 43(3): 200–204.

Olive, R. (2013) '"Making friends with the neighbours": Blogging as a research method', *International Journal of Cultural Studies*, 16(1): 71–84.

Organization for Economic Co-operation and Development (OECD) (2004) *Attracting, Developing and Retaining Effective Teachers*, retrieved from www.oecd.org/document /9/0,2340,en_2649_34521_11969545_1_1_1_1,00.html (accessed 14 December 2005).

—— (2006) *Teachers Matter: Attracting, Developing and Retaining Effective Teachers*, Paris: OECD Publishing.

Padgett, D.K. (2008) *Qualitative Methods in Social Work Research*, Thousand Oaks, CA: Sage.

Paechter, C. (2004) 'Power relations and staffroom spaces', *FORUM: For Promoting 3–19 Comprehensive Education*, 46(1): 33–35.

Paechter, C. and Head, J. (1996) 'Gender, identity, status and the body: Life in a marginal subject', *Gender and Education*, 8(1): 21–29.

Parker, P. and Martin, A. (2009) 'Coping and buoyancy in the workplace: Understanding their effects on teachers' work-related well-being and engagement', *Teaching and Teacher Education*, 25: 68–75.

Patrick, F., Elliot, D., Julme, M. and McPhee, A. (2010) 'The importance of collegiality and reciprocal learning in the professional development of beginning teachers', *Journal of Education for Teaching: International Research Pedagogy*, 36(3): 277–289.

Paton, G. (2011) 'New teachers "struggle to communicate subject knowledge"', www. telegraph.co.uk/education/educationnews/8881987/New-teachers-struggle-to-communicate-subject-knowledge.html, (accessed 27 April 2014).

Pearson, N. (2009) 'Radical hope – Education and equality in Australia', *Quarterly Essay*, 35.

Penney, D. (2007) 'Health and physical education and the development of a national curriculum in Australia. Policies, position and prospects', *ACHPER Healthy Lifestyles Journal*, 54(3/4), 17–23.

Penney, D. and Chandler, T. (2000) 'Physical education: What future(s)?', *Sport, Education and Society*, 5(1): 71–87.

Petersen, A. and Lupton, D. (1996) *The New Public Health: Health and Self in the Age of Risk*, Sydney: Allen & Unwin.

Pfeffer, J. (1981) *Power in Organizations*, Boston, MA: Pitman.

Phelan, A.M. (2005) 'On discernment: The practice of wisdom and the wisdom of practice', in G. Hoban (ed.) *The Missing Links in Teacher Education: Innovative Approaches in Designing Teacher Education Programs*, the Netherlands: Kluwer Press (pp. 57–73).

Phelan, A.M. and Sumison, J. (2008) 'Introduction: Lines of articulation and lines of flight in teacher education', in A.M. Phelan and J. Sumison (eds) *Critical Readings in Teacher Education – Provoking Absences*, Rotterdam: Sense Publishers (pp. 1–16).

Pillay, H., Goddard, R. and Wilss, L. (2005) 'Well-being, burn-out and competence: Implications for teachers', *Australian Journal of Teacher Education*, 30(2): 22–33.

Pillow, W. (2003) 'Confession, catharsis, or cure? Rethinking the uses of reflexivity as methodological power in qualitative research', *International Journal of Qualitative Studies in Education*, 16(2): 175–196.

Preston, E. (2000) *Teacher Supply and Demand to 2005: Projections and Context*, Canberra: Australian Council of Deans of Education.

Queensland School Curriculum Council (1999) *Health and Physical Education Years 1 to 10 Syllabus*, Brisbane: Education Queensland.

Ramsay, G. (2000) *Quality Matters. Revitalising Teaching: Critical Times, Critical Choices. Report of the Review of Teacher Education*, Sydney: NSW Department of Education and Training.

Richardson, L. (2000) 'Writing: a method of inquiry', in N. Denzin and Y. Lincoln (eds) *Handbook of Qualitative Research*, 2nd edn, Thousand Oaks, CA: Sage (pp. 923–948).

Richardson, P. and Watt, H. (2006) 'Who chooses teaching and why? Profiling characteristics and motivations across three Australian universities', *Asia-Pacific Journal of Teacher Education*, 34(1): 27–56.

Richmond, H.J. (2002) 'Learners' lives: A narrative analysis', *The Qualitative Report*, 7(3), retrieved from www.nova.edu/ssss/QR/QR7–3/richmond.html (accessed 23 March 2012).

Riley, D., Duncan, D. and Edwards, J. (2012) *Investigation of Staff Bullying in Australian Schools: Executive Summary*, retrieved from http://schoolbullies.org.au.

Rizvi, F. and Lingard, B. (2010) *Globalizing Education Policy*, Abingdon, Oxon: Routledge.

Rosen, L. (2009) 'Rhetoric and symbolic action in the policy process', in G. Sykes, B. Schneider and D. Plank (eds) *Education Policy Research*, New York: Routledge (pp. 267–285).

Rossi, A. (1999) *Knowledge, Identities and the Dilemmas of the Self*, unpublished Ph.D. thesis, Deakin University, Geelong, Australia.

—— (2012) 'Holly goes to school to become a PE teacher … and doesn't! A three-act play', in F. Dowling, H. Fitzgerald and A. Flintoff (eds) *Equity and Difference in Physical Education, Youth Sport and Health: A Narrative Approach*, Abingdon, Oxon: Routledge (pp. 107–114).

Rossi, A. and lisahunter (2013) 'Professional spaces for pre-service teachers: Sites of reality, imagination and resistance', *Educational Review*, 65(2): 123–129.

Rossi, T. (2000) 'Constructing knowledge and shaping identities: Dilemmas in becoming a physical education teacher', paper presented at the Pre-Olympic Congress, Brisbane, Australia, 10–14 July.

Rossi, T. and Hopper, T. (2001) 'Using personal construct theory and narrative method to facilitate reflexive constructions of teaching physical education', *Australian Education Researcher*, 28(3): 87–116.

Rossi, T., Sirna, K. and Tinning, R. (2008) 'Becoming a health and physical education teacher: Student teacher "performances" in the HPE subject department office', *Teaching and Teacher Education*, 24(4): 1029–1040.

Rossi, T., Fry, J., McNeill, M. and Tan, W.K.C. (2007) 'The games concept approach (GCA) as a mandated practice: Views of Singaporean teachers', *Sport Education and Society*, 12(1): 93–111.

Rossi, T., lisahunter, Tinning, R. and Macdonald, D. (2008) 'Initial teacher education, professional learning and the culture of the secondary school subject department: The case of Health and Physical Education', paper presented at the Australian Association of Research in Education, 30 November – 4 December.

Ryan, G. and Bernard, H. (2000) 'Data management and analysis methods', in N. Denzin and Y. Lincoln (eds) *Handbook of Qualitative Research*, 2nd edn, Thousand Oaks, CA: Sage (pp. 769–802).

Ryan, M. (2005) 'Systematic literacy initiatives: Stories of regulation, conflict and compliance', *Australian Journal of Language and Literacy*, 28(2): 114–126.

Sachs, J.G. (1999) 'The changing landscape of teacher education in Australia', *Teaching and Teacher Education*, 15: 215–227.

Sahlberg, P. (2011) *Finnish Lessons*, New York: Teachers College Press.

Sarup, M. (1996) *Identity, Culture and the Postmodern World*, Edinburgh: Edinburgh University Press.

Schempp, P., Sparkes, A. and Templin, T. (1993) 'The micropolitics of teacher induction', *American Educational Research Journal*, 30(3): 447–472.

Schirato, T. and Webb, J. (2003) 'Bourdieu's concept of reflexivity as metaliteracy', *Cultural Studies*, 17(3/4): 539–552.

Shilling, C. (2003) *The Body and Social Theory*, 2nd edn, London: Sage.

Shutt, H. (2010) *Beyond the Profits System – Possibilities for a Post-capitalist Era*, London: Zed Books.

Singh, P. (2001) 'Pedagogic discourses and student resistance in Australian schools', in A. Morais, I. Neves, B. Davies and H. Daniels (eds) *Towards a Sociology of Pedagogy: The contribution of Basil Bernstein to research*. New York: Peter Lang.

Sirna, K., Tinning, R. and Rossi, T. (2008) 'The social tasks of learning to become a physical education teacher: Considering the HPE subject department as a community of practice', *Sport, Education and Society*, 13(3): 285–300.

—— (2010) 'Social processes of health and physical education teachers' identity formation: Reproducing and changing culture', *British Journal of Sociology of Education*, 31(1): 71–84.

Smith, T. and Ingersoll, R. (2004) 'What are the effects of induction and mentoring on beginning teacher turnover?', *American Educational Research Journal*, 41(3): 681–714.

Smyth, D. (1995) 'First-year physical education teachers' perceptions of their workplace', *Journal of Teaching in Physical Education*, 14(2): 198–214.

Smyth, J. (2006) 'The politics of reform of teachers' work and the consequences for schools: Some implications for teacher education', *Asia-Pacific Journal of Teacher Education*, 34(3): 301–319.

Soja, E. (1989) *Postmodern Geographies: The Reassertion of Space in Critical Social Theory*, New York: Verso.

—— (1996) *Thirdspace: Journeys to Los Angeles and Other Real and Imagined Places*, Cambridge, MA: Blackwell.

Solmon, M. (1993) 'The interaction of school context and role identity of first-year teachers', *Journal of Teaching in Physical Education*, 12(3): 13–28.

Solmon, M., Worthy, T. and Carter, J. (1993) 'The interaction of school context and role identity of first-year teachers', *Journal of Teaching in Physical Education*, 12: 313–328.

Somerville, M. (2005) 'Working culture: Exploring notions of workplace culture and learning at work', *Pedagogy, Culture and Society*, 13(1): 5–25.

Sparkes, A. (1995) 'Writing people: Reflections on the dual crises of representation and legitimation in qualitative inquiry', *Quest*, 47: 158–195.

—— (2000) *Telling Tales in Sport and Physical Activity: A Qualitative Journey*, Champaign, IL: Human Kinetics.

Steele, S. (2006) *White Guilt*, New York: Harper Perennial.

Stok-Koch, L., Bolhuis, S. and Koopmans, R. (2007) 'Identifying factors that influence workplace learning in postgraduate medical education', *Education for Health*, 20(1): 1–8.

Stoll, L., Bolam, R., McMahon, A., Wallace, M. and Thomas, S. (2006) 'Professional learning communities: A review of the literature', *Journal of Educational Change*, 7(4): 221–258.

Strauss, A. and Corbin, J. (1998) 'Grounded theory methodology: An overview', in N. Denzin and Y. Licoln (eds) *Strategies of Qualitative Inquiry*, Thousand Oaks, CA: Sage (pp. 158–181).

Sturman, A. (1999) 'Case study methods', in J.P. Reeves and G. Lakomski (eds) *Issues in Educational Research*, Oxford: Elsevier Science (pp. 103–112).

Swabey, K. (2006) *The 1992 Australian Senate Inquiry into Physical and Sport Education: Representations of the Field*, unpublished Ph.D. thesis, University of Queensland, QLD, Australia.

Swabey, K. and Penney, D. (2011) 'Using discursive strategies, playing policy games and shaping the future of physical education', *Sport, Education and Society*, 16(1): 67–87.

Sykes, G., Schneider, B. and Ford, T. (2009) 'Introduction', in G. Sykes, B. Schneider and D. Plank (eds) *Handbook of Education Policy Research*, New York: Routledge (pp. 1–14).

Sykes, H. (2001) 'Understanding and overstanding: Feminist-poststructural life histories of physical education teachers', *Qualitative Studies in Education*, 14(1): 13–31.

Talbert, J. (1995) 'Boundaries of teachers' professional communities in U.S. high schools: Power and precariousness of the subject department', in L. Siskin and J.W. Little (eds) *The Subjects in Question: Departmental Organisation and the High School*, New York: Teachers College Press (pp. 68–94).

Talbert, J. and McLaughlin, M. (2002) 'Professional communities and the artisan model of teaching', *Teachers and Teachings: Theory and Practice*, 8(3): 325–343.

Tellez, K. (1992) 'Mentors by choice, not design: Help-seeking beginning teachers', *Journal of Teacher Education*, 43(3): 214–211.

Templin, T. and Schempp, P. (eds) (1989) *Socialization into Physical Education: Learning to Teach*, Indianapolis: Benchmark Press.

The Office for Standards in Education, Children's Service and Skills (2014) *The Framework for School Inspection*, Manchester: Ofsted.

Thomas, C., Reeve, J., Bingley, A., Brown, J., Payne, S. and Lynch, T. (2009) 'Narrative research methods in palliative care contexts: Two case studies', *Journal of Pain and Symptom Management*, 7(5): 788–796.

Thompson, G. (2003) 'A parents' case-study of a primary school athletics day', *Journal of Physical Education New Zealand*, 36(1): 42–52.

Thorpe, S. (2000). *Politics of Educational Crisis*, unpublished Ph.D. thesis, School of Scientific and Developmental Studies in Education, Deakin University, Australia.

Tickle, L. (1994) *The Induction of New Teachers: Reflective Professional Practice*, London: Cassell.

—— (2000) *Teacher Induction: The Way Ahead*, Buckingham: Open University Press.

Timperley, H. (2008) *Teacher Professional Learning and Development: Educational Practices Series 18*, Paris: UNESCO.

Tinning, R. (1984) 'The student teaching experience: All that glitters is not gold', *The Australian Journal of Teaching Practice*, 4(2): 53–61.

—— (1985) 'Physical education and the cult of slenderness: A critique', *ACHPER National Journal*, 107: 10–14.

—— (2002) 'Toward a "modest pedagogy": Reflections on the problematics of critical pedagogy', *Quest*, 54: 224–240.

—— (2004) 'Rethinking the preparation of HPE teachers: Ruminations on knowledge, identity, and ways of thinking', *Asia-Pacific Journal of Teacher Education* 32(3): 241–253.

Tinning, R. and Siedentop, D. (1985) 'The characteristics of tasks and accountability in student teaching', *Journal of Teaching in Physical Education*, 4(4): 286–300.

Tinning, R., Macdonald, D., Wright, J. and Hickey, C. (2001) *Becoming a Physical Education Teacher: Contemporary and Enduring Issues*, Frenchs Forest: Prentice Hall.

Tousignant, M. and Siedentop, D. (1983) 'A qualitative analysis of task structures in required secondary physical education classes', *Journal of Teaching in Physical Education*, Fall: 47–57.

Trost, S. (2004) 'School physical education in the post-report era: An analysis from public health', *Journal of Teaching in Physical Education*, 23(4): 318–338.

UNESCO (2008) *Oslo Declaration: Eighth Meeting of the High-level Group on Education for All*, www.teachersforefa.unesco.org/resources/Basic%20documents/oslodeclaration.pdf, (accessed 21 August 2013).

—— (2012) *UNESCO Strategy on Teachers: 2012–2015*, http://unesdoc.unesco.org/images/0021/002177/217775e.pdf, (accessed 21 August 2013).

UNESCO and ILO (2009) *Joint ILO/UNESCO Committee on the Application of the Recommendations Concerning Teaching Personnel: Report*, Paris: UNESCO.

Vertinsky, P. (1992) 'Reclaiming space, revisioning the body: The quest for gender-sensitive physical education', *Quest*, 44: 373–396.

Wacquant, L. (1989) 'Towards a reflexive sociology: A workshop with Pierre Bourdieu', *Sociological Theory*, 7(1): 26–63.

—— (1992) 'Towards a social praxeology: The structure and logic of Bourdieu's sociology', in P. Bourdieu and L. Wacquant (eds) *An Invitation to Reflexive Sociology*, Cambridge: Polity Press (pp. 1–47).

Wagner, C. (2006) 'The school leaders' tool for assessing and improving school culture', *Principal Leadership*, 7 (4), 41–44.

Walkington, J. (2005) 'Becoming a teacher: Encouraging development of teacher identity through reflective practice', *Asia-Pacific Journal of Teacher Education*, 33(1): 53–64.

Wallace, M. (1989) 'Brave new workplace: Technology and work in the new economy', *Work and Occupations*, 16(4): 363–392.

Wang, J., Odell, S. and Schwille, S. (2008) 'Effects of teacher induction on beginning teachers' teaching: A critical review', *Journal of Teacher Education*, 59(2): 132–152.

Wenger, E. (1998) *Communities of Practice: Learning, Meaning, Identity*, Cambridge: Cambridge University Press.

—— (2000) 'Communities of practice and social learning systems', *Organisation*, 7(2): 225–246.

Wexler, P. (1992) *Becoming Somebody: Toward a Social Psychology of School*, Washington, DC: Falmer Press.

Whelan, K., Huber, J., Rose, C., Davis, A. and Clandinin, D.J. (2001) 'Telling and retelling our stories on the professional knowledge landscape', *Teachers and Teaching: Theory and Practice*, 7(2): 143–156.

White, J. and Moss, J. (2003) *Professional Paradoxes: Context for Development of Beginning Teacher Identity and Knowledges*, paper presented at the New Zealand Association for Research in Education/Australian Association for Research in Education, Auckland, 29 November – 3 December.

Whitty, G. (2013) 'Educational research and teacher education in higher education institutions in England', in L. Florian and N. Pantic (eds) *Learning to Teach*, Edinburgh: The Higher Education Academy.

Williams, A. (2010) 'Informal learning in the workplace: A case study of new teachers', *Educational Studies*, 29(2): 207–219.

Willower, D.J. (1991) 'Micropolitics and the sociology of school organizations', *Education and Urban Society*, 23(4): 442–454.

Wilson, E. and Demetriou, H. (2007) 'New teacher learning: Substantive knowledge and contextual factors', *The Curriculum Journal*, 18(3): 213–229.

Witz, A. (2000) 'Whose body matters? Feminist sociology and the corporeal turn in sociology and feminism', *Body and Society*, 6(2): 1–24.

Woolgar, S. (1988) 'Reflexivity is the ethnographer of the text', in S. Woolgar (ed.) *Knowledge and Reflexivity: New Frontiers in the Sociology of Knowledge*, London: Sage (pp. 14–36).

Wrench, A. and Garrett, R. (2012) 'Identity work: Stories told in learning to teach physical education', *Sport, Education and Society*, 17(1): 1–19.

Wright, J. (2000) 'Bodies, meanings and movement: A comparison of the language of a physical education lesson and a Feldenkrais movement class', *Sport, Education and Society*, 5(1): 35–50.

Yin, R.K. (1994) *Case Study Research: Design and Methods*, 2nd edn, Thousand Oaks, CA: Sage.

—— (2003) *Case Study Research: Design and Methods*, London: Sage.

Young, M. (2000) 'Preparing English teacher educators: Defining a process', *English Education*, 32(3): 226–237.

Zeichner, K. (1983) 'Alternative paradigms of teacher education', *Journal of Teacher Education*, 34(3): 3–9.

—— (1986) 'The practicum as an occasion for learning to teach', *The South Pacific Journal of Teacher Education*, 14(2): 11–27.

—— (2003) 'The adequacies and inadequacies of three current strategies to recruit, prepare, and retain the best teachers for all students', *Teachers College Record*, 105(3): 490–519.

—— (2010) 'Competition, economic rationalization, increased surveillance, and attacks on diversity: Neo-liberalism and the transformation of teacher education in the U.S.', *Teaching and Teacher Education*, 26: 1544–1552.

Zeichner, K. and Conklin, G. (2005) 'Teacher education programs', in M. Cochran-Smith and K. Zeichner (eds) *Studying Teacher Education: The Report of the AERA Panel on Research and Teacher Education*, Mahwah, NJ: Lawrence Erlbaum Associates (pp. 645–736).

Index

Page numbers in *italics* denote tables, those in **bold** denote figures.